Maryna Romanets

ANAMORPHOSIC TEXTS AND RECONFIGURED VISIONS

Improvised Traditions in
Contemporary Ukrainian and Irish Literature

ibidem-Verlag
Stuttgart

Bibliografische Information der Deutschen Nationalbibliothek
Die Deutsche Nationalbibliothek verzeichnet diese Publikation in der Deutschen Nationalbibliografie; detaillierte bibliografische Daten sind im Internet über http://dnb.d-nb.de abrufbar.

Bibliographic information published by the Deutsche Nationalbibliothek
Die Deutsche Nationalbibliothek lists this publication in the Deutsche Nationalbibliografie; detailed bibliographic data are available in the Internet at http://dnb.d-nb.de.

COVER ILLUSTRATION:

Taras Polataiko. Kazimir Malevich: Suprematist Painting, 1995. Acrylic on canvas, 202.5 x 118.5 cm. Private collection. Photo courtesy of the artist. © Taras Polataiko.

∞

Gedruckt auf alterungsbeständigem, säurefreien Papier
Printed on acid-free paper

ISSN: 1614-3515

ISBN-10: 3-89821-576-8
ISBN-13: 978-3-89821-576-3

© *ibidem*-Verlag
Stuttgart 2007

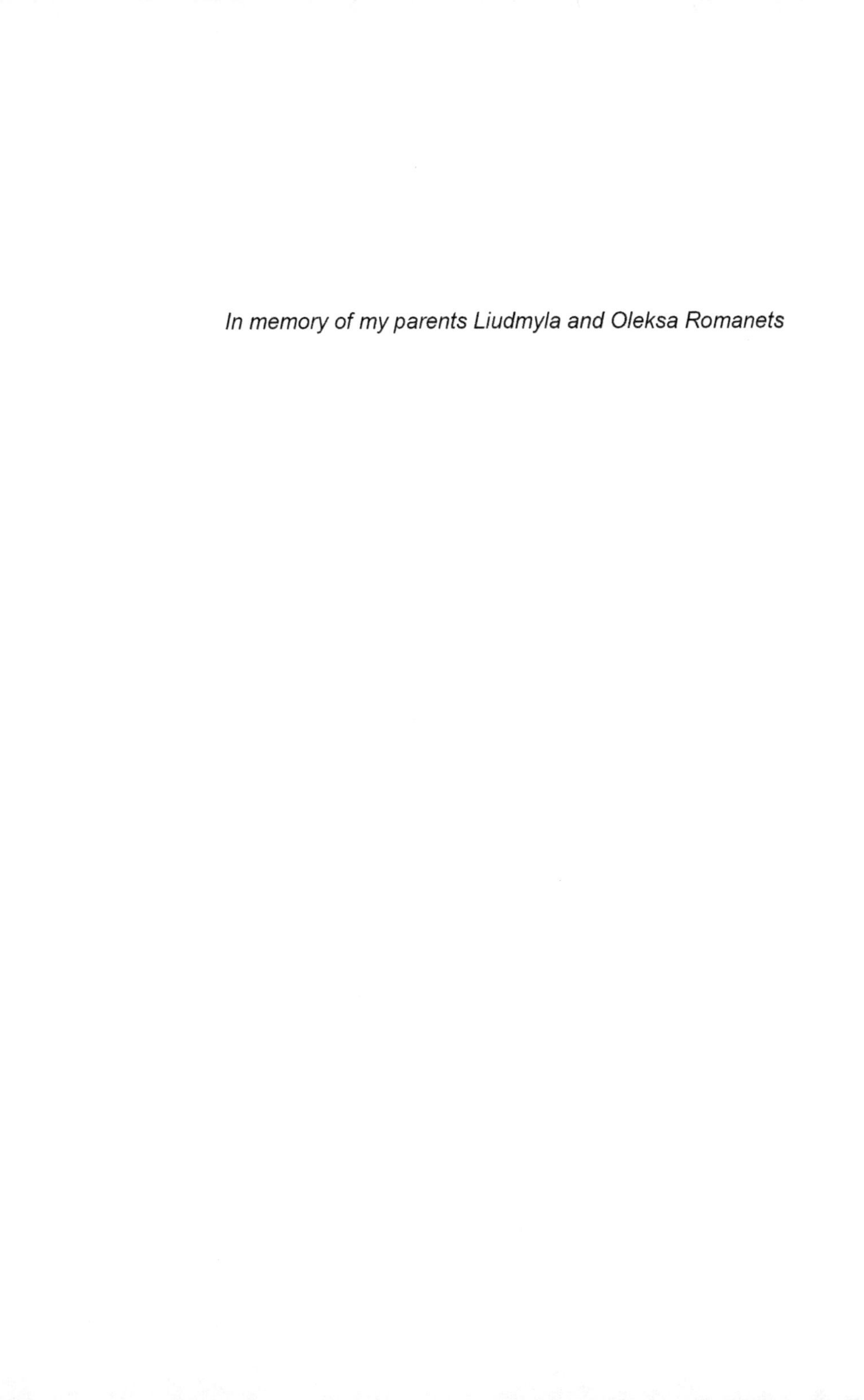

In memory of my parents Liudmyla and Oleksa Romanets

Contents

Postscript   189

Note on Translation and Transliteration

All translations of quotations from Ukrainian sources, except those from Marko Pavlyshyn's translation of *Wozzeck,* are mine. In addition to the translations included in the bilingual editions of Ní Dhomhnaill's poetry, I employ interlinear translations by Máirín Nic Dhiarmada.

Throughout the book, I use quotations in the original languages—Ukrainian and Irish—supplemented by English translations only in cases when I quote creative writing.

In the body of the book, the transliteration conventions of the Library of Congress (LC) system have been modified as follows in the reproduction of Ukrainian language material: initial "ia," "iu" and "ie" appear as "ya," "yu" and "ye"; in personal names the terminal "yi" and "ii" are rendered as "y" and "i"; and the soft sign is not transliterated. In formal references to sources, however, the LC transliteration system has been used without modification.

Acknowledgements

I would like to thank everyone who has offered unstinting insights and valuable advice, at various phases, on particular points in my book: Victor Buyniak, Roma Franko, Anthony Harding, Dee Horne, John Lavery, Carol Morrell, Mary O'Connor, Pádraig Ó Siadhaill, and Raleigh Whitinger. A sincere word of gratitude is due to Roman Senkus for his unfailing support and understanding, and to Máirín Nic Dhiarmada for her kind assistance with translations from Irish. I am especially indebted to those who were instrumental in forging the Irish-Ukrainian comparative duo: Ronald Marken, whose charisma and passion ignited my interest in Irish studies by evoking striking parallels between two cultures; and my father, Oleksa Romanets, whose encyclopedic knowledge of Ukrainian literature, history, and ethnography must have been nourishing my Ukrainian "scholarly unconscious" throughout my formative years and has proven invaluable for this venture. I am particularly thankful to Henriette Morelli for reading the entire manuscript with unremitting care and enthusiasm, and to Taras Polataiko, whose work was inspirational for my application of the representational paradigms of visual art to literary analysis. I am also grateful to Liz Albl and Darlene Shatford for their help in preparing this book for publication.

Special thanks are owed to the Social Sciences and Humanities Research Council of Canada for its generous funding of the project, and to the University of Northern British Columbia for awarding me a publication grant at the final stage.

Early versions of some ideas, as well as some substantial portions of the material—reworked, reconfigured, and hybridized in the book—appeared as journal articles and chapters in edited collections. I am grateful to the editors and publishers for permission to reprint sections from: "His Stories Becoming Histories: Lina Kostenko's Poetic Martyr-Drama," *Ca-*

nadian Slavonic Papers 65, nos. 3–4 (2003): 317–36 (adapted for Chapter I); "Degenerating the Myth of Transhistorical Masculinity: Nuala Ní Dhomhnaill's Cú Chulainn Cycle," *Nordic Irish Studies* 2, no. 1 (2003): 57–74 (adapted for Chapter II); "Erotic Assemblages: Field Research, Palimpsests, and What Lies Beneath," *Journal of Ukrainian Studies* 27, nos. 1–2 (2002): 273–85, and "Ideologies of the Second Coming in the Ukrainian Postcolonial Playground," in *Perspectives on Modern Pornography, 1800–2000*, ed. Lisa Z. Sigel (New Brunswick, New Jersey, and London: Rutgers University Press, 2005), 205–31 (adapted for Chapter III); "Cartographers of Desire: Nuala Ní Dhomhnaill Versus the Love Canon in Irish Poetry," *Canadian Review of Comparative Literature* 29, nos. 2–3 (2002): 316–36, "Travellers, Cartographers, Lovers: Ideologies of Exploratory Desire in Contemporary Irish Poetry," *Nordic Irish Studies* 3 (2004): 18–35, and "Travesties, Transvestisms, and Transgressions: Cross-dressing and Redressing in Nuala Ní Dhomhnaill's Poetry," in *Beyond Borders: IASIL Essays in Modern Irish Writing*, ed. Neil Sammells (Bath: Sulis Press, 2004), 191–202 (adapted for Chapter IV); and "Transgressive Violence, Mad Intertextuality, and Aesthetics of Convulsion," in *Discourses of Violence—Violence of Discourses: Critical Interventions, Transgressive Readings and Post-National Negotiations*, eds. Dirk Wiemann, Agata Stopinska, Anke Bartels, and Johannes Angermüller (Frankfurt on Main: Peter Lang, 2005), 41–54 (adapted for Chapter V).

Introduction

A Look from a Rear-View Mirror:
At the Elisabethplatz in Czernowitz,
November 3, 1918

A haunting, mesmerizing image—a whole book seen in an instant, a musical piece condensed in a single sound, a series of photographs compacted into one, a proliferating face fused in a sole portrait. Idris Khan (b. 1978),[1] London-based emerging artist, reinterprets preexisting books, artwork, musical scores, and photographs by rephotographing every page of a book, every photograph in a series, every self-portrait of an artist and digitally superimposing them. The end product is a seductive, synthesized image whose nebulous entirety and simultaneity both conceal and opaquely reveal each lamina of Khan's pulsating palimpsests of cultural memory. His multilayered images, compulsively overwriting themselves, seem to accumulate and measure time, delve into the repetition of history, and capture an elusive trace disruptive of any notion of absolute origin. The work of Khan, who is a composite of artist and photographer and a composite of Oriental and Occidental heritage, compellingly summons ephemeral specters of other histories and spaces.

The history of the part of Ukraine from which I come, Bukovyna, can be visualized in terms of Khan's richly overlaid textured images. After the disunification of Kyivan Rus' in the eleventh century, Bukovyna belonged to the principality of Galicia-Volhynia but was invaded by Tatars in the fourteenth century; then, in the fourteenth and fifteenth centuries, Bukovyna was integrated into Moldavia, which itself recognized the nominal supremacy of Poland until becoming a vassal-state of the Ottoman

---

[1]　For my discovery of Idris Khan, I am indebted to the publication of Geoff Dyer's article "Between the Lines" (*Guardian*, September 2, 2006, http://arts.guardian.co.uk/features/story/0,,1863044,00.html) (accessed February 3, 2007).

Empire in the sixteenth century. Having been ceded to Austria by the Turks in the eighteenth century, Bukovyna became the crownland of the Austro-Hungarian Empire during the nineteenth century. Finally, Bukovyna was annexed first by Romania and then by the USSR in the twentieth century. My historical sketch probably does not seem to be remarkable because it is indisputably true that, as David Chioni Moore states, there is no place on this planet that has not been, at one time or another, colonized: "Across Eurasia, Africa, the Americas, and more, peoples have formed and reformed, conquered and been conquered, moved and dissolved."[2] Moore's general account also brings to mind, in the context of my Irish-Ukrainian comparative study, an early example of such an interminable movement, which can be found in *Leabhar Gabhála* (*The Book of Invasions*), a core text of the mythological cycle in Irish literature that traces, through the waves of invasions, the origin of the people of Ireland from the Flood to the Middle Ages.[3] However, notwithstanding manifold foreign impositions and intrusions, which, one would expect, would have erased any sense of national belonging, it was in Bukovyna (then part of the Austro-Hungarian Empire) that people in a plebiscite—not the political elite—expressed their will to be united with other Ukrainian lands in one nation state. The Bukovynian *viche* (assembly), which took place in Chernivtsi (Czernowitz in German) on November 3, 1918, exercised people's newly granted constitutional right for self-determination.[4] Although these aspirations were defeated by Romanian occupation, the *viche* was yet another attempt to put virtually invisible Ukrainians

---

[2]   David Chioni Moore, "Is the Post- in Postcolonial the Post- in Post-Soviet? Towards a Global Postcolonial Critique," in *Postcolonialisms: An Anthology of Cultural Theory and Criticism*, ed. Gaurav Desai and Supriya Nair (Oxford: Berg, 2005), 515.

[3]   "*Leabhar Gabhála* / *The Book of Invasions*." *Royal Irish Academy* / *Acadamh Ríoga hÉireann: Library and Catalogue*, http://www.ria.ie/library+catalogue/gabh ala.html (accessed February 15, 2007).

[4]   On the history of the *Viche* in the framework of changes in the administrative structure of the Austro-Hungarian Empire based on national and territorial autonomy, see Oleksa Romanets', ed., *Narodne viche Bukovyny, 1918–1993* (Chernivtsi: Prut, 1994).

on the political map of Europe and yet another paradigmatically painful eruption in Ukrainian history. Moreover, the 1918 event acquired symbolic meaning when the second Bukovynian *viche* was held in Chernivtsi, on November 3, 2004, in support of the Orange Revolution.

Although since the Orange Revolution, Ukraine has unquestionably become an identifiable geopolitical entity, culturally it is, to a considerable degree, still unfamiliar, strange, and lost in the Bermuda Triangle of history. From the point of view of cultural encounters and exchanges, both synchronic and diachronic, Ukraine represents an exciting ambiguous and amorphous zone. It is positioned in the crack between its eastern vector charted by more than three hundred years of Russian domination, its aspirations for the future deposited in the West, and its almost forgotten inheritance of once being both a mighty medieval empire (Kyivan Rus') and an early seventeenth-century European democracy (Hetmanate).

An inquiry into some of the multiple trajectories and heterogeneous layers that comprise Ukraine's postcolonial space[5] in a comparative framework, which allows for conflating Ukrainian with another peripheral European literature that has attained a high international profile and has produced "the strongest group of writers of any English-speaking land in the twentieth century,"[6] is productive for understanding the practices of postcolonial projects that share certain tactical and symbolical forms. In his *Inventing Ireland*, Declan Kiberd points out the lack, within the area of

---

[5] My discussion of Ukrainian postcoloniality is focused on Ukraine's relationship with the Russian Empire. I am deliberately leaving the Austro-Hungarian dimension out because it represents a different type of affiliation between the imperial center and colonial periphery; the national policies of the Habsburgs were much more liberal than those in Russia since all ethnic groups could enjoy relative cultural autonomy. In addition, the former Austro-Hungarian Western Ukraine became a part of the Russo-Soviet imperial state in the 1940s. "Russo-Soviet" is the term borrowed from Moore's "Is the Post- in Postcolonial the Post- in Post-Soviet?" used to emphasize the continuity between the Russian Empire and its second "edition," the USSR.

[6] Maria Tymoczko and Colin Ireland, eds., *Language and Tradition in Ireland: Continuities and Displacements* (Amherst and Boston: University of Massachusetts Press, 2003), 16.

Irish studies, of research in comparative politics and comparative literature.[7] Similarly, David Lloyd emphasizes that the investigation of the effects that colonialism has on colonized cultures "demands" a comparative approach "so that the study of one given site may be profoundly suggestive for the understanding of another, without the two sites having to display entire congruence."[8] However, Kiberd limits himself to a conventional postcolonial geographic imagination by drawing recurrent parallels, in the domain of culture, primarily between Ireland and "the emerging peoples of the decolonizing world" in Africa and Asia,[9] with occasional references to "underdeveloped" Greece.[10] J. J. Lee's *Ireland, 1912–1985: Politics and Society*, which places Irish history in a comparative European context, was published prior to the collapse of the last European empire, the USSR, and does not stretch beyond then firmly secured Soviet borders.[11]

Since Marko Pavlyshyn's pioneering publications on Ukrainian culture and postmodernity, which opened up an entirely new discursive field,[12] the most radical development in the separation of Ukrainian cultural and literary studies from Soviet ideological orthodoxies has consisted in establishing Ukraine's subject position in a postcolonial per-

---

[7]   Declan Kiberd, *Inventing Ireland: The Literature of the Modern Nation* (Cambridge, Massachusetts: Harvard University Press, 1995), 646.

[8]   David Lloyd, "Ireland After History," in *A Companion to Postcolonial Studies*, ed. Henry Schwarz and Santeeta Ray (Malden, Massachusetts, and Oxford: Blackwell, 2000), 379.

[9]   Kiberd, *Inventing Ireland*, 135, 579, 646, 652.

[10]   Ibid., 148, 645, 776.

[11]   J. J. Lee, *Ireland, 1912–1985: Politics and Society* (Cambridge, New York, and Oakleigh: Cambridge University Press, 1992).

[12]   Marko Pavlyshyn, "Ukraïns'ka kul'tura z kutu postmodernizmu (Ukrainian culture in postmodern perspective)," in *Ukraine in the 1990s: Proceedings of the First Conference of the Ukrainian Studies of Australia*, ed. J. E. M. Clarke and Marko Pavlyshyn (Melbourne: Monash University, Slavic Section, 1992), 38–49; Marko Pavlyshyn, "Post-Colonial Features in Contemporary Ukrainian Culture," *Australian Slavonic and Eastern European Studies* 6, no. 2 (1992): 41–55.

spective.[13] Yet, the Irish experience does not come into play here. Emerging Ukrainian-Irish parallels, with rare exceptions,[14] are being consigned, for the most part, to the heated, ongoing public and legislative debates about Ukraine's bilingualism, with its troubled contexts.[15] In the process of an aggressive campaign by the pro-Russian minority to grant Russian, alongside Ukrainian, the status of the state language, thereby assigning Ukrainian an exclusively ritualistic role, a peculiar term, the "Irelandization of Ukraine," has been created. It implies that if Russian should become an official language equally with Ukrainian, Ukrainian would rapidly sink to the level of Irish in Ireland—a language confined to a few small pockets of population (*Gaeltacht*) in the West and otherwise reserved for merely state-ceremonial uses. Ireland is being summoned here, by the pro-Russian partisans, as the paragon of a desirable "normality"—where the language of the former metropolis is in the position of power, while Irish is marginalized—to validate the continuing policy of

---

[13] Oksana Zabuzhko, *Shevchenkiv mif Ukraïny: sproba filosofs'koho analizu* (Kyïv: Abrys, 1997); Oksana Zabuzhko, *Khroniky vid Fortinbrasa: Vybrana eseïstyka 90-kh* (Kyïv: Fakt, 1999); Mykola Riabchuk, *Vid Malorosiï do Ukraïny: paradoksy zapizniloho natsiietvorennia* (Kyïv: Krytyka, 2000); Mykola Riabchuk, *Dylemy ukraïns'koho Fausta: hromadians'ke suspil'stvo i rozbudova derzhavy* (Kyïv: Krytyka, 2000); Mykola Riabchuk, *Dvi Ukraïny: real'ni mezhi, virtual'ni viiny* (Kyïv: Krytyka, 2003); Vitaly Chernetsky, "The Trope of Displacement and Identity Construction in Post-Colonial Ukrainian Fiction," *Journal of Ukrainian Studies* 27, nos. 1–2 (2002): 216–32; Vitaly Chernetsky, *Mapping Postcommunist Cultures: Russia and Ukraine in the Context of Globalization* (Montreal: McGill-Queen's University Press, 2007).

[14] For the comparison of Ukrainian and Irish traditional art forms, for instance, see the doctoral dissertation by: Oleksandr Chasnyk, "Universal'ne i spetsyfichne v prostorovo-chasovii symvolitsi ukraïns'koho ta irlands'koho tradytsiinoho mystetstva (porivnial'no-semiotychnyi analiz)" (Candidate diss., Kharkivs'ka derzhavna akademiia kul'tury, 2001).

[15] See, for example, *Stenohrama hromads'kykh slukhan' vid 5 hrudnia: obhovorennia zakonoproektu "Pro rozvytok i zastosuvannia mov v Ukraïni."* 10.12.2003 | 10:42 | Upravlinnia zv'iazkiv z hromadskistiu SKMU, http://www.kmu.gov.ua/control/uk/ publish/article?art_id=3646619&cat_id=38176 (accessed February 1, 2007); Oleh Romanchuk, "Derzhava *contra* kul'tura," *Universum*, http://www. universum. org.ua/journal/2004/rom_3.html (accessed February 1, 2007).

what Mykola Riabchuk terms "linguistic apartheid" carried out in a variety of disguises in postindependence Ukraine.[16]

By attempting a comparative Irish-Ukrainian analysis across the field of postcolonial studies, I will thus be mapping another, essentially untouched, area of the typology in cultural decolonization. Although I am fully aware that the signification of existing similarities between two countries "may yet differ," as Lloyd suggests elsewhere, "in their distinct contexts,"[17] my emphasis here will be on the comparative element. Though situated within the boundaries of white Christian Europe, Ukraine and Ireland, located as they are at Europe's extreme Eastern and Western fringes, its frontier regions of sorts, are on the periphery of Eurocentric ideology, and the gravitational pull of the center does not hold them steadily in its orbit. Being subjected to counter-centripetal forces determined by the "non-modern" rhythms incapable of blending into the linear, progressive, and "onward flow of history,"[18] these cultures are best conceptualized as running counter to the metropolitan models of the major European states. Simultaneously, Ukrainian and Irish literatures, as part of European tradition, inevitably indulge in the "vices" of binarisms, dichotomies, dualities of Western thought, analytical frameworks and systematizing perspectives so much opposed by certain postcolonial theorists. These contradictory factors contribute to my project of destabilizing the idea of homogeneous Eurocentricity as a paradigm adopted and utilized by a considerable part of postcolonial critique in its attempt to reassert the epistemological value and agency of the non-European world.

Furthermore, Ireland and Ukraine have a similar psychohistorical legacy that is determined in part by a traumatic sense of history in which

---

[16]   Mykola Riabchuk, "Ukraine without Ukrainians?" in *Towards an Intellectual History of Ukraine: An Anthology of Ukrainian Thought from 1710 to 1995*, ed. Ralph Lindheim and George S. N. Luckyj (Toronto: University of Toronto Press, 1996), 401.

[17]   Lloyd, "Ireland After History," 391. Lloyd's work explains in detail the dynamics of comparative and differential practices in postcolonial projects.

[18]   Ibid., 377.

Irish "funerary" obsession[19] matches the Ukrainian sense of being left "only a heritage of crosses and grave mounds."[20] Both nations experienced enormous human losses, as a result of the Great Hunger (1845–1847) in Ireland and of successive, artificially induced waves of *Holodomor* (Famine) (1932–1933 and 1946–1947) in Ukraine and of extensive, economically forced emigration to the New World.[21] Although Ukrainian Cossacks were renowned as the "defenders of Christendom" who saved Europe from devastation by the Ottoman Empire[22] and insular, learned Irish monks successfully spread wisdom and Christianity in the then largely "uncivilized" European mainland, in the history of European expansion, both Ukraine and Ireland were turned into arenas for colonial exploitation. Moreover, the colonization of Ireland seems to have provided a valuable template for Russian colonial endeavors: Tsar Peter I (1672–1725) regarded the British subjugation of Ireland as a valuable operative model for his colonial strategies in Ukraine.[23] In their turn, as some scholars contend, "almost all promoters of schemes for settlement in Ireland drew comparisons between their plans and those of their con-

---

[19] Cheryl Herr, "The Erotics of Irishness," *Critical Inquiry* 17 (1990): 6.

[20] Borys Antonenko-Davydovych, "Shadows of Forgotten Days," in *Before the Storm: Soviet Ukrainian Fiction of the 1920s*, ed. George Luckyj, trans. Iurii Tkacz (Ann Arbor: Ardis, 1986), 250.

[21] Lloyd proposes that although displacements of population have been "a common experience of virtually all colonized peoples," Ireland occupies a special place regarding the impact of emigration comparable to that of the slave trade on West Africa, and it is "emigration as the distinctive form of disciplining that differentiates the Irish colonial experience from most others" ("Ireland After History," 387). Ukraine here can provide a missing parallel outside of the slave trade framework because in addition to a considerable labor emigration from Ukraine at the turn of the twentieth century, Ukrainians were subjected to mass deportations to prison camps and forced settlement areas in Siberia and the Far East under Stalinism, with no less "pedagogical" rationale; for details see one of the earlier publications on the issue, Robert Conquest's *The Nation Killers: The Soviet Deportation of Nationalities* (New York: Macmillan, 1970).

[22] Orest Subtelny, *Ukraine: A History*, 3rd ed. (Toronto, Buffalo, and London: University of Toronto Press, 2000), 111–13.

[23] Ibid., 165.

temporaries who were projecting settlement among the North American Indians."[24]

Common political and socioeconomic features in the fate of Ireland and Ukraine were so obvious that the instigator of the Bolshevik revolution in Russia and the designer of the Soviet state, Vladimir Lenin (1870–1924), declared in his 1914 speech in Switzerland that Ukraine "has become to Russia what Ireland was for England: exploited in the extreme and receiving nothing in return."[25] After the 1917 Russian revolution, however, such analogies with Ireland appeared threatening to the state apparatus; this speech was never included in the Soviet edition of Lenin's *Complete Collection of Works*, which is hardly surprising since Lenin also wrote that a blow against the British Empire in Ireland would have been of "a hundred times more significance than a blow of equal weight in Asia or in Africa."[26] Curiously enough, it was the publication of Dmytro Doroshenko's (1882–1951) *Про Ірляндію* (*On Ireland*) by the Kyiv cultural society "Просвіта" (Enlightenment) that served as a formal reason for the Russian imperial successor, the Soviet government, to ban the society[27] in the 1920s.

Some points in Irish and Ukrainian history offer striking chronological parallels in the evolving system of colonial domination. Since the military agreement with Muscovy (1654), Ukraine lost in succession its autonomous elective monarchy of Hetmanate, its Cossack regimental civil order, its traditional legislative procedures, its independent military force, and its educational system.[28] In 1775, the Russian army destroyed the greatest symbol of ancient Cossack liberties, the Zaporozhian Sich.

---

[24]   Stephen Howe, *Ireland and Empire: Colonial Legacies in Irish History and Culture* (Oxford and New York: Oxford University Press, 2000), 23.

[25]   R. Serbyn, "Lenine et la question ukrainienne en 1914: le discours 'separatiste' de Zurich," *Pluriel* 25 (1981) : 83.

[26]   Quoted by Kiberd, *Inventing Ireland*, 197.

[27]   *Narys istoriï "Prosvity"* (L'viv, Kraków, and Paris, 1993), 134.

[28]   Zenon E. Kohut, *Russian Centralism and Ukrainian Autonomy: Imperial Absorption of the Hetmanate, 1760s–1830s* (Cambridge, Massachusetts: Harvard University Press, 1988).

In 1800, an edict issued by Tsar Paul I (1754–1801) signaled the "final isolation of Ukraine from Europe and its absorption by the Russian Empire."[29] Similarly, the Cromwellian conquest and clearances, the Restoration land settlement, the civil war of 1689–1693, the Penal Laws passed between 1691 and the 1720s, and the 1790s revolutionary war against imperial England declared by Wolfe Tone (1763–1798) all escalated the reduction of Ireland to colonial status.[30] The violent repression of the 1798 insurrection followed by the abolition of the Irish parliament, and the Act of Union in 1800 signified Ireland's submergence into a larger supranational, imperial community.[31]

Domineering powers, in their exploration and subjugation of the peripheral territories, exercised coercion that signaled their status as occupiers and introduced bloody correctives into the natural landscapes that were later to become the symbols of patriotic topography. In the Ireland of 1798, after the disastrously lost Battle of Vinegar Hill, every tree along the roads leading from Wexford became a gibbet: "[T]he slaughter of the rebels was proceeding so methodically that at least one gaoler felt the need to invent for himself a gallows which would hang thirty at a time."[32] In the Ukraine of 1708, after the ill-fated military alliance of Ivan Mazepa (1639–1709) with Sweden against Peter I of Muscovy in the Great Northern War (1700–1721), the Russians razed to the ground the Hetman's capital, Baturyn, and diked the River Seim with dead bodies after slaughtering, with unprecedented cruelty that shocked Europe, all the defenders and inhabitants of the city. *Gazette de France*, *Lettres historiques*, *Mercure historique et politique*, and *Clef du Cabinet*, for example,

---

[29] Leonid Zalizniak, "Ukraïna—Rosiia: Rizni istorychni doli," *Starozhytnosti*, November 1991, no. 10: 6.

[30] J. C. D. Clark, *The Language of Liberty, 1660–1832: Political Discourse and Social Dynamics in the Anglo-American World* (Cambridge: Cambridge University Press, 1994), 73.

[31] Liam de Paor, ed., *Milestones in Irish History* (Cork and Dublin: Mercier, 1986), 76.

[32] Robert Kee, *The Most Distressful Country*, vol. 1 of *The Green Flag: A History of Irish Nationalism* (London: Quartet Books, 1976), 132.

revealed "horrific massacre," "women and children on sabers' edges," "inhumane customs of the Muscovites," and their "barbarity."[33]

The figures of the eighteenth-century historical doppelgängers, Wolfe Tone and Ivan Mazepa, who attempted to resort to respectively French and Swedish aid in their struggles for independence, exhibited tragic signs of inability to break through a vicious imperial circle. A succession of failures accompanied by violent phlebotomies and the political decapitation of both to-be-nations created a psychological matrix of defeatism and a sense of being on the verge of annihilation. Both countries, with ancient cultures, paroxysms of agrarian violence, and the considerable psychological hold of historical memories on the minds of many people, seemed destined to become "the missing people," to use Gilles Deleuze's expression, who did not get to parade in the imperial progressive march of history and whose own history was erased. This erasure was not complete, however; history returned to haunt them as ghostly apparitions from their pasts—the Irish existing under the "curse of Cromwell," the Ukrainians in "пропащий час" ("the lost time"). In these historiographic metaphors both William Butler Yeats (1865–1939) and Mykhailo Drahomanov (1841–1895) identified the crucial points that signified the fatal fall of their countries. The first was Oliver Cromwell's (1599–1658) brutal campaign of 1649–1650 in Ireland; the second, the infamous 1654 Pereiaslav Treaty with Muscovy.[34] In both countries, traumatic experiences overlaid a historical national identity and resulted in fragmentation, duality, or even multiplicity of the contemporary one. The latter factor produced a sense of dislocation and dispossession that in their extreme manifestations generated a state of hysteria and insanity exposed in the figures of Jonathan Swift (1667–1745) and Nikolai Gogol

---

[33] For more details on Ukrainian-Swedish alliance and military campaign against Muscovy, see Il'ko Borshchak and Rene Martel', *Ivan Mazepa: Zhyttia i poryvy velykoho het'mana,* trans. Mykhailo Rudnyts'kyi (Kyïv: Radians'kyi pys'mennyk, 1991), 110.

[34] The chronological framework is specified in the subtitle "Українці під Московським царством (1654–1876)" ("Ukrainians under the Muscovite Tsardom, 1654–1876"), published in 1909.

(1809–1852), and Edmund Burke (1729–1797) and Mykhailo Drahomanov. Both Irish and Ukrainian historical memories and the repetitive
character of British and Russian policies of extermination in Ireland and
Ukraine respectively that turned into bloody rituals prevented the collective lapses of memory in the colonized. They enhanced the process of
reclamation of the past reinterpreted as "heritage" and the creation of a
"mythic" heritage model of national identity that served as protection
against the complete absorption by the metropolitan culture.

British policy in Ireland, according to Seamus Deane, "failed to
recognize the cultural *differences* between the two islands."[35] Since both
Ukraine and Ireland were racially undistinguishable from their colonizing
powers, the most prominent, visible, or rather audible, demarcation line
between them ran along the linguistic axis. Matthew Arnold (1822–1888),
for example, in his "modest proposal" on the language issue, explicitly
expressed British views on Anglo-Irish relations that excluded any possibility of a politically independent future for Ireland, whose language he
regarded as a token of defeat. He saw its decline and ultimate extinction
as beneficial because the "fusion of all the inhabitants of these islands into one homogeneous English-speaking whole ... [and] the swallowing up
of separate provincial nationalities, is a consummation to which the natural course of things irresistibly tends."[36] While the nineteenth-century
British Empire's policy of linguistic assimilation in Ireland was aided by
"natural" factors because the post-Famine demographic decline severely
reduced the number of Irish-speakers, and the surviving ones were
abandoning Irish in favor of English as "a means of literal survival,"[37] the
Russian Empire conducted a persistent and blatant discriminative policy
concerning the Ukrainian language. This strategy of consecutive bans on

---

[35]   Seamus Deane, *A Short History of Irish Literature* (London: Hutchinson, 1986),
        144.
[36]   Matthew Arnold, *Lectures and Essays in Criticism* (Ann Arbor: University of Mi-
        chigan Press, 1962), 296.
[37]   Tymoczko and Ireland, eds., *Language and Tradition*, 12.

language culminated in the notorious Valuev Circular (1863),[38] which stated "there was not, there is not, and there cannot be any separate Little Russian[39] language."[40] This decree was followed by the no less infamous 1876 Ems Edict that prohibited all publications in Ukrainian and the import of Ukrainian-language books from abroad (this again was unconditionally reiterated in the 1894 Addition).[41]

The process of assimilating Ukrainians and Irish into the dominant cultural formation was further accelerated through the imperial homogenizing educational systems that allowed for a strict state supervision of school curricula and academic publishing. Public education was thus deprived of its independent momentum, and its highly subversive force—in both countries, school teachers, especially in rural areas, successfully and devotedly disseminated national sentiments[42]—was restricted. National Schools, set up by the British government in Ireland in 1831, forty years prior to those in the rest of the British Isles, admitted neither Irish history nor the Irish language.[43] Correspondingly, the 1864 Statutes on Primary School in Russian school policy stated that the instruction in schools should be conducted exclusively in Russian, thus demoting the history and culture of Ukraine.[44] The nineteenth-century Russian Empire deliberately ignored, and worse, relentlessly denounced, cultural distinc-

---

[38] On the impact of the circular, see Johannes Remy, "The Valuev Circular and Censorship of Ukrainian Publications in the Russian Empire (1863–1876): Intention and Practice," *Canadian Slavonic Papers* 49, nos. 1–2 (2007): 87–110.

[39] The name Little Russia for Ukraine (as opposed to Great Russia) was officially introduced in 1722 with the elimination of the Hetmanate as a form of Ukrainian autonomous governance and the establishment of Little Russian Collegium by Peter I. See Arkadii Zhukovs'kyi and Orest Subtel'nyi, *Narys istoriï Ukraïny* (L'viv: Naukove tovarystvo imeni T. Shevchenka, 1992), 53.

[40] Quoted by Roman Smal'-Stots'kyi, "Do povnoho obrusieniia (Peresliduvannia ukraïns'koï movy Moskvoiu)," *Slovo*, February 1992, no. 1: 3.

[41] Ivan Kryp'iakevych, *Istoriia Ukraïny* (L'viv: Svit, 1990), 273, 445.

[42] Lawrence W. McBride, ed., *Reading Irish Histories: Texts, Contexts, and Memory in Modern Ireland* (Dublin: Four Courts Press, 2003), 93.

[43] Ibid., 88–94.

[44] Stephen Velychenko, "Identities, Loyalties and Service in Imperial Russia: Who Administered the Borderlands?" *The Russian Review* 54, no. 2 (1995): 198–99.

tions, having the far-reaching goal of appropriating the Ukrainian culture and history of the period of Kyivan Rus' in order to construct a simulacrum model of the millennium-long history of Russia through "historiosophic expansion."[45]

In addition, while attempting to legitimize colonial enterprise, imperial historiography presented a precolonial past of the colonized as "bloody stasis, a tract of time without history or civility"[46] dominated by the "wild" natives. As early as 1596, Edmund Spenser (1552–1599) justified the idea of the extermination of the Irish on the grounds that they were barbaric Scythians.[47] Although the Russian colonial discourse has been recurrently referring to the part of Ukraine that used to be called *Dyke pole*[48] (Wild Steppe)—and belonged to Scythia in the seventh century BC to third century AD—as a showcase of a successfully humanized and colonized former uncultivated and uninhibited land, the Scythian period in Ukrainian culture was embraced by the imperial metropolis as soon as it was made "Russian." Having been promptly established as a stage in the pedigree of the "Scythian Rome," the idea also captured the imagination of writers—one of the fin-de-siècle groups of Russian poets called itself Scythians, and among a plethora of avant-garde magazines published during the Silver Age of Russian literature, one titled itself *The Scythians* (1917–1918).[49]

It is noteworthy, though, that unlike the majority of colonized nations, both Ireland and Ukraine, prior to the imposition of colonial rule,

---

[45] Vasyl' Iaremenko, "Zrada: Shel'muvannia istoriieiu v ukraïns'komu varianti," *Slovo*, September 1992, no. 14: 2.

[46] Norman Vance, *Irish Literature: A Social History. Tradition, Identity and Difference* (Oxford: Basil Blackwell, 1990), 6.

[47] Edward E. Said, *Culture and Imperialism* (New York: Vintage Books, 1993), 222.

[48] The territory between the Don, upper Oka, and left tributaries of the Dnipro and Desna Rivers. Although the name was considered to be out of circulation at the end of the eighteenth century ("Dyke pole," in *Ukraïns'ka radians'ka entsyklopediia*, 2nd ed., vol. 3 [Kyïv: Holovna redaktsia URE, 1979], 344), contemporary Russian neocolonialists use it to assert their claims on certain regions of Ukraine.

[49] Thais S. Lindstrom, *A Concise History of Russian Literature*, vol. 2 (New York: New York University Press, 1978), 2.

had extensively developed literary traditions. Literature in Gaelic used to occupy the position of power, being "arguably the richest vernacular literature in medieval Western Europe."[50] Poets, highly trained professionally for up to twelve years, "stood second only to chieftain" in social hierarchy.[51] Similarly, Ukrainian Baroque writers demonstrated virtuoso usage of poetic devices in a wide variety of poetic forms, such as, for example, technically intricate *carmina curiosa.*[52] Under the bardic order, Irish poets acquired the status of visionaries and prophets; they were foretellers empowered by *imbas forosna.* In Irish, *file* traditionally meant seer, one who possesses second sight, who sees into, beyond, and more than others do and thus transcends the normal boundaries of time and space. Irish prophetic poets, according to Seamus Deane, created their verses in "their windowless rooms, in darkness."[53] Ukrainian *kobzari*, who both performed at the courts of nobility[54] and participated as minstrels in Cossacks' military campaigns, often voluntarily blinded themselves in order to see with the "eyes of the soul."[55] They opposed the impediments passed to them in and by darkness to the "monocular vision" of the world of those who can physically see. Blindness, either inborn or inflicted in the case of *kobzari* or imitated in the case of *filí*, ensured freedom from a cognitive confinement within the visible world and generated visionary powers where prophetic vision exceeded those of a mortal sight. As Jacques Derrida writes in *Memoirs of the Blind*, the blind explore and seek "to foresee there where they do not see, *no longer* see, or do *not yet* see. The space of the blind always conjugates

---

[50]   Tymoczko and Ireland, eds., *Language and Tradition*, 5.

[51]   Declan Kiberd, *Irish Classics* (London: Granta Books, 2001), 4.

[52]   L. Ie. Makhnovets', ed., *Davnia literatura (XI–persha polovyna XVIII st.)*, vol. 1 of *Istoriia ukraïns'koï literatury* (Kyïv: Naukova dumka, 1967), 454–56.

[53]   Deane, *A Short History*, 15.

[54]   Leopol'd Iashchenko, *Derzhavna zasluzhena kapela bandurystiv Ukraïns'koï RSR* (Kyïv: Muzychna Ukraïna, 1970), 5.

[55]   Nelli Korniienko, "Les' Kurbas i zasady ukraïns'koho avanhardu," *Dzerkalo tyzhnia*, February 3–9, 2007, http://www.zn.kiev.ua/ie/razdel/633/3730/ (accessed February 4, 2007).

these three tenses and times of memory."[56] The figure of a poet, a prophet and keeper of condensed collective memories in both cultures, became symbolic of the cultural rebirth that countered the colonial model of precolonial underdevelopment and savagery.

The nineteenth-century Revivalist movements in both countries represented times prior to colonization from a perspective diametrically opposite the colonial portrayals of primitive "natives." Escape to precolonial times, romantically viewed as a golden age, was also a way of setting moral and heroic *exempla* for the present and coming generations and of avoiding colonizers' cultural tutelage. This strategy in defying anti-nationalist cultural imperialism had a considerable impact on the formation of respective national identities; however, it could also become a way of entrapping actuality within a national myth that acquired the hypnotic power of a demonic mirror over the present. The image in this mirror, however attractive it was supposed to be and whatever stereotypes it intended to smash, did not grant access to the "purity" of precolonial times as it was inevitably hybridized throughout a shared history of the colonizer and colonized. The myth of a glorious past was also refracted in the prism of an accumulated experience of defeat and domination by a more powerful neighbor, creating a detrimental consciousness of "dolorous patriotism" when, according to Lady Augusta Gregory (1852–1932), the writer was "in touch with a people ... whose heroes have been the failures ... who went out to a battle that was already lost."[57] Lesia Ukrainka (1871–1913) realized that constant contemplation on people's thralldom, on frustration of losses, and on abortive efforts and the creation of a national "sanctuary" was traumatic for national con-

---

[56]   Jacques Derrida, *Memoirs of the Blind: The Self-Portrait and Other Ruins*, trans. Pascale-Anne Brault and Michael Naas (Chicago and London: University of Chicago Press, 1993), 5–6.

[57]   Augusta Gregory, "The Felons of Our Land," *Cornhill Magazine*, May 1900, no. 47: 634.

sciousness and provided an escape for a certain part of the Ukrainian intelligentsia into a paralyzing discourse of complaint.[58]

The issues related to nineteenth-century revivalist processes in Ireland and Ukraine resurface in the contemporary ongoing negotiations of the ideas concerning identity and its cultural construction and redefinition. Taking what some scholars call "the identity-obsession"[59] as a symptom of unresolved dependence, one must go back to the "foundational fictions" and "mythic" subtexts of national development established by respective national Revivals in order to understand the contemporary literary strategies of revision and renewal of previously existing literary systems, codes, and forms. These strategies are employed by contemporary writers who draw imaginary lines in literary tradition that link blank spaces and are instrumental in overcoming colonial aporias.

Revivalism evolved from the antiquarian movement of the eighteenth century, which was partially motivated by a nostalgically desperate desire to document and register the remnants of what seemed then to be almost extinct cultures, and attempted to contextualize local aristocracy, severed from history, by reconstructing its genealogy. Liah Greenfield concurs that European "elites whose status was threatened or who were prevented from achieving the status they aspired to" turned to nationalism since only national identity could guarantee "status with dignity to every member of whatever is defined as a polity or society."[60] Antiquarianism was bridging discontinuities, thus turning out to be politically dangerous for imperial systems as it ultimately provided for fundamentals of future national and cultural identity based on collective identities of the past. Having started as one whose gaze was retrospective, the

---

[58] See Dmytro Dontsov, "Poetyka ukraïns'koho Risordzhimentu (Lesia Ukraïnka)," in *Ukraïns'ke slovo: Khrestomatiia ukraïns'koï literatury ta literaturnoï krytyky XX st.*, vol. 1, ed. Vasyl' Iaremenko and Ievhen Fedorenko (Kyïv: Ros', 1994), 149–83.

[59] Herr, "The Erotics of Irishness," 6.

[60] Liah Greenfield, "Transcending the Nation's Worth," in *The Worth of Nations: The Boston, Melbourne, Oxford Conversazioni on Culture and Society*, ed. Claudio Véliz (Boston: Boston University, University Professors, 1993), 45.

movement became much more radical and less romantic, catalyzed by the 1840s Famine in Ireland,[61] a succession of Russian bans and repressions in Ukraine, and the breakout of revolutions throughout Europe in 1848, signifying the "springtime of the peoples."[62]

Studies in history, ethnography, language and literature and publications of historical chronicles and documents, initiated in the eighteenth century, were of great importance both for Ireland and Ukraine in resisting the tendency common to all the imperial states where "colonialism did not merely force itself and its laws onto a people's present and future, but also on to their past, distorting, mutilating and annihilating it."[63] Resistance to the cultural erasures of the past materialized in Charlotte Brooke's (1740?–1793) *Reliques of Ancient Irish Poetry* (1789) and *Fairy Legends and Traditions of the South of Ireland* (1825), published by Thomas Crofton Croker (1798–1854); *Irish Minstrelsy* (1831) by James Hardiman (1782–1855); *The Lays of the Western Gael* (1864) by Samuel Ferguson (1810–1886); and other publications that launched into cultural circulation the aristocratic heroic age of legends and sagas of pagan Ireland. A number of translators from Irish—James Clarence Mangan (1803–1849), Aubrey De Vere (1814–1902), and Standish Hayes O'Grady (1832–1915), among others, engaged in the project of "materializing" Ireland[64] through the conversion of Irish-language literature, culture, and history into the Anglo-Irish tradition. The Gaelic League, founded in Dublin in 1893, undertook the publication of a vast amount of Irish poetry and prose. Standish James O'Grady (1846–1927) revitalized the heroic past of the nation in *History of Ireland: The Heroic Period* (1878), *Cuchulain and His Contemporaries* (1878), *History of Ireland: Critical and Philosophical* (1881), and *The Story of Ireland* (1894). *Dublin University*

---

[61] R. F. Foster, *Modern Ireland, 1600–1972* (London: Penguin, 1989), 316.

[62] Jonathan Sperber, *The European Revolutions, 1848–1851* (New York: Cambridge University Press, 1994), 116.

[63] Ruth Fleischmann, "The Insularity of Irish Literature: Cultural Subjugation and the Difficulties of Reconstruction," in *The Internationalism of Irish Literature and Drama*, ed. Joseph McMinn (Gerrards Cross: Colin Smyth, 1992), 311.

[64] Kiberd, *Inventing Ireland*, 624.

Magazine (founded in 1833) and *Dublin University Review* (1885) also promoted national cultural revival.

The publications of Ukrainian folklore, initiated in the eighteenth century, were continued by Nikolai Tsertelev's (1790–1869) *Опыт собрания старинных малороссийских песен* (*Experience in Gathering Ancient Little Russian Songs*) (1819), *Малороссийские песни* (*Little Russian Songs*) (1827), and *Украинские народные песни* (*Ukrainian Folk Songs*) (1834); Mykhailo Maksymovych's (1804–1873) *Сборник украинских песен* (*Collection of Ukrainian Songs*) (1849); and Izmail Sreznevsky's (1812–1880) six volumes of *Запорожская старина* (*Zaporozhian Antiquity*) (1833–1838). The recovery of the glorious and tragic past was undertaken with the publication of *История Руссов* (*History of the Ruses*) (written in 1770s; published in 1848), and the Cossack chronicles by Samiilo Velychko (4 vols., 1848–1864) and Hryhori Hrabianka (1854). The Fundamental *История Малой России* (*History of Little Russia*) (1822) and *Источники малороссийской истории* (*The Sources of Little Russian History*) (1858) by Dmytro Bantysh-Kamensky (1788–1850); Mykola Markevych's (1784–1860) *История Малороссии* (*History of Little Russia*) (5 vols., 1842–1843); and Mykola Kostomarov's (1817–1885) works on Ukrainian hetmans,[65] among others, had a great impact on the (re)construction of Ukrainian history. *Записки о Южной Руси* (*Notes on Southern Rus'*) (1856–1857), edited by Panteleimon Kulish (1819–1897); the monthly *Киевская старина* (*Kyivan Antiquity*), established in 1882; and the serial publication *Етнографічний збірник* (*Ethnographic Collection*), edited by Volodymyr Hnatiuk (1871–1926) in Austrian-ruled Western Ukraine, made a considerable contribution to studies on the political, social, and cultural history of Ukraine.

---

[65]   *Иван Свиргговский, украинский гетман XVI века* (*Ivan Svyrhovsky, A Ukrainian Hetman of the Sixteenth Century*) (1855), *Богдан Хмельницкий и возвращение Южной Руси к России* (*Bohdan Khmelnytsky and the Return of Southern Rus' to Russia*) (1857), *Гетманство Выговского* (*Vyhovsky's Hetmancy*) (1861), and *Руина* (*The Ruin*) (1879–1880).

Reclaimed history and visionary mytholograms inscribed and encoded in literature were among the factors instrumental in selecting, compressing, reinterpreting, and popularizing those events and ideas that were to comprise a composite, foundational national mythology. This resistance mythology was essential for cementing national consciousness and for cultivating the feeling, or the illusion, of homogeneity. The totality of the myth of national history, identity, and memory was indispensable in crystallizing the philosophy of national self-determination and of culturally distinct nations. The nation could come into being if it was organized around the national myth as the very point of its identity. The more monolithic the construct was in the face of the colonizer, the more viable and successful it was. In this case, homogenizing and essentializing practices, with their formulaic fixities and invariabilities on the part of the colonized, fall into the category of what Gayatri Chakravorty Spivak calls "strategic essentialism," whose tactical and deliberate use communicates "a scrupulously visible political interest"[66] and is unavoidable in identitarian grouping.[67]

It is also worthwhile mentioning that in the time when the boundary between scholarship and national mythology was rather bendable, Irish history and culture of the past were systematized and institutionalized through the publications of many notable texts by the Royal Irish Academy (1785), which was the center of research into Irish civilization; the Gaelic Society of Dublin (1807); the Iberno-Celtic Society (1818); the Ossianic Society (1853); the Celtic Society amalgamated with the Irish Archaeological Society in 1853; and the Irish Text Society (1898). Since there were no state or community funded institutions of the kind in Ukraine, Ukrainian scholars were working in the framework of imperial structures. For example, the Archaeological Committee, founded in Kyiv in 1843, published four volumes of *Памятники* (*Monuments*), thirty-five

---

[66] *The Spivak Reader*, ed. Donna Landry and Gerald MacLean (London and New York: Routledge, 1996), 214.

[67] Neil Lazarus, ed., *The Cambridge Companion to Postcolonial Literary Studies* (Cambridge: Cambridge University Press, 2004), 209.

volumes of *Архив Юго-Западной России* (*Archive of Southwest Russia*) (1859–1914), and other materials on Ukrainian history of great historiographic value. Most such institutions established by the center were closely connected with its imperial policy. At the beginning of the 1870s, the founding of the Southwestern Department of the Russian Geographic Society (as a subdivision of the Russian Geographic Society) played an important role in proving the "Russianness" of Ukraine in the Russian-Polish territorial disputes. Similarly, the publication of the Ukrainian chronicles *История Руссов* (*History of the Ruses*), mentioned earlier; *Летопись Самовидца* (*Eyewitness' Chronicle*) (1846); and other important documents by the Russian Historical Society were aimed at supporting the concept of Russian-Ukrainian sameness. The Society carried out fundamental publications and organized the Archaeological Congress in Kyiv (1874), which promoted scholarly achievements in Ukrainian studies and thus surpassed its primarily defined functions. Russian tsar Alexander II (1818–1881) ordered the Society's closure because it was turning into the main center of Ukrainian scholarly life[68] and allegedly fuelling separatist sentiments.[69] This very much resembled the reaction of the British government to the publication of the materials of the Irish Ordinance Survey set up by the House of Commons in 1824. The colonial enterprise was "undermined" by an ardent revivalist George Petrie (1790–1866), who directed its historical section and selected the team of enthusiastic scholars and poets that included John O'Donovan (1809–1861), Eugene O'Curry (1796–1862) and Charles Mangan, providing each set of maps with a comprehensive memoir of a corresponding county. However, as John Hutchinson argues, after the "publication of the first volume on the County of Londonderry in 1839, funding for the historical section of the survey was ended by the government, reportedly

---

68   Dmytro Doroshenko, "Rozvytok nauky ukraïnoznavstva u XIX–na pochatku XX st. ta ïi dosiahnennia," in *Ukraïns'ka kul'tura*, ed. Dmytro Antonovych (Kyïv: Lybid', 1993), 31.

69   David Saunders, "Russia's Nationality Policy: The Case of Ukraine (1847–1941)," *Journal of Ukrainian Studies* 29, nos.1–2 (2004): 409.

concerned at the nationalist implications of this revival of the Celtic past...."[70]

Revivalist undertakings were crucial both for Ireland and Ukraine as they were marked by "negotiations on all cultural fronts for personal and national identities,"[71] mapped out conceptual fields, and opened up the possibility of constructing continuous histories, resulting in the concept of cohesive national cultures. Anthony D. Smith emphasizes the central role of lexicographers, philologists, and folklorists in the struggle for political and cultural self-identification: "By creating a widespread awareness of the myths, history and linguistic traditions of the community, they succeeded in substantiating and crystallizing the idea of an ethnic nation in the minds of most members."[72]

Literary revivals at the turn of the twentieth century drew their myth-making energies from opened-up repositories of history, folklore, and mythology of heroic ages; they integrated myth and actuality, producing a matrix for a future literary process. Yeats, who turned to Irish folklore, legend, and mythology in *Wanderings of Oisin and Other Poems* (1899) and initiated the Celtic Twilight, emphasized the importance of folklore for the realization of both nationality and literature.[73] He found mythic ways for the emerging poetic consciousness in Ireland to reenact "the ancient drama between artistic imagination and national allegiance."[74] The Yeatsian metaphor of twilight implying a diffused and obscured vision in literature's becoming reciprocates Lesia Ukrainka's image in "Досвітні

---

[70] John Hutchinson, *The Dynamics of Cultural Nationalism: The Gaelic Revival and the Creation of the Irish Nation State* (London: Allen & Unwin, 1987), 86.

[71] Betsey Taylor FitzSimon and James H. Murphy, eds., *The Irish Revival Reappraised* (Dublin: Four Courts Press, 2004), 14.

[72] Anthony D. Smith, *National Identity* (Reno: University of Nevada Press, 1991), 12.

[73] Kiberd, *Inventing Ireland*, 138–39.

[74] Ronald Schuchard, "The Legacy of Yeats in Contemporary Irish Poetry," *Irish University Review* 34, no. 2 (2004): 293.

34   MARYNA ROMANETS

огні" ("Dawn glow").[75] Not unlike Yeats's, Ukrainka's oeuvre "rememo-rizes" the climactic points of Ukrainian culture: medieval masterpieces with the elements of late Gothicism; Baroque mythic consciousness, with its emotionally tense feeling of the irrational; and cosmogonist *feriae* of folk culture. Both Yeats and Ukrainka's poetry and drama grew out of the tension between tradition and modernity, the idea of the regeneration of their cultures by an awareness of their past mythologies and practices that embraced a wider European context, the complex symbolism and shadowy beauty of Neoromantic sensibilities, and an understanding of the dark, submerged forces of the suppressed people. As iconic revival-ists, they transcend established boundaries by iconoclastically overlaying actuality, mythology, and history and by turning present reality into some-thing open, ponderable, and available for further revisions and interpre-tations. This is "a habit of mind" created, as Seamus Deane sees it, by the Revival "which found the conjunction between myths of the past and the actualities of the present an appealing structural device both in poetry and in fiction."[76] Both Ukrainian and Irish writers engaged in the (re)for-mulation and (re)signification of received traditions through radical inter-textual appropriations and transpositions, thus carrying on the process of cultural negotiations in which cultural differences between the metropolis and periphery became increasingly politicized.

The commitment of literature to the formation of a national con-sciousness, to the construction of nationhood and a nation-state identity, also offers similarities in both countries. Both literatures were involved in what Deleuze sees as the political task of art: the invention of "missing," "unborn" people, who, according to his concept of the revolutionary po-tential of minor literatures, were entering into the condition of becoming

---

[75]   Oksana Zabuzhko draws a brief parallel between Ukrainka and Yeats, alongside other modernist poets, related to their search for a new, "terrible beauty," in her *Notre Dame d'Ukraine: Ukraïnka v konflikti mifolohii* (Kyïv: Fakt, 2007), 461–64.

[76]   Deane, *A Short History*, 200.

and did not yet have a language[77] for enunciation. Deleuze and Guattari's *Kafka: Toward a Minor Literature* reveals the dynamics between "major" (mainstream, metropolitan) and "minor" (marginalized, peripheral) literatures and complex mechanisms, which force minor literatures—within imperial literary systems characterized by universalist preoccupations—into the sphere of politics:

> Everything in them [minor literatures] is political. In major literatures, in contrast, the individual concern (familial, marital, and so on) joins with other no less individual concerns, the social milieu serving as a mere environment or a background…. Minor literature is completely different; its crumpled space forces each individual intrigue to connect immediately to politics. The individual concern thus becomes all the more necessary, indispensable, magnified, because a whole other story is vibrating with it. In this way, the family triangle connects to other triangles—commercial, economic, bureaucratic, juridical—that determine its values.[78]

Deleuze and Guattari also state that everything in minor literatures takes a collective value, a collective utterance that constitutes an act of resistance and is positively charged with revolutionary, volatile energies.

Irish writers were fully aware of the ominous power of resurrected past in bringing the modern nation to a consciousness of itself. Kiberd writes that "[m]any exponents of Gaelic revivalism had remarked that their texts were even more potent than bullets and had been surprised that no attempt was made by the authorities to block their dissemination."[79] Irish cultural movement, followed by a political one, did culminate in the 1916 Easter Rising. Russian authorities were much more alert in this respect, fearing, for example, even the spirit of the dead. In 1914, they banned the centennial celebration of Taras Shevchenko (1814–

---

[77] Gilles Deleuze, *Essays Critical and Clinical*, trans. Daniel W. Smith and Michael A. Greco (Minneapolis: University of Minnesota Press, 1997), xlii.

[78] Gilles Deleuze and Félix Guattari, *Kafka: Toward a Minor Literature*, trans. Dana Polan (Minneapolis: University of Minnesota Press, 1986), 17.

[79] Kiberd, *Irish Classics*, 418.

1861),[80] whose politically subversive poetry made him a national icon and a symbolic substitute for tradition; he, very much like Yeats in Ireland, was a figure overshadowing the literary landscape far into the next century after he was arrested because of the revolutionizing power of his work and subjected to a particularly severe punishment—ten-year-long military service as a private in Asia, with a special order that he be forbidden to write, draw, and paint while in military exile.

Having provided a genealogically useful past for the Irish and Ukrainian people, the cultural initiatives of the nineteenth and the beginning of the twentieth century generated a process of cultural identification on the next turn of the spiral and inescapably overlapped with political and revolutionary developments, thus facilitating, in part, crucial sociopolitical changes, which present an almost identical chronological outline for both countries:

1916	Easter Rising, declaration of the Irish Republic;
1917	Bolshevik revolution in the Russian Empire, declaration of Ukrainian independence and the creation of the Ukrainian National Republic (UNR) in central Ukraine; 1918—establishment of the Western Ukrainian National Republic (ZUNR) in Galicia, northern Bukovyna, and Transcarpathia; 1919—act of union between the UNR and the ZUNR;
1918	Sinn Féin win the elections;
1919	Foundation of Dáil Éireann, the Irish Parliament;
1917–1921	Russian-Ukrainian War;
1919–1923	Anglo-Irish War;
1922	Anglo-Irish Treaty and the establishment of the Irish Free State, a dominion of the British Commonwealth, in the twenty-six southern counties of Ireland, "while

---

[80] S. Cherkasenko, "Z ukraïns'koho zhytia," *Literaturno-naukovyi vistnyk* 17, no. 65 (1914): 582–95.

leaving a self-governing northern statelet in the remaining six counties"[81]

1922   Establishment of the USSR by the Russian Federa-
            tion and the neighboring areas of its military occupa-
            tion: Ukraine, Belarus', and Transcaucasian Federa-
            tion. Although each of the constitutive republics for-
            mally had its own parliament and constitution that
            granted the right of secession from the Union, the
            domination of the refurbished Russian Empire in
            Ukraine lasted for another seven decades.

While Ireland successfully gained its independence and completely
severed its ties with the Commonwealth, declaring itself a republic in
1949, Ukraine tragically failed by falling to the Bolsheviks after a short
period of sovereignty, which was reclaimed only in 1991. The process of
breaking away from colonial control was traumatic for both countries.
Ireland experienced a painful partition of its Northern part, with bloody
and humiliating wounds inflicted by an aggressive enmity and hostilities
between pro- and anti-treaty forces. Robert Kee writes that the "division
of the civil war continued to scar Irish political life for nearly half a century. In the course of that half century, Ireland, or rather the greater part of
her, evolved into a totally independent sovereign republic, technically a
realization of all the most extreme nationalist had ever dreamed of."[82]
The formative processes of a nation state in Ireland were not so complicated by geopolitical factors as they were in Ukraine,[83] which was dis-
membered, fragmented, possessed, and repossessed by different states
for centuries, being divided between Muscovy and Poland from 1667, be-

---

[81]   Prem Poddae and David Johnson, eds., *A Historical Companion to Postcolonial
       Thought in English* (New York: Columbia University Press, 2005), 245.
[82]   Robert Kee, *Ourselves Alone*, vol. 3 of *The Green Flag: A History of Irish
       Nationalism* (London: Quartet Books, 1976), 174.
[83]   According to John Breuilly's classification, Ireland belongs to the reform type of
       state, with a "fit" between ethnic and state boundaries, while Ukraine belongs to
       the unificatory one, being fragmented between several states. See his *Nationa-
       lism and the State* (Manchester: Manchester University Press, 1982), 243, 250.

tween the Russian and the Austro-Hungarian Empires (after the partition of Poland in 1770s), and among the Soviet Union, Poland, Romania, and Hungary in 1918 until its Western territories were annexed by the USSR in 1939 under the Molotov-Ribbentrop pact.

Ireland, which was one of the earliest decolonized nations, has provided a blueprint for later developments in postcolonial cultural politics. In Ukraine, which finally became independent after the break-up of the Soviet Union, the processes of decolonization are still in the making; thus, it is a laboratory in which to explore the typology of decolonizing strategies, as well as the limitations of the current models of postcoloniality. Although politically liberated, Ireland and Ukraine are still bound—culturally and economically—to the colonizer. While Ukraine struggles to escape the steel embraces of the Russian "elder brother," trying to fight back its history and culture, the discussion of incomplete decolonization is still ongoing in Ireland.[84] Continued neocolonial influences in both Ireland and Ukraine are enhanced by their physical proximity to former metropolis—the British who suffer from the "Continent of Britain delusion" and the Russians who experience a perpetual imperial phantom limb syndrome. Both countries have to deal with the political consequences of colonization: the issues of Northern Ireland and those of the rift between Western (pro-European, Ukrainophone) and Eastern (pro-Russo-Soviet, Russophone) Ukraine that has been recurrently exploited by politicians, most ferociously during the 2004 presidential and the 2006 parliamentary campaigns. Today's continuing and painful process of identity-shaping involves countertendencies of both magnetic attraction and repulsion necessary to forge new definitions and configurations, which are routed through identitarian political and cultural discourses including literature.

Each essay in this book attempts to explore various lines of flight in inventing and reinventing such definitions and the broken traditions of people once stripped of history through an incessant dialogue with various precursor texts, many of which were recovered and rearticulated by

---

[84]   Howe, *Ireland and Empire*, 1.

cultural Revivals of the past. The works under study mark blank spots and interruptions, which otherwise cannot be filled, by constructing historiographic metafictions (Lina Kostenko), revising epic and mythology (Nuala Ní Dhomhnaill), rereading symbolic representations and *topoi* of literary conventions (Nuala Ní Dhomhnaill, Paul Muldoon, Seamus Heaney, Richard Murphy, Michael Longley, Ciaran Carson, and John Montague), inventing erotic narratives (Oksana Zabuzhko, Yuri Pokalchuk, Les Poderviansky, and Yuri Vynnychuk), and reemplotting "mad" intertexts as the sedimented consequences of colonialism (John Banville and Yuri Izdryk via Georg Büchner) while negotiating between reality and fiction, past and present, compliance and transgression, and creating a discursive space for enunciation, where the defacements of history are recast to make the future survivalable.

My analysis draws on the intersections of such analytical approaches as postcolonialism, representation, gender (cross-gender), intertextuality, and cross-cultural studies. In addition, I eclectically utilize a considerably flexible body of critical materials—history, folklore, mythology, philosophy, fine arts, and music—to serve my purpose as the texts under study resemble a radical system that forms a vast field for interpretive variants. Heterogeneous critical equipment allows for avoiding the dictatorial power established by the ultimate authority of a monotheory, which limits possible conceptual space by pretheorized reading. I am interested in the ways contemporary Ukrainian and Irish writers call into question the procedures of representation implemented by canonical traditions, as well as in gender dynamics of such revisionary endeavors in cases when traditionally male master texts are under the scrutiny of women writers; in the mechanisms of reshaping an entire territory within which signs and images circulate; and in the channels of cultural psychohistory which nourish them. I believe that the examination of convergences and divergences in several distinct cultures, combined with the study of gender differences within national cultural systems, contributes to an internationalizing of national situations in general and of minoritarian discourses in particular.

While attempting to position Ukrainian literature in a wider post-colonial context, my book delineates some of the aspects of the contemporary Ukrainian literary process aimed at resisting imperializing cultural systems. It might be instrumental in breaking through the exclusivity of critical practices which confine to inferiority and invisibility texts and traditions left out of hegemonic literary and critical discourses, as well as of postcolonial counterhegemonic critique which claims Third World countries as its special provenance. Furthermore, my approach opens up fissures in supposedly homogeneous European foundations by acknowledging varied histories and imbalances in power. Attractive though binary paradigms—center-margin / Europe-Third World—have been to some postcolonial theorists, the evidence suggests a more complex dialectic operating along a postcolonial continuum. I trust that my work expands the framework of postcolonial and gender studies and includes literally "liminal" spaces on the discursive postcolonial map.

Unlike Irish literature, which has been propelled into postcolonial critique by Edward Said's "Yeats and Decolonization"[85] and since has been steadily penetrating the secured borders of postcolonial studies within the last decade, although not without controversy,[86] Ukrainian literature has not yet been made visible in the field. In fact, it was Said who excluded the Russian Empire, with all of its colonies, from the range of his discussion because "[u]nlike Britain or France, which jumped thousands of miles beyond their own borders to other continents, Russia moved to swallow whatever land or peoples stood next to its borders, which in the process kept moving father and father east and south."[87] So

---

[85] Said, *Culture and Imperialism*, 220–39.

[86] For the debate about Ireland's colonial status, see Lloyd, "Ireland After History," 377–95; Howe, *Ireland and Empire*, 1–6; Glen Hooper and Colin Graham, eds., *Irish and Postcolonial Writing: History, Theory, Practice* (Basingstoke: Palgrave Macmillan, 2002).

[87] Said, *Culture and Imperialism*, 10. Moore critiques Said's explanation because it not only "excuses" Russian violent colonial enterprise by adjacence but also "grants odd primacy to water" ("Is the Post- in Postcolonial," 525). Moore's article emphasizes the necessity of breaking the silence of postcolonial studies on the subject of the former Soviet-controlled countries, as well as the necessity for

far, among the high priests and priestesses of the postcolonial canon, only Homi K. Bhabha once fleetingly referred to "the central European steppes."[88] It is not that the only driving force behind my argument here is either to expose Bhabha's geographic error or to reclaim the Ukrainian steppe from "central" Europe and return it to where it belongs, the southeast. Who would fight over a metaphor for void? However, I hope my book might contribute to the understanding of this and other of Ukraine's metaphoric "inscape[s] of national identity,"[89] to borrow Bhabha's phrase. The steppe is a territory that is traversed, a tangible, intricate, accumulated palimpsest on the cross-roads with multidirectional vectors of becoming, a place for the nomads to pass through, move on, and emerge as Persians, Anglo-Saxons, Celts, or Greeks, leaving visible and invisible traces. However, the trace of signifying chains, the "original"—prealphabetic, prelinguistic and prehistoric—has been disrupted and infinitely deferred under the multilayered inscriptions of myths and histories and is only looming like a ghost in the vast void of enormous, horizonless, open spaces of steppe and text.

---

scholars from these countries to conceptualize their condition in postcolonial terms.

[88] Homi K. Bhabha, "DissemiNation: Time, Narrative, and the Margins of the Modern Nation," in *Nation and Narration*, ed. Homi K. Bhabha (London and New York: Routledge, 1990), 291.

[89] Ibid., 295.

I   A Baroque Optical Fold:
Lina Kostenko's Phantasmagoria of Ukrainian History[90]

The fate of Marusia Churai, a legendary Ukrainian Baroque woman poet and singer, has been recounted throughout the nineteenth and twentieth centuries in numerous versions[91] and has led to the creation of a multi-layered cloak of myth, propagated both from within and without Ukraine. The specular reproduction of the story of fatal love, betrayal, witchcraft, revenge, and murder, brought to the surface by a romantic wave of Ukrainian Revival and monopolized by male authors, stimulated Lina Kostenko's imaginative history and was instrumental in her rethinking and reseeing the past (1979).[92]

Marusia became a symbolic progenitress for Kostenko, who was self-exiled into a sixteen-year-long silence, and was instrumental in restoring the poetic voice of her twentieth-century counterpart. In her recurrent dialogue with history and with various precursor texts, Kostenko resurrects the spirit of the "Ukrainian Sappho" to construct and reconstruct both national and personal symbolic lineages, as well as literary history.

---

[90]   I am alluding here to the Deleuzian operative concept of the Baroque as the Fold, the former being the infinite work or process, the latter being that which embraces material and immaterial folds, an expressive matter that determines and materializes form. See Gilles Deleuze, *The Fold: Leibniz and the Baroque*, trans. Tom Conley (Minneapolis and London: University of Minnesota Press, 1993), 14–38.

[91]   In 1839 the Russian playwright A. Shakhovskoi published a historical novella *Маруся—малороссийская Сафо* (*Marusia—Little Russian Sappho*), and in the 1880s a historical drama by H. Borakovsky appeared, *Маруся—українська піснетворка* (*Marusia—Ukrainian Bard*), followed by works by L. Borovykovsky, S. Rudansky, V. Samiilenko, B. Zaleski, K. Topolia, O. Hroza, A. Aleksandrov, P. Biletsky-Nosenko, I. Onopriienko-Shelkovy, M. Starytsky, O. Kobylianska, I. Mykytenko, L. Zabashta, V. Luchuk, and others.

[92]   Lina Kostenko, *Marusia Churai: Istorychnyi roman u virshakh* (Kyïv: Dnipro, 1982); hereafter cited parenthetically in the text.

Among her rewriting strategies is one of shifting from the frontal relationship with master texts to a displaced perspective; as in a Baroque anamorphosic painting, an image appears hidden beneath the apparent
amalgam of themes. Kostenko's Neobaroque text creates a martyr-drama (both of Ukrainian history and of Marusia's way to her Self) that
reveals the mechanisms of conversion whereby histories are erased but
resurface as symptoms on the colonized body politic to be reread, reinterpreted, and rewritten.

Preoccupation with history and memory runs through Kostenko's
oeuvre. In her lecture, *Гуманітарна аура нації або дефект головного
дзеркала* (*Cultural Aura of a Nation, or a Defect in the Main Mirror*)
(1999), Kostenko uses the metaphor of optical illusion to call attention to
the urgency of cultural self-determination in postindependence Ukraine.
She sees Ukrainians being still entrapped in a system of rhetoric and
representation that forces them to face sets of ready-made images
manufactured, hierarchically ordered, and imposed by colonial rule: "reverberations of old imperial mirrors, with flaking amalgam."[93] Her statement echoes James Joyce's unerring definition of the subservient identity
of the colonized as that being reflected in the "cracked looking-glass of a
servant."[94] Kostenko emphasizes a malfunction of the imperial optical
system that, on the one hand, causes the distortion and, on the other, if
one develops her metaphor further, ostensibly fixes the image of the
peripheral Other in a *trompe-l'oeil* mirror that offers a concocted "portrait"
of this abject degenerate otherness, designed to validate the metropolitan culture's superiority, both for domestic and worldwide use. The

---

[93] Lina Kostenko, *Humanitarna aura natsiï abo defekt holovnoho dzerkala: Lektsiia,
prochytana v Natsional'nomu universyteti "Kyievo-Mohylians'ka akademiia" 1 veresnia 1999 r.* (Kyïv: KM Academia, 1999), 31.

[94] Robert F. Garratt provides the following explanation of this metaphor: "Joyce's
apt image implies two fundamental problems of Irish literature: the distortion of
any reality caught in a cracked mirror and the servitude inherent in literature written for export to entertain foreign readers with Irish wit and humour" (*Modern Irish
Poetry: Tradition and Continuity from Yeats to Heaney* [Berkeley and Los Angeles: University of California Press, 1989], 11).

acceptance and internalization of this image by the colonized signifies the ultimate loss of subjectivity and identity and an advance towards what Jean Baudrillard calls "the subject of a mirror object" where what is supposed to be a surface of reflection turns out to be a bewitching surface of absorption, and the onlookers lose themselves in an illusory image that has "the irony of too much reality."[95]

For Kostenko the major task of Ukrainian intellectuals, in the aftermath of empire, consists in dismantling the deficient system of colonial mirrors, with their essentializing tendencies of representation, and in reclaiming agency and significance for people:

> The Ukrainians are a nation that has for centuries been under pressures forcing it out of existence.... It is a great miracle that this nation still exists today; it could have been leveled and could have disappeared long ago. As a matter of fact, we are a rarity, a nation that feels so lonely on its own land in its vast social space, and even lonelier in the cosmos of humanity. The phantom of Europe that, only by the end of the century, started to turn into something real for the rest of the world.[96]

Kostenko's work is concerned with refocusing the colonial readings of Ukrainian history, with making visible the experience which imperial historical accounts used to write off as extraneous, with tracing the extremities and atrocities of history, and with outlining counterhistory to intervene in the painful, colonially induced amnesia that marks contemporary Ukraine. Kostenko has her own version of history that has been articulated in an impressive body of poems[97] to culminate in another historical novel in verse, *Берестечко* (*Berestechko*) (1999), which deals with one of the most devastating tragedies in Ukrainian past: the battle at Berestechko (1651). The novel was written during the years of Kostenko's

---

95 Jean Baudrillard, *Seduction*, trans. Brian Singer (New York: St. Martin's Press, 1979), 61.

96 Kostenko, *Humanitarna aura*, 30.

97 "Drevlians'kyi tryptykh," "Liutizh," "Chadra Marusi Bohuslavky," "Kniaz' Vasyl'-ko," "Horyslava—Rohnida," "Chumats'kyi shliakh" in the collection *Nepovtornist'* (1980); and *Skifs'ka odiseia* (1983–1986) and *Duma pro brativ Neazovs'kykh* (1984), published in *Sad netanuchykh skul'ptur* (1987).

internal emigration (1966–1967) and turned into an ongoing project, being rewritten several times. Its apocalyptic vision of the last defeat is terrifying and translates into Kostenko's philosophy of history, defeat, and failure,[98] thus becoming a cautionary tale of history obsessively repeating itself and of the scars of the past making themselves felt in the present. In this, *Берестечко* (*Berestechko*) is both a sequel and prequel to *Маруся Чурай* (*Marusia Churai*) as they reciprocally reveal that any attempt to retrieve and repossess history will inevitably be haunted by that which can never be recovered.

Written at the ebb tide of the Ukrainian literary movement known as *shistdesiatnyky* (the generation of the 1960s), which signified a political thaw and enabled the emergence of works less restricted by censorship, *Маруся Чурай* (*Marusia Churai*) generated vast critical response. Numerous reviewers and scholars emphasize the historicity of the novel and point out that Kostenko's innovative approach consists of her refusal to limit herself to her protagonist's private life but to interweave it successfully into the sociopolitical situation of seventeenth-century Ukraine.[99] However, defining Kostenko's novel as exclusively historical leads to a considerable reduction of its scope, forces it into a strict discursive grid, and suggests a monocular reading. The poet's idiosyncratic polyvocalities, which undercut multiple deeper strata in rearticulating the symbolic meaning of appropriated and reworked texts, allow us to regard *Маруся Чурай* (*Marusia Churai*) primarily as a work of foundational fiction in postcolonial terms. Nonetheless, *Маруся Чурай* (*Marusia Churai*) also encompasses the characteristics of a philosophical novel, a *Künst-*

---

[98]   For a detailed analysis of the novel, see Oksana Weretiuk, "Filozofia porażki: Beresteczko Liny Kostenko," *Przegląd Humanistyczny*, 2006, no. 1: 123–36.

[99]   For example, V'iacheslav Briukhovets'kyi, *Lina Kostenko: Narys tvorchosti* (Kyïv: Dnipro, 1990), 152–182; Anatolii Makarov, "Istoriia—sestra poeziï," *Ukraïns'ka mova i literatura v shkoli* 10 (1980): 31–32; D. H. Struk, "The How, the What and the Why of *Marusia Churai:* A Historical Novel in Verse by Lina Kostenko," *Canadian Slavonic Papers* 32, no. 2 (1990): 156; D. H. Struk, "Istorychnyi roman Liny Kostenko," *Suchasnist'*, 1990, no. 5: 26–41; Volodymyr Smyrniv, "Istorychna poetyka Liny Kostenko," *Journal of Ukrainian Studies* 12, no. 2 (1987): 6; Liudmyla Taran, *Enerhiia poshuku* (Kyïv: Radians'kyi pys'mennyk, 1986), 108.

lerroman, a mythological novel, a psychological novel, an *Erziehungs-roman*, a romance novel, a social novel, or a criminal novel. I will argue that the essential difference in Kostenko's recomposed, reframed narrative consists in her reterritorialization of history. The narrative's many lines of flight, formed by heterogeneous elements, stretch in different directions and shatter the linear unity by their cyclicality. What surfaces in the process of Marusia's struggle through the experience of void, silence, and horror disturbs the ideological constructs of Soviet historiography, with its enforced celebration and glorification of the "reunification" of Ukraine with Russia (1654) aimed at blocking out any "separatist" ideas. This glossed myth of unity was both actively promoted as the focal point of the period (and the starting point of Ukrainian history proper) and relentlessly reduplicated in ideologically sanctioned heroic grand narratives, producing an institutionally regulated collective memory. However, imperfect erasures in the subaltern peripheral past form a basis for the production of alternative spaces of signification. *Маруся Чурай* (*Marusia Churai*) represents the return of the profoundly repressed tradition of the anonymous eighteenth-century *Історія Русів* (*History of the Ruses*), which was never published in the Soviet Union because of the explosive energies of its antiauthoritarian stance. Kostenko bends the straight line of imperial history, with its homogeneity of narratives and memories, into vicious circles to expose both its fictionality and the political dogma surrounding it. Her textual strategies go beyond the transparencies of subject matter by evoking Baroque culture, with its violent contrasts and contortions, as a contextual and conceptual framework for Marusia's history. The author conversely projects this culture, which was provoked all over Europe, as Maravall contends, by a social crisis of a major magnitude during the seventeenth century[100] and which represents one of the most turbulent periods in Ukrainian history, onto the present. Kostenko's text, which forms a rhizome with the world and concurrently deterritorializes it, refuses the assumption of a single focus, one that would

---

[100] José Antonio Maravall, *Culture of the Baroque: Analysis of a Historical Structure*, trans. Terry Cochran (Minneapolis: University of Minnesota Press, 1986), 24–29.

regard the "objective" reality of its operation. As if complying with the representational techniques of the period that was also "the great age of anamorphosis,"[101] Kostenko chooses the oblique angle, rejecting a frontal plane of "projection," to recapture and form anew the seventeenth-century poet's image. This disturbing Baroque aspect of her novel creates its magnetic field and assimilates the broken and diffuse vision into the real.

Kostenko presents a fundamental modification of master narratives,[102] for her text unfolds in a complex mosaic, starting with the moment of extremity, Marusia's trial, which is comprised of a polyphony of voices reconstituting Marusia's crime. The only figure that remains silent is the heroine herself, wrapped in her muteness that alienates her from the judges, the witnesses, the crowd, her factionaries, and ill-wishers. Marusia's silence makes her a figure out of context and at the same time the center of that context. She is under the "lethargic rays" of melancholia—"Black Sun," compelling one "to silence, to renunciation."[103] This sequence is structured by the exertions of Marusia's memory and its regressive and retrospective movement in depth. Her love story and isolated islets of her previous life surface during three nights in jail before the execution and form an intricate web of a multilayered interior monologue. The concentric narrative circles and the stratification of narrative perspectives, refracted in Marusia's recollections, delineate the claustrophobic space of her captivity.

---

[101] Peter C. Sutton, "Artificial Magic," in *Dalí's Optical Illusions*, ed. Dawn Ades (New Haven and London: Wadsworth Atheneum Museum of Art in association with Yale University Press, 2000), 34.

[102] The nineteenth-century master narratives presented this story of fatal passion in chronological order: Marusia and Hryts' fall in love; he departs and they are separated; he returns and betrays his beloved by marrying another woman; Marusia grieves; she makes up her mind to take revenge upon him by witchcraft; he dies by the poisonous drink prepared and administered by Marusia; she appears at the funeral ceremony and publicly confesses in the church; she is sentenced to death and is at the point of being executed; she is miraculously released because of the Hetman's interference; she repents and decides to go to the monastery.

[103] Julia Kristeva, *Black Sun: Depression and Melancholia*, trans. Leon S. Roudies (New York: Columbia University Press, 1989), 3.

In the opening stanzas related to the 1658 fire of Poltava when the city was burnt to the ground, the thematic leitmotif of the novel emerges: the loss of texts, documents, traditions, and continuities that make up the body of history. The key image of fire—intensified by references to burning, melting, flames, ashes, destroyed papers, municipal books and judicial registers, which, as Kostenko suggests, might have contained the case of Marusia Churai—sets up the intensity of the following narrative. Endless fires and their aftermaths produce a disturbed field of vision, which is dimmed by the obscurity of the centuries and by the film imprinted on the retina by recurrent outbursts of combustion. Fire becomes the substance that generates the revisionary impulse to embark on a symbolic detour to the past.

After Marusia's last-moment amnesty at the site of execution, Kostenko sends her on a quest journey to Kyiv. Utilizing the structure of quest in one of the segments of *Маруся Чурай* (*Marusia Churai*), Kostenko reenacts the geography of devastation caused by the lethal encounters between the invaders' violence and the counterviolence of the resisters. Her voyage induces epic horror, the contour of her discursive space being created by pestilence, plague, death, and blood. The landscape is inhabited by the spectral presence of the dead and tormented. Marusia is haunted by an apocalyptic vision of phantasmagoric candles, offered to some unidentifiable satanic power, to which she compares the colonnades of pales. This brief reference to the pales has far-reaching implications, familiar to all Ukrainians: pales were the instruments of diabolic torture in which a sharpened stick was forced up the anus, slowly causing death by tearing viscera as the impaled person slid down:

> Аж ген за обрій—далі, далі, далі!—
> Усе мені ввижаються ті палі.
> Над плином років, паростю ялин,
> жовтогарячим дивом горобин,
> ще й досі кості торохтять зотлілі,
> і на вітрах рукава лопотять,
> і чорні свити на козацькім тілі
> за вороннням ніяк не одлетять … (90)

> Far away over the horizon—further, further, further!—
> all the time those pales appear to me [as in a dream].
> Over the flow of years, sprout of fir trees,
> fire-yellow wonder of ash trees,
> even now decomposed bones are rattling,
> and in the winds the sleeves are flapping,
> and black cloaks on a Cossack's body
> cannot fly off after flocks of ravens ...

The visual endlessness of these sanguinary perpendicular forms, emphasized by the repetition, stretches far beyond the horizon of memory and time. Familiar objects of clothes, remnants of somebody/something that once was human, acquire arresting power, creating surrealistic images of deathly levitation. The conglomeration of a successive imagery of death, torture, and desolation supercharges the atmosphere to the point when it is no longer an actual journey from Poltava to Kyiv, but a descent into the Inferno, into a shadowy collapsed universe without God.

There is yet another textual dimension introduced by the dichotomy of the plane of nature—vibrant and beautiful—and the human stratum. This contrast runs throughout the novel and reveals Kostenko's pantheistic world-view, so explicitly expressed in Marusia's fundamentally pagan confession to the sun and in numerous descriptions of natural scenery reminiscent of the Baroque *topos ut pictura poesis*. Kostenko's landscapes also parallel an aestheticized richness typical of the luxuriant vegetative ornamentation of Ukrainian Baroque polygraphy, with its obtrusive desire to retain whimsical natural beauty and to infuse it into human spaces of the text. From this point of view, Kostenko's nature provides a contrasting frame in which a violently cut-in window opens onto a mute abyss of horror. In this, her discourse swings from one extreme to the other in its chromatic repertory, from the abundant color spectrum of nature to the almost monochromic representation of people. Such violent tension produced by colliding extremeness is seen by Maravall as a psychological action "closely bound to the assumptions and goals of the Baroque."[104]

The image of the candle, the generator of Marusia's macabre hallucinations, reappears again, reterritorialized from the metaphoric plane to a literal one. A mysterious shimmering in the distance creates an optical delusion; what Marusia thinks to be a yellow glowworm or the glimmering of moldy stumps belonging to the natural realm, at a closer look become the tokens of human existence—candles. The impulses of light are located in a complete darkness and void, and people are semi-alive. It is a mysterious Baroque game of playing intense light against very dark backgrounds, whose dramatic effect heightens the tragic meaning of the narrative. A possible encounter with warmth and light turns into a horrific encounter with near corpses lying on the grass. The whole area, and by extension, the whole country of unburied carrion becomes an open and enormous graveyard, with recurrent allusions to lifeless bodies, the smell of decay, and funeral rites:

> На жовті пальці обпливає віск.
> Обличчя гострі …
> Горять свічки.
> І сосни пахнуть ладаном. (98)

> On yellowed fingers wax is dripping.
> Faces [are] sharp …
> Candles burn.
> And pines smell of incense.

The vision is blurred and obscured by the restless disposition of glittering lights and shadows, whose theatrical use introduces motion into the Baroque-like scene, so that space becomes unlimited—"a broad and floating world"[105]—and extends into the dimension of time folding and unfolding it. Objects merge into one another, and one never knows exactly what or where anything is in this chiaroscuro of silence and candles. This is a moment of transition between visible and invisible,

---

[104] Maravall, *Culture of the Baroque*, 210.
[105] Deleuze, *The Fold*, 124.

death and life, as well as that which precedes death: a livid, vampiric sphere where specters, apparitions, and ghosts enshroud the atmosphere. The visible field is progressively extinguished to the minimal difference between black and black. A black invisibility erases everything, including the people in the liminal zone, on the frontier of life and death. The silence of the mortuary is disturbed by a minimalistic dialogue structured to parallel the minimalism of the color by incomplete sentences, whispered, stammered, and deformed diction, barely audible at the edge of the mutism of death.

After the terrors of Marusia's journey, Kyiv first appears in all its grandeur in a diffraction of sunlight from golden domes. Kostenko leads her protagonist from the state of momentary blindness that she experiences after the amnesty to a metaphoric recovery of sight which plays tricks, generating phantomlike, eclipsed visions. The city she sees is a mirage sharpened for an instant into *trompe-l'oeil* images, but when the anamorphic ghost disappears, she again encounters a gothic reversal of illusionary beauty, the gruesome reality of calamitous destruction. The landscape is emblematically unmasked and resolved in death; the whole scene is enveloped in silence. Marusia recurrently encounters empty spaces that were once inhabited but now are completely erased. She is haunted by the void. A mystical permanence of this recurrent ocular deception raises to the mythic level: hell, deprived of its counterpart, heaven, becomes the only point of fixation. Its only alternative is a mock paradise envisioned by the vagabond cleric, Marusia's fellow pilgrim on the way to Kyiv, an abandoned cemetery, the Garden of Eden of Hell, where Marusia and the old cleric are Adam and Eve (99). Kyiv is depopulated, suffocated in ashes after three days of infernal fire. Kostenko superimposes various perceptual registers, as if exploring the limits of the representable, their exchange producing condensed images. Marusia hears what she sees and smells what she hears. A pervasive suffocating smell of charred ruins, "із випаленою душею" (103, "with a burnt-out soul"), combined with the image of the lost moon, leafing half-burnt books with its cold finger (103), evinces an ambiguous lapse into time-lessness.

Marusia seems to move in concentric circles until she reaches the Lavra (the Kyivan Caves Monastery), which, with its intricate layout, is a city within a city, a labyrinth for the surrealistic wanderings of bodiless souls and soulless bodies, inhabited by its own fears, domineering and alienating. The Lavra is guarded by Brueghelian creatures—primordially enigmatic, disfigured, and distorted—which merge into the main gates to form a fanciful, fantastic Baroque design. These figures, elements of feverish hallucinations, are petrified shadows of pilgrims who endlessly stream to the Lavra. Some of them die on their way, while others occupy intermediate states in transition from human beings to quasi-material objects. The design of bodily assemblages replicates the whimsicality of the Lavra, situated not only on the surface but also in the depth of the ancient caves. In their impenetrable darkness, one finds oneself beyond life and death, and the bodies of pilgrims turn into ironic doubles of the mummified remains of canonized saints in the caves. This is a gruesome mirror reflection of the other world, of the world which is permeated with deadly stillness and silence, of the space of vertiginous catalepsy punc-tuated by a dash, a gasp, an aphasia: "Дзвіниця мертва—обгоріли кро-ни. / І все німе—і гори, і Поділ" (102, "The belltower [is] dead—the tree canopies have burnt away. / And everything is mute—both the hills and the lower town"). The toll of looted bells in the capital is substituted by a throbbing, primordial beat of a solitary gong. Kostenko's devoiced, deprived of bells Kyiv reciprocates Marusia's fortified silence as if all tragedies and traumas exceed articulation or as if Kostenko's poetics of aphasia emphasizes the limits of the recovery of unrecorded histories.

In general, the sounds of Kostenko's bells that come from every-where in Poltava are interwoven into a fugal composition of the novel. Their reiterated booming voice synthesizes an apocalyptic music through systematic melodic imitations and repetitions. These repetitions in the phonic textures and syntagmatic structures contribute to a metrical pulsa-tion characteristic of seventeenth-century Ukrainian *partesy*, polyphonic concertos. The mighty sounds of the bells put the whole world off balance through an alarming vibration of alliterative [dz]: "І дзвонять дзвони, / дзвонять, дзвонять дзвони …" (29, "And toll the bells, / toll, toll the bells …"). Kostenko's bells perform the function of *basso continuo* in the architectonics of the novel, which resembles the Monteverdian *stile concitato*, characterized "by rhythmic subdivisions of repeated notes" meant to evoke "agitation and terror."[106] This undercurrent in polyphonic structural dynamic is emphasized by Deleuze when he defines some of the principle traits of Baroque music, in his study of Leibniz, as "melody and counterpoint that change their nature (luxuriant counterpoint and continuo homophone); continuous bass, preparing or consolidating a tonality that the accords include and in which they are resolved, but also submitting the melodic lines to the harmonic principle."[107] The sound parallel to Baroque counterpoint that signified the departure from earlier pure linear melodic arrangements provides yet another module in Kostenko's conceptualizing the disjunctive history of Ukraine. The desired but unattainable harmony folds into a nearly deathlike calm in the world that no longer can be conveyed in sonorous accords; the sounds of the bells have almost been extinguished, but not completely. An eclipsed auditory motif is unfolded and refolded at the end of the novel: the feeble tolling of a graveyard church bell, the voice of the city still alive.

Kostenko's fugue of disaster perfectly matches her gothicized pictorial iconography. These elements form a split frame; on one side there is silence and a languageless presence, on the other, the voids of space and devastation. The buildings, open spatial structures that reach upwards and neglect the laws of gravity, are the only remaining witnesses of the tragedy. Mute survivors, they make up her ghostly cities and towns: "Лиш на валах необгорілі вежі / стирчать у небо. Попіл стережуть" (102, "Only on the ramparts, unburnt towers / jut into the sky. They guard the ashes"). There is hell wherever Marusia goes; terror is within

---

[106] Nicholas Anderson, *Baroque Music: From Monteverdi to Handel* (London: Thames and Hudson, 1994), 23.

[107] Deleuze, *The Fold*, 136.

and outside her, and she is magnetized on all sides by the terrific evil engraved in Ukraine's past and present and in her personal experience. Terrible hallucinations also reverberate in the death of her father, taken prisoner and executed with other Cossack officers by the Poles who ordered the decapitated heads to be placed on the pales at the regimental cities. The image of her father's head becomes obsessively haunting in a circling vortex of personified death, a twirling and hovering "страшна хуртовина" (35, "frightful snowstorm/tempest"), as uncontrollable as any natural phenomenon. Death appears in different masks and disguises, here as a blustering snowstorm, where snow is associated both with original mysteries of the distant and primeval night of the soul, and with the lunar world of nocturnal madness. Elsewhere in the novel, death wanders around with a bloody scythe (106). This, a fiery-scythed Death, multifaceted and blind,[108] is one of the favorite images both of Baroque writers and of Ukrainian folktales where Death is depicted as a skeleton with a sharp scythe, usually in feminine attire. The feminine as the image of death implies an ambivalent linking of life-giving and destruction that become interchangeable and blur in a chimeral, cataclysmal circular motion. The macabre pagan dance also has diabolic associations because in Ukrainian folklore, snowstorm and whirlwind are metaphorized as the weddings of evil spirits.[109] The dance comes to a dead point with the introduction of a Biblical allusion. Marusia's memories, choked with blood, thus acquire another dimension of horror because, as Annie le Brun suggests, "latent or manifest violence [is] contained in Christian imagery, whose depictions of torture, martyrdoms and crucifixions rival each other in intensity, inventiveness and realism."[110] Paganism and

---

[108] L. O. Sofronova, "Kyïvs'kyi shkil'nyi teatr i problemy ukraïns'koho barokko," in *Ukraïns'ke literaturne barokko*, ed. O. V. Myshanych (Kyïv: Naukova dumka, 1987), 114.

[109] V. P. Myloradovych, "Zametki o malorusskoi demonologii," in *Ukraïntsi: narodni viruvannia, povir'ia, demonolohiia*, ed. A. P. Ponomariova, T. V. Kosmina, and O. O. Buriak (Kyïv: Lybid', 1992), 417.

[110] Annie le Brun, *Sade: A Sudden Abyss*, trans. Camille Naish (San Francisco: City Light Books, 1990), 15.

Christianity become woven together, stretching the poetic connotations into prehistoric times:

> Танцює, хижа і п'яна,
> Льодистими сережками трясе.
> Як голову криваву Іоанна
> Над білим світом Іроду несе ... (35)

> She dances, ravenous and drunken,
> shaking icy earrings.
> As if carrying John's bloody head
> Across the wide/white world to Herod ...

Furthermore, the images of predatory violence, a severed head and Herod, are also reminiscent of the conceptual and thematic repertoires of the European drama of tyranny and of the Baroque martyr-drama, with its sufferings, torments and physical agony. As Walter Benjamin argues in *The Origin of German Tragic Drama*, these two genres are always interrelated and hidden in each other. Herod, presented throughout seventeenth-century European theatre as the embodiment of the tyrant,[111] becomes one of Kostenko's structural images, reappearing in the poem "Був Ірод, і була Іродіада" ("There was Herod, and There was Herodias"), where Salome, intoxicated by blood, performs her terrifying, licentious dance.[112]

Horror becomes inescapable in the doubling of the external and internal. In Lubny, Marusia witnesses the signs of past disaster, the focal figure of which is Yarema Vyshnevetsky (Jeremi Wiśniowiecki) (1612–1651). He has become an icon of monstrosity in Ukrainian history for persecuting the Ukrainian Orthodox population and for suppressing the 1637 Cossack rebellion with unprecedented cruelty, particularly in Volyn. Kostenko describes him as "упир з холодними очима" (88, "a vampire with cold eyes") who paved his way with corpses and marked it with pales. Vyshnevetsky's cruelty matches that of Vlad Tepes the Impaler

---

[111]   Walter Benjamin, *The Origin of German Tragic Drama*, trans. John Osborne (London: NLB, 1977), 70.

[112]   Lina Kostenko, *Nepovtornist': Virshi. Poemy* (Kyïv: Molod', 1980), 160.

(1431–1476), the legendary count Dracula. Reference to vampires and to impaling, Dracula's favorite torture method, makes this parallel more substantial. Such "dark assemblages," co-functioning by contagion, stir, as Deleuze and Guattari state, what is deepest in human being: "becoming-animal"; the entire multiple becomings "spread contagion. There is a complex aggregate: the becoming-animal of men, packs of animals, elephants and rats, winds and tempests, bacteria sowing contagion. A single Furore. War contained zoological sequences before it became bacteriological. It is in war, famine and epidemic that werewolves and vampires proliferate."[113] Again, the image of the instigator and master of bloody ceremonies and orgies of decapitation, spreading horror like an infectious disease, is correlated with a biblical reference to Judas (91). Similarly, in the reference to pales, Kostenko fuses the terror of an unparalleled and persistent torture and the image of God, Vyshnevetsky's private God of Evil who has turned everything into a horrifying void. A boundless dread, still visible and felt, is engraved in the memory and in the landscape, in a sweeping enumeration of tortures and a monotonous repetition of "карав" ("tortured"). Such a reiterative pattern becomes recurrent in the novel; it sounds like an endless, rhythmic incantation expressive of a sinister inevitability under the spell of evil, with death inscribed in the mechanized drive of repetition.

The scene is laid among the terrestrial wounds of ruins which bridge the past and the present, delineating the temporal and historical movement down the axis to death and destruction. Painfully decipherable messages from bygone days, the ruins are set against the background of wild vegetation, which is untouched by the eroding hand of time and constantly regenerates in this fearful setting of human haematomania and decay. Once again Kostenko superimposes the natural onto the human in a striking metaphor, "козацьких тіл кривавий живопліт" (90, "a bloody hedge of Cossacks' bodies"), and inhibits her landscape of terror

---

[113] Gilles Deleuze and Félix Guattari, *A Thousand Plateaus: Capitalism and Schizophrenia*, trans. Brian Massumi (Minneapolis: University of Minnesota Press, 1987), 242.

with the restless soul of Vyshnevetsky's mother, Raina, sobbing and wailing among the ruins. A strange, hypnotic, almost homonymic relationship exists between *руїна* [ruïna] (ruin), *Раїна* [raïna], the tyrant's mother, and *Руїна* [ruïna] (the Ruin), the name for the late seventeenth-century period of Ukrainian history characterized by the disintegration of statehood and general decline.

Kostenko's historical vectors are projected both into the bloody past and no less bloody future, combining *before, during,* and *after.* Continuously displacing her narrative through disjunctive forms of temporal representation, Kostenko initiates a strategy of repetition that disperses the homogeneous, linear time. In her meditations on her native city, Marusia goes far back into history. She moves into the tragic depth of the lethal flight of Polovtsian nomadic arrows and the devastation of the Tatar-Mongol invasion to the times of Lithuanian grand duke Vytautas (1350–1430), who prayed to his own gods, and of the alien king Sigismund Vasa (1566–1632); through the reign of the "executioner" Jeremi Wiśniowiecki; to Bohdan Khmelnytsky (1595–1657), who guided the Ukrainian popular uprising against Poland. All these waves of violence became genetically encoded in the organism of the city to develop a capacity for regeneration: rebirth from ashes and continuous resurrection. At the moment of Marusia's meditations, Poltava's freedom is threatened—the city is again under siege. Marusia's visions, in which the demarcation lines between the real and the imaginary blur, are materialized in the disposition of those who besiege the city. Ghosts from hell, they appear to become the symbols of the satanic lusts found in human cruelty, rapacious shadows in purple reflections of fire (128).

Alongside the flashback technique, Kostenko uses flashes forward, *parabasis*, a disruption of the time continuum when the authorial voice interrupts the narrative to address the reader.[114] Kostenko inserts textual retardations, which act as enhancements in her infrastructure of time,

---

[114] Tejaswini Niranjana, *Siting Translation: History, Post-Structuralism, and the Colonial Context* (Berkeley, Los Angeles, and Oxford: University of California Press, 1992), 95–96.

during Marusia's trial. These stoppages introduce different characters and events: Lesko Cherkes, who tries to fight the injustice of the court with his saber, will perish on the Don; colonel Pushkar's head will be given to Vyhovsky on a spear seven years later; fearless Ivan Iskra will die while returning from a diplomatic mission to the Muscovite tsar (22). All of these allude to what will happen in the future, after the "reunification" with Russia, adding yet another chapter to the history of failures accompanied by ferocious suppression of Ukraine's national movement. Such systematic use of violence efficiently implemented tactics of terror that were aimed at achieving control for several centuries.

Another essential plot line in Kostenko's representation of history is the character of the nameless vagabond cleric and philosopher who becomes Marusia's guide and mentor on the way from Poltava to Kyiv. He provides the historical retrospective and interpretation for Marusia's experience and contributes to her revelations and enlightenment. He brings together the past and the present and is himself both a seismograph of history and a symbol of its tragic unrecorded transitoriness. "А хто напише, або написав, / велику книгу нашого народу?!" (93, "And who will write or has written / a great book of our people?!") is the question that forms the articulatory axis around which his discourse revolves. The Word, the building block of history, is the one constant of his numerous speculations structured on strings of negations that culminate in "Неназване, туманом пойнялося. / Непізнане, пішло у небуття" (94, "Unnamed, it has been obscured by fog. / Unrecognized, it has gone into nonbeing"). These fusions of variously configured negative grammatical forms reflect history's confinement to the inevitability of oblivion. The cleric's own manuscript, in which he tries to address this question and has invested years of his life, has been stolen. He reiterates the idea that Ukrainian history is engraved into the landscape and embodied in ballads and songs expressed earlier in the novel in Khmelnytsky's amnesty. The songs become relevant instruments of historiographic survival when everything else is subjected to amnesia and annihilation:

> Історії ж бо пишуть на столі.
> Ми ж пишем кров'ю на своїй землі.
> Ми пишем плугом, шаблею, мечем,
> піснями і невільницьким плачем.
> Могилами у полі без імен,
> дорогою до Києва з Лубен! (94)

> For histories are written at a desk.
> But we write with blood on our land.
> We write with plough, saber, sword,
> with songs and slave lament.
> With nameless graves in the field,
> along the road to Kyiv from Lubny!

The cleric's extended metaphors produce the effect of seventeenth-century patristic writing, which blends Biblical style with the rhetorical tradition of late antiquity. His speech abounds in aphoristic symbols, in Biblical allusions, and in parallels to ancient Greek and Roman history and mythology, which are combined with anaphoric constructions and rhetorical questions. His Biblical references are worded by traditional, elevated stylistic clichés and by transpositions of Old Slavonic lexis, producing a mixture of the alien and the familiar. Such lexical shifts between Middle and Modern Ukrainian create what Douglas Robinson calls an "authoritative word."[115] Further stylistic similarities with Ukrainian Baroque rhetoric are enhanced by antithetic structures both within a single figurative unit and on the semantic level of the cleric's discourse. When the cleric goes through the hagiographic sanctuary in a *Patericon* of the Kyivan Caves Monastery, he establishes the iconoclastic juxtaposition of ecclesiastically authorized saints with the brutal actuality of the lives of uncanonized martyrs to create a parable of Ukrainian history in his own martyrology. Although the migrant philosopher is one of those schooled at the Academy, his perception of the world is close to that of writers representing a tradition of "low Baroque," which developed the genre of burlesque poetry as a reaction to the official ecclesiastic litera-

---

[115] Douglas Robinson, *Translation and Taboo* (DeKalb, Illinois: Northern Illinois University Press, 1996), 118.

ture.[116] This tendency is explicit in the cleric's visualizing of the cemetery as the Garden of Eden and in his caustic explanations in the caves of Lavra while he and Marusia are observing sacred remains. His preoccupations with the matters of "this world" also indicate his opposition to the elitist "high Baroque" poetry whose poetic methods caused a particular cultural point of view: the world appearing to acquire a somnambulistic character far out of reach. However, in their highly conditional and ideal forms comprised by mythologemes, philosophical abstractions, exotic toponyms, allusions, symbols, extended metaphors, and parables,[117] the words, according to the cleric, are dead because professional poets "складають віршики святочні, / а в селах ридма плачуть кобзарі" (92, "compose ceremonial verses, / and in the villages, *kobzari* lament violently"). Here Kostenko's rhetorical strategy is consistently structured on a binary basis, constantly swinging between opposites and extremes: low vs. elitist, written vs. oral, sound vs. silence. Her cleric presents a "reversed translation" of mythologized texts, firmly anchoring them in the land where even the voice shouting in the wilderness would have seemed to be more audible than in Ukraine. The devastated land needs voice and naming; it needs a Word. The cleric, himself anonymous, having appeared from nowhere, disappears into the void like a figment of the imagination.

The reverberations of a tragically disharmonious Baroque world, sounded by Kostenko, are not limited to the character of the cleric. Khmelnytsky's proclamation of Marusia's amnesty contains direct intertextual references to seventeenth-century literature and literary theory. The Hetman's comparison of Marusia's songs to multiprecious pearls evokes the title of Kyrylo Trankvilion-Stavrovetsky's (?–1646) book *Перло многоцінноє* (*Pearl Multiprecious*) (1646), and his allusion to "земні марноти" (81, "earthy vanities") reflects the pathetically tragic Baroque experience of *vanitas*. Moreover, while analyzing the cleric's character,

---

[116] Anatolii Makarov, "Krasa barokko," *Khronika 2000: Ukraïns'kyi kul'turolohichnyi al'manakh*, 1992, no 1: 100.

[117] Ibid., 90–95.

Viacheslav Briukhovetsky notes that the cleric's "seditious faculty" is close to the "spirit of freedom and restlessness" of Hryhori Skovoroda[118] (1722–1794), indefatigable wanderer, the last philosopher and writer of the late Ukrainian Baroque. Kostenko's affinities with Skovoroda reveal themselves in her collection *Сад нетанучих скульптур* (*The Garden of Unmelting Statues*) (1987), which includes a poem-dialogue, set during a chimerical walk through time of the poet and a stone figure of the philosopher (similar to Marusia's and the cleric's journey through history). This establishes a supratextual relation with Skovoroda's *Сад божественних пісень* (*The Garden of Divine Songs*) (1785), the book which sums up the development of the *topos* of the garden, one of the key images of Ukrainian poetry at the end of the sixteenth to the middle of the seventeenth centuries and also one of Kostenko's recurrent images, where all later depositions are superimposed upon the Baroque *florilegium*.

The cleric's stories summon numerous historic phantoms onto a ghastly stage. Affected by his tragic vision of Ukraine's past and present, Marusia appropriates the epic *Пісня про Байду* (*Song About Baida*) and thus reenacts the heroic death of the Volynian prince Dmytro Vyshnevetsky (Baida) (?–1563), the first Cossack hetman and the founder of the Zaporozhian Sich. Kostenko establishes an historical continuum by resurrecting Yarema Vyshnevetsky's glorious ancestor who was captured by the Turks during one of his military campaigns and put to an atrocious death in Istanbul by Süleyman the Magnificent (1495–1566). Kostenko's Marusia actualizes and remodifies the ballad. The scene in her version is already laid, not in Istanbul, but in Poltava, and the order to execute Baida's exhumed apparition, who has decided to descend from Heaven to see how his family in the third generation are doing, is given, not by the Oriental despot, but by his perversely cruel descendent, Yarema Vyshnevetsky. Kostenko's is an exact replica of the death order in the original epic and logically concludes Yarema Vyshnevetsky's gallery of mutilated corpses in the cleric's history. This piece is an imaginative

---

[118] Briukhovets'kyi, *Lina Kostenko*, 173.

reconstruction of Marusia's creative process. When Kostenko uses Marusia Churai's actual ballads, she does so subtly, introducing them in reported speech, interweaving phrases of Marusia's songs into her text so that they are organically blended into the novel.

Against a wider historical perspective, Marusia establishes her own lineage, her individual prehistory through her father. The spectral vision of his decapitation punctuates the narrative. His death provides a bloody landmark in counting off the time against the background of all the calamities and becomes iconic, for the insane raging of ultimate power, which was pushed to the extreme, followed an inviolable ritualistic pattern: torture, death, dismemberment, and public exhibition of body parts.[119] His death also becomes an impulse to an essentially new turn in Marusia's development as a poet. The associative row of her memory includes the performance of a ballad about Hryhori Churai by a minstrel, a *kobzar*, in Poltava. At the moment the song starts, Marusia grows dumb; this muteness will come upon her again and again, forming a paradigm for her voice to be able to find its expression in a metaphoric simile based on a binary, contradictory, oxymoronic logic which fuses dumbness and voice to characterize Marusia's state: "як той німий, що в камені кричить" (44, "like that mute who shouts in the stone"). Metaphorically signifying her death drive as a Freudian return to the inorganic state, Marusia's condition is simultaneously presented as a moment of revelation, an insight caused by pain, suffering and, ultimately, sorrow. Marusia is thus led to the realization of the eternity of the Word, with which her silence was pregnant, by which it was awoken, and in which it reverberated, the Word that ultimately ensures her own long-lasting afterlife.

The tragic rhythm of death and resurrection is captured in the scene of Marusia's execution, which becomes her *rite de passage*. Kostenko does not traditionally place the scaffold in the public square but carries it out to the void of the steppe that is a distinct marker of Ukraini-

---

[119] *Istoriia Rusiv*, trans. Ivan Drach (L'viv: Atlas, 1991), 97.

an national topography. It is the site of Zaporozhian free lands, furrowed with toponymic reminders of Cossack victories and defeats, and with numerous burial mounds since Scythian times. It is a peculiar and chimerical steppe, a recurrent symbolic image of Ukrainian poetry since time immemorial. Its open space is a zero territory, the territory of Marusia's initiation and becoming and the starting point of her quest journey. In addition to the specifically Ukrainian cultural implications of the steppe, Marusia's violent expulsion unto death is staged according to archetypal sacrificial scenarios, which traditionally included, according to René Girard, the public exposure of criminals, sometimes accompanied by a procession through the streets of the community; significantly, criminals had to be displayed "at the frontiers of the country."[120] In Ukrainian history, the steppe used to be literally the frontier region, the war theatre for the defense from Tatar and Turkish raids.

The steppe is also an ideal setting for Kostenko's drama of phantasms, for its haze makes things rise and fall and people levitate as if suspended on a rope. A horizon of Marusia's solitude and her transcendence, the steppe becomes the vantage point that mesmerizes and magnetically attracts people. The instinctual drive of the crowd in the novel is intertextually related to Kostenko's earlier poem "Брейгель. Шлях на Голгофу" ("Brueghel. The Road to Golgotha"), a textual conversion of Brueghel's passions, where Kostenko constantly juxtaposes the visual exteriority of a spectacle-thirsty mob and the tormented interiority of Maria Magdalene, the Mother of God, and the poetic persona. Similarly, in *Маруся Чурай* (*Marusia Churai*), the populace forms a procession to the gallows floating in the steppe like a ghost, "оті ворота в небуття" (76, "those gates to nonexistence"). The gallows are no longer paraphernalia for execution but become the symbol of tragic continuity—an explicit parallel to Christ's crucifixion, on a universal level, and to the fate of Marusia's father, on the personal. The scene acquires a ritualistic sense: the flat horizontal plane of the steppe, pierced with the sharp

---

[120] René Girard, *Violence and the Sacred*, trans. Patrick Gregory (Baltimore: John Hopkins University Press, 1979), 298.

verticality of the gallows, can function as a "mythic operator," in the sense of Levi-Strauss, in Marusia's becoming the object of sacrifice in an almost chthonic rite where, as Girard writes in *Violence and the Sacred*, the "woman qualifies for sacrificial status by reason of her weakness and relatively marginal status. That is why she can be viewed as a quasi-sacred figure, both desired and disdained, alternately elevated and abused."[121] The reaction of the crowd in Kostenko's novel matches the above statement in that Marusia's upward movement against the petrified line of people arouses confusion, the polarity of clashing attitudes, and a sense of witnessing something much larger in scale than the capital punishment of a murderous witch (79).

One of the key points in the execution scene is Khmelnytsky's proclamation of amnesty. As Leonid Kaufman explains, two nineteenth-century versions of Marusia's release exist. On the one hand, Shakhovskoi asserts that Marusia was granted her life because the Hetman took into consideration the execution of her father by the Poles in Warsaw. A. Shkliarevsky, on the other hand, asserts that the amnesty was very much influenced by her songs.[122] Kostenko combines these two versions while creating the lost document that becomes the site of the hybridity of histories. However, her imaginary text extends far beyond the proposed limits, starting with the preamble that stylizes the manner in which documents of the time were written and establishing a completely different frame of reference from those suggested in the existing master narratives. Kostenko's proclamation refracts and focuses many of the novel's tenors, embracing both a devastating historical situation and the poet–song–national spirit–history relationship. Indeed, Kostenko regards the songs as documents of unrecorded history and symbolic repositories of national identity:

> Про наші битви—на папері голо.
> Лише в піснях вогонь отой пашить.

---

[121] Ibid., 141–42.

[122] Leonid Kaufman, afterword to *Divchyna z lehendy: Marusia Churai* (Kyïv: Dnipro, 1974), 103.

Таку співачку покарать на горло,—
то це ж не що, а пісню задушить! (81)

About our battles the paper is bare.
Only in songs does that fire blaze.
To execute such a singer by hanging her—
is no less than strangling a song!

The violent metaphor of strangled song here imposes a new accent, which becomes recurrent in Kostenko's reflections on her own poetic voice: "часом я—це мовчання задушеної вільної людини"[123] ("sometimes I am the silence of a strangled free human being"). What formally was a just verdict turns into judicial murder, into murder of poetry and murder of history, because silence does not have history. Kostenko's choice of the type of death penalty—death by hanging (other authors use decapitation)—adds to the symbolic order she constructs since hanging is the type of death met in various initiation myths.[124] The Ukrainian archaic expression used by Kostenko, "покарати на горло" ("execute by the throat"), which is synonymous to hanging, refers directly to the organ where the sound is produced and where it can be extinguished. The expression implies suffocation, which is murderous to sound; death occurs at the site of voice, an absent signifier in Marusia's silence. The verdict to put Marusia to death by hanging, which was supposed to be the most merciful execution, turns out, in this particular context of song–singer, to be much more maleficent than the brutality and spectacularity of decapitation. Besides, the vertical axis of the gallows (as opposed to the horizontal one of the scaffold) intensifies the association with the

---

[123] This phrase comes from Kostenko's talk at the roundtable discussion of her work at the Kyiv-Mohyla Academy in 2005 and was used as a title for the account of the event in *Vechirnii Kyїv*. See Oleksandr Balabko, "Lina Kostenko: 'Chasom ia—tse movchannia zadushenoї vil'noї liudyny,'" *Vechirnii Kyїv*, March 23, 2005, http://www.vechirka.kiev.ua/article.php?id_article=3461 (accessed February 11, 2007).

[124] Eva Cantarella, "Dangling Virgins: Myth, Ritual, and the Place of Women in Ancient Greece," in *The Female Body in Western Culture: Contemporary Perspectives*, ed. Susan Rubin Suleiman (Cambridge, Massachusetts, and London: Harvard University Press, 1985), 61.

cross/crucifixion and with the place of martyrdom. Kostenko thus adds another dimension to her visual vertical lines of crosses, poles, and pales, among other elements of death's heraldry in her tragic iconography, which play the role of markers of historical and textual continuity in the novel and provide for its rhythmic divisions.

Kostenko's quest voyage, with human sacrifice and tortures staged by the head-hunters of Ukrainian history against the background of a gigantic spatial void, is undertaken in the dark and infernal regions of the sensibilities of *genre noir.* This descent into Hell—into the subterranean depth of horror—ultimately becomes both an initiation and a quest for immortality. Marusia constantly feels the breath of death on her shoulders during her pilgrimage; she earlier confronts death without dying but by almost crossing the line between the world of the living and the world of the dead and only miraculously escaping punishment by death. She descends into the "Kingdom of the Night," as Mircea Eliade writes elsewhere, and reemerges alive.[125] This is the act of creation of the Self, which begins quotidian time acquiring another, historical dimension. Kostenko lets loose the knot of official historiography, releasing the destructive demons of chaos. She positions her history in a multidimensional and fluid space, enlarged and complicated by the back-and-forth, up-and-down spatiotemporal scale, which is not homogeneous but contrapuntal, running counter to an official progressive "March of History." In Kostenko's novel, the historical web is inhabited by the protagonist, who is connected to it by different strings: genealogical, poetic, emotional, and national.

The evocation of the Baroque passion of signs through motifs, images, and modes of representation is an essential moment that distinguishes Kostenko's novel from numerous utilizations of the legend. Baroque "wanderings of poetic imagination" between real and imaginary worlds are deprived of stable temporal and spatial significations. This

---

[125] Eliade suggests that the pattern mentioned here is characteristic of both the initiation rite and the quest for immortality (*Symbolism, the Sacred, and the Arts* [New York: Crossroad, 1986], 9).

global and universal continuum, wavelike or cyclic time, is similar to Kostenko's spatiotemporal strategies, which are alien to analytical fragmentation of the world. Alongside intricate ornamentation and the ornate eulogies of Baroque poetry, an inclination to somber poetics appears, signifying the presence of something "dark" in all the spheres of human existence, which becomes palpable in Kostenko's tragic rhythms of history. While defining the distinctive features of Ukrainian Baroque, Anatoli Makarov suggests that the combination of the elitist and the popular, characteristic of Ukrainian cultural tradition in general, was initiated during the Baroque period when professional poets, who wielded skilful poetic techniques but did not have access to printing presses, migrated into the domain of anonymous folklore.[126] Does Marusia Churai's fate as a poet reflect this state? Although throughout the nineteenth and early twentieth centuries the reality of her existence was not in dispute, Soviet scholarship, which was preoccupied with purposeful and ideological "objectivity" based on historical evidence, considered her to be "a fruit of the previous century writers' and poets' imagination," a combined character created by folk fantasy.[127] With all the constitutive complexities of her life and historical background, the "Ukrainian Sappho" has been transformed into a ghostly reflection looming in the twilight zone between reality and fiction and displaced to the realm of romance, which denies her positioning in an "official" history.[128] Marusia Churai's categorical negation by

---

[126] Makarov, "Krasa barokko," 93.

[127] Kaufman, afterword, 85.

[128] In postindependence Ukraine, a number of publications attempting to prove the existence of Marusia Churai appeared; among the most recent ones, see, for example, El'vira Zahurs'ka, "Lehendy pro Marusiu Churai: Pravda i domysly pro ukraïns'ku narodnu poetesu," *Den'*, December 16, 2006, http://www.day.kiev.ua/1 74196/ (accessed February 11, 2007); Mykhailo Stepanenko, "Kolo Marusi Churai: Trahedia bezsmertnoï ukraïnky," *Den'*, January 27, 2007, http://www.day. kiev.ua/176126/ (accessed February 11, 2007). In addition, the city of Poltava built the monument to their famous cocitizen in 2005 to celebrate the 375th anniversary of her alleged birth. However, Marusia Churai still retains the status of a legend in Ukrainian literary history; see Valerii Shevchuk's fundamental two-volume work on the Ukrainian Baroque, *Renesans. Rannie baroko*, vol. 1 of *Muza Roksolans'ka: Ukraïns'ka literatura XVI–XVII stolit'* (Kyïv: Lybid', 2004),

certain critics manifests, on the one hand, recognizable tendencies in the Soviet ideological practices that denied any continuity in the Ukrainian literary process prior to the nineteenth century outside the framework of folk culture. On the other hand, this refutation reflects distinctively misogynistic attitudes in society, resulting in the positioning of a woman author in the anonymous domain of folklore and, thus, exiling her to a "fossilized" cultural zone, to the periphery of peripheral literature. In Kostenko's novel, which invigorates and revitalizes collective memories, the power of mighty words that have passed unnoticed within the oral tradition is transformed into the power of the written text.

Furthermore, Ukrainian Baroque literature was either completely ignored, underestimated, misrepresented, or treated with considerable suspicion by Soviet literary criticism under the influence of its sociological critical dogma, derived straight from the nineteenth century, that denounced the "political deafness and unlimited egotism" of Baroque clerical writers.[129] An even more ideologically subversive role was assigned to Ukrainian Baroque architecture, which has long been regarded as a symbol of the separate entity of Ukraine and as a repository of national sentiments. Thus, in 1800, the Russian tsar Paul I prohibited building cathedrals in the "Ukrainian Baroque style,"[130] and in the 1930s, Baroque buildings (many of them associated with the symbolic name of Mazepa) were systematically destroyed because such architecture "was conducting anticommunist work."[131] The exquisite beauty of Ukrainian Baroque edifices also corrupted the purity of the designated colonial monuments of achievement. Stephen Slemon analyzes the symbolic significance of the monuments of Empire thus:

> [C]olonised cultures must always remain uninscribed.... [T]heir cultural acts of self-definition and resistance, are written out of the record; and in the process, subjugated peoples are "troped" into

---

107; and *Rozvynene baroko. Piznie baroko*, vol. 2 of *Muza Roksolans'ka: Ukraïns'ka literatura XVI–XVIII stolit'* (Kyïv: Lybid', 2005), 459, 686.

[129] Anatolii Makarov, *Svitlo ukraïns'koho baroko* (Kyïv: Mystetstvo, 1994), 220–21.

[130] Zalizniak. "Ukraïna—Rosiia," 6.

[131] Makarov, *Svitlo ukraïns'koho baroko*, 225.

> figures in a colonial pageant, "people without history" whose capacity to signify cannot exceed that which is demarcated for them by the semiotic system that speaks for the colonising culture.[132]

The simple fact that Kostenko handled Baroque material in the Soviet Union was a challenge in itself but was ultimately so elusive that Soviet ideology and class-blocked criticism did not even notice it.

In Kostenko's novel, the employment of the frame of a solar year (the novel begins in summer and progresses through autumn and winter to spring), with its periods of bloom, decay, and rebirth, synchronizes human and natural energies, establishing a pattern of rotation and creating the text's narrative rhythm. The recurrent return is also duplicated in textual circular structures through repetitions, both paradigmatic and syntagmatic; in circlings, which provide points of stability in cosmic chaos; in framing by textual blocks; in the recurrence of small textual units, phrases and separate words; and in an alliterative rhythm. These elements comprise a total structure of significance, which is reflected in the mythic mode, and also represent what Bhabha terms "a specifically postcolonial performance of repetition,"[133] simultaneously regenerating the phonic umbilical cord with the orality of Marusia Churai's poetry.

Marusia's metaphoric voyage is envisioned as a displacement in space, which is doubly obscured by history and legend. Thus, the "projective past," whose symbols start functioning as the "sign" of the present, emerges and introduces, according to Bhabha, a "necessary split between the time of utterance and the space of memory. This 'lagged' temporality is not some endless slippage; it is a mode of breaking the complicity of past and present in order to open up a space of revision and initiation."[134] While (re)writing history, Kostenko poses the problems of national memory, of the split identity and its distorted character under the colonial status, and of the traumatic experience of unrecorded his-

---

[132] Stephen Slemon, "Monuments of Empire: Allegory/Counter-Discourse/Post-Colonial Writing," *Kunapipi* 9, no. 3 (1987): 5.

[133] Homi K. Bhabha, "Freedom's Basis in the Indeterminate," *October* 61 (1992): 50–51.

[134] Ibid., 57.

tory. Her reclaimed text breaks through systematically cultivated amnesia and collective lapses of memory enhanced and manipulated by the repressive regime. The writer thus deprives imperial historical metanarrative of its authority by constructing a competing story that points to the fact that history is narrativization and not an "objective" truth. While placing Marusia Churai in heterogeneous contexts and writing her into tradition and history, Kostenko establishes her own poetic lineage, picking up the loose end of the line of Ukrainian women's literature to keep it going.

II   A Convexo-Concave Vision:
Nuala Ní Dhomhnaill's Cú Chulainn Cycle

"The Irish Renaissance had been essentially an exercise in translation, in carrying aspects of Gaelic culture into English, a language often thought alien to that culture,"[135] writes Kiberd in *Inventing Ireland*. Evocatively exploring and appropriating an entire literary tradition, with its former glories and pagan energies, the Celtic Twilight was forging a new, Anglo-Irish literary identity by incessantly meandering between the two cultures. Certain scholars seem to celebrate the contemporary merger of the Anglo-Irish duo, stating that "[t]wo cultural traditions once separate have become blended and hybridized, with artists in particular moving freely back and forth across linguistic and cultural boundaries, creating and configuring their individual patternings and amalgams from the varied and rich cultural fields they inherit."[136] Nuala Ní Dhomhnaill, however, has a much less optimistic view of Ireland's bilingualism and of both poetic mobility and visibility within an ambivalent Irish cultural matrix that is characterized by asymmetrical power relations: the inter-crossings and frictions between Anglo-Irish cultural mainstream and literature in Irish, which is relegated to opaque zones of peripherality.

Ní Dhomhnaill chooses to write in Irish, a minoritized language in Ireland whose status she defines as "precarious" in her aptly titled article "Why I Choose to Write in Irish, The Corpse That Sits Up and Talks Back."[137] Together with this language of awesome beauty and infinite tonalities, she has inherited contrapuntal symbolic territories of the Gaelic tradition, with its multilayered psychohistorical and sociocultural patterns deposited in literature. While commenting on years spent in the library

---

[135]   Kiberd, *Inventing Ireland*, 624.
[136]   Tymoczko and Ireland, eds., *Language and Tradition*, 20.
[137]   Nuala Ní Dhomhnaill, "Why I Choose to Write in Irish, The Corpse That Sits Up and Talks Back," *The New York Times Books Review*, January 8, 1995, 3.

and studying ancient Irish manuscripts, she mentions that this material works for her on two levels:

> First is when I revel in the well-turned phrase or nuance or retrieve a word that may have fallen into disuse. To turn the pages of these manuscripts is to hear the voices of my neighbours and relatives—all the fathers and grandfathers and uncles come to life again. The second interest is more thematic. The material is genuinely ineffable, like nothing else on earth.[138]

The poet's dialogic engagement with the Gaelic tradition, released from multiple layers of amnesia and aphasia, represents one of the constitutive trajectories in the heterogeneous, often conflicting lines of flight in present-day Irish culture, charged with the violent history of colonial rule, continuous struggles against the powerful historical dysfunctions of society, and the formation of a variegated social imaginary in the face of empire. A writer of enviable emotional intensity and range, Ní Dhomhnaill makes the past flow through the present by evoking the seductive powers of Gaelic culture to produce new conjunctures. In the process, she surveys a vast array of contemporary textual production by subversively deploying its transmigrating imagery, motifs, and tropes. Conceptualized by Kiberd as "an *Irish* translation of the Irish past,"[139] her poetic

---

[138] Ibid., 28.

[139] Kiberd, *Inventing Ireland*, 626. Kiberd suggests that Ní Dhomhnaill's English-language translators were captivated by her seditious and dynamic reimagining of Gaelic tradition and translated her work "in order to derive from the experience a sense of greater abandon in the presence of Gaelic material" (ibid., 602–603). Here Gaelic culture seems to function, for translators, as a phantom limb, or rather a phantom body, palpable, painful and irrevocably lost, and this sense of loss entices them into negotiating between what Spivak calls "the trace of the other" (the foreignness of Irish) and "the trace of the other in the self" (the recovery of its nativeness through the act of translation) (*Outside in the Teaching Machine* [New York and London: Routledge, 1993], 179). Kiberd's idea of intralingual translation, however, seems to position Ní Dhomhnaill's poetry as an interim copy of Gaelic "originals"—the specter of specters in the Irish-language shadowland—to be further encoded in and assimilated into the target language idiom and culture. From this point of view, the bilingual editions of Ní Dhomhnaill's poetry provide another page in the metaphoric "translation" of Ireland; in the process, the island's two languages have been unremittingly "ghosting" each other (Michael

reverberations that involve an exuberant interplay along both synchronic and diachronic axes destabilize culturally recognizable significations and open up the possibility for further iconoclastic readings and meanings.

In contemporary Irish cultural politics, a virtual warfare between the sexes, deeply rooted in literary tradition, has been transposed onto the plane of representation, having thus become a battle between oppressive and subversive representational codes. Ní Dhomhnaill lays siege to certain traditionally masculinist strongholds founded on a cultural pattern of the male/female dichotomy by recomposing and reassembling master narratives and themes. She calls into question the tired, distinctive division of male and female spheres of influence expressed in the conceptual metaphor, "marriage is to the woman what war is to the man,"[140] which seems to epitomize cultural consensus on the issues of dominance of men over women and, correspondingly, masculinity over femininity. This division reflects a "universal" construct of gendered power dynamics in patriarchal societies where, as Sam Keen writes, "[h]istorically, the major difference between men and women is that men have always been expected to be able to resort to violence when necessary. The capacity and willingness for violence has been central to our self-definition. The male psyche has not been built upon the rational 'I think; therefore I am,' but upon the irrational 'I conquer; therefore I am.'"[141]

Ní Dhomhnaill launches an offensive against one of the most prevalent myths, the aggressive myth of nationalist masculinity, by going back to male/female rivalry in Celtic mythology, with its warrior cult representing virility that is inspired, protected, and ruined by the female, belligerent supernatural powers—the war-goddesses. Ní Dhomhnaill summons fierce, militant women of the pagan past endowed with "aggression, blatant sexuality, a tendency to speak their minds, and a habit of

---

Cronin, *Translating Ireland: Translation, Languages, Cultures* [Cork: Cork University Press, 1996], 4).

[140] Deleuze and Guattari, *A Thousand Plateaus*, 236.

[141] Sam Keen, "The Rite of War and the Warrior Psyche," in *Gender Images: Reading for Composition*, ed. Melita Schaum and Connie Flanagan (Boston and Toronto: Hougton Mifflin Company, 1992), 617.

tossing spears at men."[142] The poet incongruously appropriates *Táin Bó Cuailnge (The Cattle Raid of Cooley)* saga and sets her counternarratives in motion through systematic misrepresentation of the foundational text. In her Cú Chulainn cycle,[143] mythology is dismantled from within its own structures and is changed from something fixed to something modifiable and endlessly open. By perusing the discursive field within which the Cú Chulainn myth continues to operate, Ní Dhomhnaill engages in a combative relationship with the canonical text. Her redirected reflections of cultural image systems disturb conventional spaces of representation, and the reconfigured collages of assorted stereotypes contain disruptive possibilities of anamorphoses.

The retrieval of the Cú Chulainn figure by contemporary writers has essential ramifications. Spellbound stories about his legendary feats comprised the core of revivalist cultural enterprise, drawing on the Cú Chulainn heroic paradigm that allowed for identifying with the ferocious martial hero who "glorified both individualism and action on behalf of the tribe."[144] By employing Cú Chulainn as a symbol, late-nineteenth- and early-twentieth-century cultural nationalists "sought to contrast a new essentially Irish identity"[145] with the one from the colonial past. Featured prominently in the inventory of revivalist icons, Cú Chulainn personified the mythos of Gaelic militaristic masculinity and thus played a significant role in identitarian politics. The latter is related, primarily, to the restitution

---

[142] Lisa M. Bitel, *Land of Women: Tales of Sex and Gender in Early Ireland* (Ithaca and London: Cornell University Press, 1996), 212.

[143] I term a number of Ní Dhomhnaill's conceptually coherent poems this way to allude to the Yeatsian famous cycle of plays about Cú Chulainn. Ní Dhomhnaill's cycle includes: "Labhrann Medb" ("Medb Speaks"), "Cú Chulainn I," "Cú Chulainn II," "Agallamh Na Mór-Riona Le Cú Chulainn" ("The Dialogue of the Great Queen with Cú Chulainn"), "Labhrann An Mhór-Rion" ("The Great Queen Speaks"), and "An Mhór-Rion ag Cáiseamh na Baidhbhe le Cú Chulainn" ("The Great Queen Berates the Badhbh to Cú Chulainn"), published in her *Selected Poems / Rogha Dánta*, trans. Michael Hartnett (Dublin: Raven Arts Press, 1988).

[144] Maria Tymoczko, *Translation in a Postcolonial Context: Early Irish Literature in English Translation* (Manchester: St. Jerome Publishing, 1999), 79.

[145] Elizabeth Frances Martin, "Painting the Irish West: Nationalism and the Representation of Women," *New Hibernia Review* 7, no. 1 (2003): 31.

and reinvention of Irish "manliness" by cultural nationalists in order to counterpose a widely spread colonial strategy of representing colonized males as effeminized and the Irish in general as an "essentially feminine race."[146] Cú Chulainn's hypervirility became instrumental in contesting the reformulation of the colonial power dynamics in terms of already existing gender relations because it provided a perfect model for historicizing Gaelic manliness. While examining internalizations of the discourse of colonial masculinity by the Irish nationalist movement, which resulted in the resurgence of a physical and quasi-militaristic culture, Kiberd explains:

> Cuchulain provided a symbol of masculinity for Celts, who had been written off as feminine by their masters. A surprising number of militant nationalists accepted that diagnosis and called on the youth of Ireland to purge themselves of their degrading femininity by a disciplined programme of physical-contact sports. The Gaelic Athletic Association had been founded in 1884 to counter such emasculation and to promote the game of camán (hurling) beloved of the young Cuchulain.[147]

The proponents of the new nationalism had taken up the warrior ideal of manliness with vigor, for such a conception of masculinity seemed indispensable to national survival. David Cairns and Shaun Richards see a direct connection between the revival of the Cú Chulainn cult of heroic acts, which suggests violence, confrontation, and rivalry, and the compulsion to forge and ensure the stability of Irish hypermasculine identities through enforcing women's subaltern status.[148] This may explain why "many nationalist groups, including the parliamentarians and the Ancient Order of Hibernians, were determined to resist the enfranchisement of women."[149] Although the campaign launched by the proponents of wom-

---

146 David Cairns and Shaun Richards, *Writing Ireland: Colonialism, Nationalism and Culture* (Manchester: Manchester University Press, 1988), 46–49.

147 Kiberd, *Inventing Ireland*, 44.

148 David Cairns and Shaun Richards, "Tropes and Traps," in *Gender in Irish Writing*, ed. Toni O'Brien Johnson and David Cairns (Milton Keynes, Philadelphia: Open University Press, 1991), 131–32.

149 Ibid.

en's suffrage succeeded, and the 1922 Constitution granted women full voting rights, Éamon de Valera's Constitution of 1937 redefined woman's role "in purely maternal and domestic terms."[150] Whereas one may argue that Article 41 of the Constitution could be read as the acknowledgement of the importance of women's household work and the assertion of their right not to work outside the home, the ban on married women in the professions and the repressive laws with respect to deserted wives, widow's allowances, and the rights of single mothers severely limited women's freedoms.[151] In addition to utilizing the colonial homology between sexual and political dominance, Irish nationalism, similarly to its counterparts in other decolonizing countries, "authenticated itself through female custodians of spiritual domesticity."[152] This attitude has augmented the promotion of certain cultural patterns and meanings, as well as the duplication of conventional male poetic models of a submissive womanhood, and the advancement of idealized representations of Irish woman "as the vessel of the race."[153]

In the context where male dominance has become a pervasive cultural, psychological, and social phenomenon, the concept of female sovereignty becomes one of the focal points in Ní Dhomhnaill's assertion of her poetic identity. The writer, whose primeval, hypnotic poetic world is populated by the phantoms of eternal goddesses, earthy passions, furious desires, cruelty, tenderness and frank sexuality, fights "éiric atá míle uair / níos luachmhaire, mo dhínit"[154] ("for an honour-price / a thousand times more precious— / my dignity," 111). In an interview with Dominic Larkin, Ní Dhomhnaill explains the incentives of her creative impulses: "I wrote a lot of those poems out of states of extreme rage. And I think that

---

[150]   Kiberd. *Inventing Ireland*, 403.

[151]   Ibid., 403–404.

[152]   Leela Gandhi, *Postcolonial Theory: A Critical Introduction* (New York: Columbia University Press, 1998), 98.

[153]   Martin, "Painting the Irish West," 32.

[154]   Ní Dhomhnaill, *Selected Poems / Rogha Dánta*, 110; hereafter cited parenthetically in the text.

the level of rage is part of feminine experience of our time."[155] Hers is the rage of the writer who holds "the opposites together" to create the pressures explicit both on the thematic level of the text and in its lexico-semantic composition.

Ní Dhomhnaill bridges the temporal abyss between Irish mythology and the present in "Labhrann Medb" ("Medb Speaks"). The poem, which is the author's negotiation of her relationship with her ancestors, deepened and widened by the introduction of an entirely new vantage point, ultimately demythologizes and reshapes traditional myth. Ní Dhomhnaill uses mythological thematic textures, assimilating past and present, herself and Medb, the Great Queen, and the Badhbh, who make their prophetic utterances ingraining fear and destruction in their male adversaries. In "An Mhór-Rion ag Cáiseamh na Baidhbhe le Cú Chulainn" ("The Great Queen Berates the Badhbh to Cú Chulainn"), the most liminal of the Morrigán poems that becomes a nexus of values significant to the poet, Ní Dhomhnaill leaps back and forth from ancient atrocities to a casual conversation on the phone between the Badhbh and the Great Queen; Ní Dhomhnaill's calamitous Badhbh keeps swelling corpses under her bed and maneuvers in high heeled slippers through the heaps of bones. Likewise, when Ní Dhomhnaill makes Cú Chulainn toss stones at passing trains in "Cú Chulainn II," her past and present, myth and reality, play a shuttle game, shifting so fast that it is difficult to say which is more real. She creates her personal continuum primarily by manipulating the existent conceptualization of time and by intentionally colliding multiple temporal layers. After the crash, a pluridimensional, atemporal universe appears, in which past, present, and future coexist simultaneously. Ní Dhomhnaill's deliberate confusion of different spatiotemporal laminations erodes the epic tradition and reduces its sacred values by fastening the shadows of the glorious past onto modern routine and, thus, removing them from a distanced horizon to a zone of maximal proximity and familiarity. In his analysis of the constitutive features of the epic as a genre,

---

[155] Nuala Ní Dhomhnaill, "Dominic Larkin Interviewing Nuala Ní Dhomhnaill," *An Nasc* 3, no. 1 (1990): 26.

Mikhail Bakhtin says, "the represented world of the heroes stands on an utterly different and inaccessible time-and-value plane, separated by epic distance."[156] Ní Dhomhnaill radically restructures and violates mythic boundaries and crosses various limits and thresholds; she contemporizes the "absolute" past of goddesses, gods, and heroes, finished and closed in a circle; and represents it, to use Bakhtin's phrase, "on a plane equal with contemporary life, in an everyday environment, in the low language of contemporaneity."[157] Such parodic stylization of canonized characters and events makes Ní Dhomhnaill's poems revisionist travesties—a simulacrum of an heroic paradigm; although her images circulate in the epic milieu, she desecrates them by annihilating epic distance. By representing the traditional myth in a contemporary setting, the poet dislocates its truth-value and adopts the powers of representation by miming them against themselves.

"Labhrann Medb" ("Medb Speaks") starts with a bold line that is looted from the *Táin* and is repeated verbatim or with minor lexical variations, continually recharging itself by circulating within the poetic structure:

> Fógraim cogadh feasta
> ar fhearaibh uile Éireann ... (110)

> War I declare from now
> on all the men of Ireland ... (111)

This line becomes the element of a syntagmatic repetition in the verse structure. The initial statement of the first stanza, "Fógraim cogadh" ("War I declare"), encircles it with the last line, which contains an insertion of an emphatic epithet—"is fógraím cogadh cruaidh feasta" ("a terrible war I will declare")—to express the speaker's determined and everlasting enmity. The next stanza opens similarly with "Fógraím cath gan truamhéil" ("Merciless war I declare") and ends—"is fógraím cath gan

---

[156] Mikhail Bakhtin, *The Dialogic Imagination: Four Essays*, trans. Caryl Emerson and Michael Holquist (Austin and London: University of Texas Press, 1981), 14.
[157] Ibid., 21.

truamhéil orthu" ("a merciless war I will declare"). The last stanza syntactically repeats the first: "Tabharfad fogha feasta" ("I will make incursions") and, correspondingly: "is fógraím fogha fíochmhar feasta" ("I will make fierce incursions"). The repetition also provides a rhythmic frame by means of its cyclic recurrence of position. It plays both a metronomic and a semiotic function by emphasizing particular lexical units through their occurrence in identical metrical positioning.

The key words "cruaidh" ("terrible"), "gan truamhéil" ("without pity"), and "fíochmhar" ("fierce") modify this war for dignity against male aggression on female pride. The framing by repetition creates an intensive lyrical and semantic exertion. Its strict rhythmic organization opens the poem's pattern and puts it in perpetual motion of constant departures and arrivals, rotating around its conceptual, emotional, and semantic stem, "Fógraim cogadh" ("War I declare"). Paradoxically, the repetition, with its inevitable restriction of lexical elements, appears to be a means of liberating and opening the poetic structure. Simultaneously, it provides an invariant frame that contains variable actualities causing Medb's crusade. It encompasses the joint between past and present, whereby the present takes up and repeats the past and functions as the locus of temporal intersections and conceptual tensions. Medb's adversary is "all the men of Ireland," regardless of their age, a generic male whom Ní Dhomhnaill calls elsewhere *Masculus Giganticus Hibernicus*. The poet attacks this symbol of hypermasculinity consistently promoted by militant nationalists who, since the Revival, "emulated the muscular imperial ethic with their own Cuchulanoid models."[158] She also declaims an instrumental view of women traditionally regarded as sites of contest and, in this particular case, of sexual conquest, and to take it further—rape. The latter association is elicited by the reference to honor-price, a specific term pertinent to rape in the Early Irish legal apparatus, which had to be paid as a penalty by a rapist not to the victim but "to the highest-ranking man

---

[158]   Kiberd, *Inventing Ireland*, 44.

in the tribal or familial unit to which the woman belongs."[159] Moreover, the rapist was liable only in the case of what was classified as forced rape, and if the woman was not perceived as having resisted enthusiastically enough, she had to repay her husband the bride-price and his honor-price as well.[160] Reworking the scene of national epic, Ní Dhomhnaill mingles the existing codes by making Medb claim a traditionally male prerogative, her honor-price. Interestingly, Medb led the *táin* against Conchobor mac Nesa, the king of Ulster, who was one of the first of Medb's royal consorts. When she left him for another husband, an avenging Conchobor stalked her en route to the feast of Temair and raped her.[161]

Turning to Medb, the queen of Connacht, Ní Dhomhnaill shifts the emphasis of the battle for property rights in the *Táin* to a wider sphere where Medb figures prominently as a female voice for independence and sovereignty, for she is at war with men over the issues of mastery, submission, and control. The poet's insurgent Medb rebels against the subordinate position of women in Ireland. She negates the patriarchal code, once mythologically established by, among others, heroic acts of Cú Chulainn, "who checks / sword with shield / for cattle and women."[162] The idea of the abduction of women is a part of a male warfare scheme in which sexual domination of the female symbolically stands for aggression and conquest, penetration of a woman's body mirroring penetration of a weapon into an adversary's flesh. Women and cattle, both as material and symbolic prizes for victory, are interlinked through the text of the *Táin*, and the pairing of "cows and women" is reiterated from different perspectives—in Ailill's address to Fergus (161), in Cú Chulainn's report

---

[159] Lisi Oliver, "Forced and Unforced Rape in Early Irish Law," in *Proceedings of the Harvard Celtic Colloquium, 13, 1993*, ed. Barbara Hillers, Pamela Hopkins, and Jerry Hunter (Cambridge, Massachusetts: Harvard University Press, 1993), 98.

[160] Ibid., 103.

[161] Bitel, *Land of Women*, 214.

[162] The *Táin*, trans. from the Irish epic *Táin Bó Cuailnge* Thomas Kinsella (Oxford: Oxford University Press; Dublin: Dolmen Press, 1969), 159; hereafter cited parenthetically in the text.

to Conchobar (113, 265), or in the passage wherein "the women and maidens and half the cattle" are sent to the hero (endn. 121, 266). Ní Dhomhnaill's rejection of such status for women is expressed decisively through an anaphoric structure:

"ach le teann fearaíochta" ("but showing off with pride")

(stanza I);

"ach iad ag lorg iarraim cúis" ("but them looking for a chance")

(stanza II);

"ach éiric atá míle uair" ("but for compensation that is a thousand times")   (stanza III).

The syntactic anaphora, like one of concentric circles, is embraced by the overall parallelism of war imagery. The pattern is based on the opposition introduced by "ach" ("but") and is concluded in both semantic and grammatical negation:

is ní tarbh a bheidh á fhuadach,
ní ar bheithígh a bheidh an chlismirt ... (110)

not just to steal a bull
not over beasts this battle ... (111)

Ní Dhomhnaill's war for dignity has deeper connotations in the sociopolitical situation where Irish women have been experiencing the curtailment of their rights since independence. The strategy of employing sharper polarization between masculinity and femininity and between the spheres of men and women's activities resulted in the political marginalization and constitutionally sanctioned domestic subordination of Irish women well into the late twentieth century. Until the reemergence of the women's movement in the 1970s, which culminated in the divisive divorce and abortion nationwide referenda of the 1980s, the issues related to women's social status and roles in Irish society were not widely discussed. The outcomes of the 1980s referenda indicated no changes in public views; they upheld the ban on divorce and upgraded abortion from illegal to unconstitutional.[163] In the second divorce referendum in 1995, the proposal to end the sixty-year-old constitutional ban on divorce won by the "narrowest of margins."[164]

Running counter to the promoted gospel of domesticity, "Labhrann Medb" ("Medb Speaks") establishes a revisionist frame of reference for "Cú Chulainn I"; "Cú Chulainn II"; "Agallamh Na Mór-Riona Le Cú Chulainn" ("The Dialogue of the Great Queen with Cú Chulainn"); "Labhrann An Mhór-Rion" ("The Great Queen Speaks"); and "An Mhór-Rion ag Cáiseamh na Baidhbhe le Cú Chulainn" ("The Great Queen Berates the Badhbh to Cú Chulainn"). These poems make a sequence in which Ní Dhomhnaill places the precursor text into continuous variation. The latter three deal with Cú Chulainn's encounters and ambiguous relationship with the Great Queen, the Morrigán, who incites violence and bloody combats between men. The war-goddess, Phantom Queen, Queen of Demons, is multifaceted and combines different aspects, being closely associated with destruction, fertility, and sovereignty.[165] Though Thomas Kinsella writes in the introduction to his conjectural English translation of the *Táin* that "the greatest achievement of the *Táin* and the Ulster cycle is the series of women, some in full scale and some in miniature, on whose strong and diverse personalities the action continually turns,"[166] he sometimes compresses and abridges the text in cases that are considered to be interpolations in the earlier narrative. This is what happens to the Morrigán. In Kinsella's version, she arrives unidentified: "Cúchulainn beheld at this time a young woman of noble figure coming toward him, wrapped in garments of many colours" (132). Compare this very

---

[163] Mary O'Connor, "Breaking the Rules: Nuala Ní Dhomhnaill's Language Strategies," in *Cross-Addressing: Resistance Literature and Cultural Borders*, ed. John C. Hawley (New York: State University of New York Press, 1996), 74.

[164] Anthony Breadley and Maryann Gialanella Valiulis, eds., *Gender and Sexuality in Modern Ireland* (Amherst, Massachusetts: University of Massachusetts Press, 1997), 275.

[165] Miranda Green, *Celtic Goddesses: Warriors, Virgins and Mothers* (New York: George Braziller, 1996), 41–43.

[166] Thomas Kinsella, introduction to *The Tain*, trans. Thomas Kinsella (Oxford: Oxford University Press; Dublin: Dolmen Press, 1969), xiv-xv.

modest appearance with the Morrigán's spectacular show in Lady Gregory's version, *Cuchulain of Muirthemn*: "a chariot, and a red horse yoked to it, and a woman sitting in it, with red eyebrows, and a red dress on her, and a long red cloak that fell on to the ground between the two wheels of the chariot, and on her back she had a grey spear."[167] The enchanting seductress is persistently marked by the royal red of both passion and otherworldliness, of love and of death. Unlike Kinsella and Lady Gregory's versions, in which the Morrigán's discourse is curtailed, Ní Dhomhnaill's "Agallamh Na Mór-Riona Le Cú Chulainn" ("The Dialogue of the Great Queen with Cú Chulainn") presents a discourse of supreme authority and empowerment. The Morrigán's vocabulary of power is established by a functional lexical net of synonyms for the semantic nucleus "tire" ("country"). The Morrigán comes to Cú Chulainn as a goddess of sovereignty in whom the internal and external landscapes coincide:

> le go mbronnfainn ort cumhacht
> agus flaitheas tíre,
> an dúiche inmheánach
> ina hiomláine,
> críocha uile an anama
> i nóiméad aimsire,
> a bhforlámhas uile
> is a nglóir siúd
> mar is ar mo láimh a tugadh é
> chun é a bhronnadh
> ar cibé is áil liom.
> Thugas chughat mo sheoda
> is mo chuid eallaigh. (116)

> to grant you power
> and kingdoms
> all the internal country
> all the territory of the soul

---

[167] *A Treasury of Irish Myth, Legend, and Folklore: Fairy and Folk Tales of the Irish Peasantry*, ed. William Butler Yeats; *Cuchulain of Muirthemne: The Story of the Men of the Red Branch of Ulster*, trans. Lady Isabella Augusta Gregory (New York: Avenel Books, 1986), 555.

> in one second
> power over all this
> and much glory
> for it was given to me
> to bestow on whom I wish
> I brought you jewellery
> and chattels. (117)

The Goddess offers to confer kingship on her prospective consort. Ní Dhomhnaill's Morrigán is a stunning beauty, as opposed to the traditional, well-known symbols of sovereignty: repulsive, futile hags, inhabiting the stories of early Ireland, who needed a royal aspirant to have sex with and thus be transformed into gorgeous young women.

Ní Dhomhnaill manipulates the double-valenced power of the Goddess, combining her generative agency and destructive agency, the erotic and the horrific, by giving prominence to either of the divine aspects. The Morrigán also reappears in disguise in an erotically explicit "Dúil" ("Desire"). The poet does not reveal her character's identity, thus creating zones of ambiguity, only to resolve the ambivalence at the end of the poem by the act of naming, "Mór ar lár" (30, "Mór is down," 31). However, this disclosure is still not complete, for the name pulls a string of associations: the Mór of the poem, placed in extratextual context with Ní Dhomhnaill's constant warping between the present and Irish mythology and legends, may acquire a number of ancient doubles. First of all, it is Mór, the Mór-Ríon (the Great Queen), unruly Mór, with excessive sexual desire, who is uncontrollably hatching in "Mór Goraí" ("Mór Hatching"). Next, there is Mór Muman, a hag who turns into an astounding beauty after spending the night with a king. Then there is Mór of Munster whom Proinsias Mac Cana indirectly equates with the sovereignty deity by comparing her to Medb of Connacht.[168] This Mór is the queen of the province of females. Ní Dhomhnaill thus slides down the temporal axis to the primeval world and the place of origin. All this provides an extended network of multiple connotations, implications, and possible interpreta-

---

[168] Proinsias Mac Cana, *Celtic Mythology* (London: Hamlyn, 1970), 120.

tions in her pluridimensional spaces. Thus, the present and prehistoric past close up, and the sexualities of a modern speaker and her archetypal counterpart are matched. Ní Dhomhnaill's outspoken sensuality and her recurrent allusions to the Irish goddesses of sovereignty, associated with fertility, contradict the iconic use of women by cultural nationalists as "signifier[s] of moral purity and sexual innocence."[169] Catherine Nash suggests that such signifying use of women—alongside the continuous use of the notion of Ireland as female, against which male poets assert both personal and national identities—endorses "their erosion from Irish history, and their contemporary silencing"[170] and facilitates the control over women's body by the state and the Catholic church.

The multifaceted nature of Ní Dhomhnaill's goddesses is accompanied by their potential polymorphism. This quality also manifests itself in the fluidity of her poetic landscape, for shape-shifting occurs on different levels of her texts: in images, in voices, in structures, and in concepts. The Morrigán—the greatest transmogrifier among Ní Dhomhnaill's deities—can transform herself both along the bipolar temporal axis (young beautiful maiden—hideous old hag) and along the species line (an eel, a grey wolf, a hornless red heifer, a crow, a raven). It is noteworthy that the war-goddess undergoes further transformations in later folk tradition, reappearing in a changed form. As Bríona Nic Dhiarmada writes, "[t]he Goddess went underground, into the Sí, from which she emerged in various guises and manifestations such as the 'Spéirbhean' or woman from the 'lios', the 'bean sí', or the withered old hag."[171] This conceptual metamorphosis takes place when Ní Dhomhnaill aligns the Morrigán, who sexually "bestows" herself on the Celtic cavalier, with witches by turning the Goddess into a dangerous castrating female. Such

---

[169] Catherine Nash, "Remapping the Body/Land: New Cartographies of Identity, Gender, and Landscape in Ireland," in *Writing Women and Space: Colonial and Postcolonial Geographies*, ed. Alison Blunt and Gillian Rose (New York and London: Guilford Press, 1994), 235.

[170] Ibid., 239.

[171] Bríona Nic Dhiarmada, "Tradition and the Female Voice in Contemporary Gaelic Poetry," *Women's Studies International Forum* 11, no. 4 (1988): 391.

a liaison is established through Cú Chulainn's fear of the Morrigán's *vagina dentata*, which belongs to one of the core areas of practical witchcraft, ligature. The toothed vagina deprives "man of his virile member," according to the definition in the notorious *Malleus Maleficarum* (1486).[172] Thus, the pagan Goddess acquires another, diminished, human shape, that of a heretic witch.

The aftermath of the Morrigán's amorous offer and its refusal by Cú Chulainn in Ní Dhomhnaill's poem is the same as in the *Táin*, but it is structured differently. In the myth, it is a dialogue in which each of the Goddess' threatening utterances is counterpoised by the hero's prospective counteraction. The stream of her intimidations is broken by contrapuntal arrangement so that it has to gain its momentum after each separate clause. In this verbal contest, Cú Chulainn's violent remarks to a triple menace are targeted at mutilation of all bodily parts of his divine opponent: "I'll … crack your eel's ribs … burst the eye in your head … shatter your leg" (133). Each of his responses has a syntactically and semantically identical refrain that becomes the center of the structure: "and you'll carry that mark forever unless I lift it from you with a blessing" (133). This specific lexical and grammatical organization undermines the authority of the Morrigán's statements by employing violent reciprocity. Ní Dhomhnaill opposes this architectonics in her poem. Although the title, "Agallamh Na Mór-Riona Le Cú Chulainn," translates "The Dialogue of the Great Queen with Cú Chulainn," which implies certain roles in the staging, Cú Chulainn in the poem is completely devoiced (Michael Hartnett eliminates this ironic discrepancy by interpreting the title as "The Great Queen Speaks. Cú Chulainn Listens"). The author creates a monolithic monologue, terrifying in its passion and outrage, which violates the traditional construct. Its emotional tension has been built in the initial stanza, boiling with the wrath of Cú Chulainn's rejection. The enumeration of the Morrigán's vengeful acts, which follow in swift progression when almost each line begins with the action expressed by the

---

[172] Charles Alva Hoyt, *Witchcraft*, 2nd ed. (Carbondale and Edwardsville: Southern Illinois University Press, 1989), 50–51.

future tense, evolves into a crescendo and abruptly freezes in the present: "Seo foláireamh dóite dhuit, / a Chú Chulainn" (118, "There's my hot harangue for you / *Cú* Chulainn," 119). While the hero is fixated on his own feat, on an invariable model that is iterated again and again, the Goddess possesses the power of metamorphosis.

The Morrigán reappears in "Labhrann An Mhór-Rion" ("The Great Queen Speaks"), transformed into a repulsive old hag. While in the *Táin* she comes to Cú Chulainn as "a squint-eyed old woman" (136), in Ní Dhomhnaill's poem her body is virtually freed from human physicality as if trespassing the very anatomy of living things and breaching one of the most fundamental laws of the universe, symmetry. This asymmetrical creature acquires a distinct Fomorian aspect through the repetition of "leath" ("half"), which becomes the first component of three compound adjectives: "Táim ar leathcheann, / leathshúil, leathchois" (120, "I'm half-witted / one-eyed, one-legged," 121). This transcendence of symmetrical balance is also symbolized in the imagistic and structural triplicity of the poem.

In the next stanza, the Great Queen receives her missing "halves" back under Cú Chulainn's triple blessing. Ní Dhomhnaill deviates from the chronological arrangement of the events in the myth and includes a flashback description of the injuries inflicted upon the Goddess by Cú Chulainn when she attacks him three times in zoomorphic forms. Her trifold assault is targeted at each of Cú Chulainn's three births: he is conceived from three hypothetic fathers, Lug mac Ethnenn, Conchobor, and Sualdam mac Roich. The symbolism encapsulated within "threeness" also operates on different levels of metric multiplicity; Cú Chulainn's appearance (triple-braided hair), his heroic acts (he kills his adversaries in groups of three), and the general plot structure ("threefold killing")[173] are all established in the Irish oral tradition. This symbolic significance of the number three, the most magical of all numbers in Celtic mythology

---

[173] Miranda Green, *Dictionary of Celtic Myth and Legend* (London: Thames and Hudson, 1992), 214.

and a conventional literary formula,[174] is reflected in the composition of Ní Dhomhnaill's poem. The first three stanzas are based on triplism and represent the following succession: effect—its annihilation—cause. The recurrence of structural elements in the poem and their complete or partial duplication cut across phonological and lexico-semantic levels of textual construction. These constituting elements of repetition are systematic. Interrelated and interdependent, they form the compositional level on which the multiplication is based on the principle of either identity or antithesis. Together they make up the expressiveness of a thematic structure of the text.

The Great Queen and Cú Chulainn's encounter is also triple. Moreover, the triadic pattern is essential to the nature of Celtic war-goddesses who have many common features and are interchangeable, thus concurrently functioning as one goddess and three: "the entity of the Morrigán may be tripled, or Badbh, Nemhain and Morrigán may be combined to become the triadic Morrigna."[175] When the Great Queen and Cú Chulainn meet for the third time, the prophetic Morrigán, who foretells either victory or death, pronounces Cú Chulainn's death sentence. According to Miranda Green, the Morrigán "tried to prevent him from going into battle by breaking his chariot-shaft, but in vain."[176] Ní Dhomhnaill fundamentally recasts the dynamics of their relationship. This is the rancorous Phantom Queen who is speaking in "An Mhór-Rion ag Cáiseamh na Baidhbhe le Cú Chulainn" ("The Great Queen Berates the Badhbh to Cú Chulainn"). She again refers to an infamous episode in her unsuccessful amorous advances. The hero's blind basic male fear of extinction in the vagina during the sex act is explained here from the psychoanalytical point of view, in terms of castration anxiety experienced by males at the sight of female genitals. In addition, Ní Dhomhnaill conflates this omnipresent Freudian concept with popular beliefs of witch lore, whose imaginary constructs peculiar to the discourse of neurotic men are reflected in

---

[174] Ibid.

[175] Green, *Celtic Goddesses*, 41–42.

[176] Ibid., 45.

numerous legends of a toothed vagina that cuts the penis, a medieval fabulous vagina with snakes, or witches mutilating the penis while having sex.[177] The Goddess attacks culturally pervasive penile synecdoche with a pejorative ardor:

> Eagla, siúráilte, go gcoillfí tú
> go mbeadh fiacla bréige ar mo phit,
> go meilfí tú idir mo dhá dhrandal
> mar a dhéanfaí le coirce i muileann
> is cíor mhaith agam chun do mheilte. (122)

> Fear, certainly, of castration
> fear of false teeth in my cunt
> fear my jaws would grind you
> like oats in a mill
> me having a good comb to tease you ... (123)

Here the Morrigán, who demonstrates an enviable expertise in male sexual phobias, is endowed with the gaze of a psychologist, a traditionally male instrument of objectification. She transgresses the ancient dictum that women should not direct anything, neither a gaze nor a voice. In addition to the assumed power of the gaze, the Goddess is also empowered by psychoanalytical discourse, with all its phallogocentricity and culturally situated chauvinism, using it as a template for asserting her own subject position and expressing her scopic drive, as well as for defining Cú Chulainn's masculinity. In her revisionary effort, the Morrigán becomes a proto-Cixous-Irigaray-Kristeva figure of sorts.[178]

By employing certain elements of the highly debatable analysis of female sexuality in psychoanalysis, the poet redirects the speculum to present a rival image of Cú Chulainn's sexual prowess. Like many other mythic heroes, the Cú Chulainn of the source text abstained from sexual intercourse before the battle for professional reasons because it pre-

---

[177] Jean Markale, *Women of the Celts*, trans. A. Mygind, C. Hauch, and P. Henry (London: Gordon Cremonesi, 1975), 67.

[178] The works of Hélène Cixous, Julia Kristeva, and Luce Irigaray contributed significantly to the reevaluation of psychoanalysis from feminist perspective; see, for example, Patricia Waugh, ed., *Literary Theory and Criticism: An Oxford Guide* (Oxford: Oxford University Press, 2006), 332–37.

sumably alleviated vital energies, drained a body of the life force essential for warfare, and potentially caused defeat and death. Ní Dhomhnaill's speaker renders the ancient hero-terminator, the most manly of men, a hopeless impotent, making him a predecessor of sexually frustrated descendants who apparently require convincing proofs of their sexual capacity through identification with phallic mastery and who are desperately "ag maíomh gur iníon rí Gréige / a bhí mar chéile leapan aréir acu" (110, "boasting that / last night they bedded / a Grecian princess," 111). The poet constructs this exemplar of seeming hypermasculinity in terms of obsessive projections and anxieties by exploring continuities between the present literary praxis and myth. Her ironic treatment of psychoanalytical stereotypes also reveals itself in Cú Chulainn's preoccupation with the question of his paternity ("Cú Chulainn II"). The author mocks what Deleuze calls infantilization or psychoanalization in literature when a reductionist Oedipal structure is projected onto the real or interjected into the imaginary: "In this infantile conception of literature, what we seek at the end of the voyage, or at the heart of the dream, is a father."[179] It is noteworthy that Diana Fuss, in her discussion of Deleuze and Guattari's *Anti-Oedipus*, emphasizes the connection between the historical emergence of "oedipalization" in psychoanalysis and colonial endeavors, stating that both "participate in a double ideological operation where each serves effectively to conceal the political function and purpose of the other."[180] In addition, the hero's anxiety is the retroaction of what has been looming on the Irish literary landscape for decades, the obsession with the father-son relationship that deepened, according to Kiberd, with "each succeeding generation of male authors"[181] since the establishment of a new state. The scholar considers that "a nervously patriarchal psychology" of Irish society has resulted from the uncertainty of new leaders about that state's legitimacy, about a genealogical line that seems to be

---

[179] Deleuze, *Essays Critical*, 2.

[180] Diana Fuss, *Identification Papers: Readings on Psychoanalysis, Sexuality, and Culture* (London and New York: Routledge, 1995), 158.

[181] Kiberd, *Inventing Ireland*, 407.

"delegitimized" by multiple legacies.[182] Ní Dhomhnaill mutilates the structural constancy of myth, leaving Cú Chulainn's question unanswered; she amputates a part of the *Taín* that gives a detailed account of the hero's birth (23). By problematizing Cú Chulainn's parentage, the poet questions the validity of the myth of origins of Irish manliness. At the same time, there is yet another implication to her strategy that characterizes postcolonial writing in general. As John Thieme writes in his study of intertextuality in postcolonial literature, dubious parentage becomes one of its major tropes: "[T]he genealogical bloodlines of transmission are frequently delegitimized by multiple ancestral legacies," and postcolonial texts rarely offer "comfortable solutions" as to the purity of characters' lineage.[183] In this, Ní Dhomhnaill's Cú Chulainn, once a mythological hero of both human and divine origin, joins a remarkable catalogue of postcolonial bastards and orphans examined by Thieme.

The representation of Cú Chulainn in "An Mhór-Rion ag Cáiseamh na Baidhbhe le Cú Chulainn" ("The Great Queen Berates the Badhbh to Cú Chulainn") echoes that in "Cú Chulainn I." Ní Dhomhnaill picks up what Medb of the *Taín* says about Cú Chulainn to incite Loch by juxtaposing the two males: "Surely a peppery overgrown elf like him [Cú Chulainn] can't resist the fiery force of a warrior like you [Lock]" (134). The poet takes this particular point of view, which is unique in the canonical text, because all other descriptions of the hero abound in superlative degrees demonstrating his superiority. An exemplary case is Fergus's portrayal of Cú Chulainn to Medb. The powerful epic beauty and elemental force of the passage are expressed in its solemn cumulative monotonousness that is achieved through syntactically limited verbal textures consisting of several, separate, and syntactically typological textual blocks. The first one is comprised of nouns and adjectives in a comparative degree: "You'll find no harder warrior against you—no point more sharp, more swift, more slashing; no raven more flesh-ravenous, no hand

---

182 Ibid., 406.
183 John Thieme, *Postcolonial Con-Texts: Writing Back to the Canon* (London and New York: Continuum, 2001), 8.

more deft, no fighter more fierce" (75–76). The second one is constituted of nouns only: "You will find no one there to measure against him—for youth or vigour; for apparel, horror or eloquence; for splendour, fame or form" (76). The enumeration of Cú Chulainn's merits goes on and on, but all these armigerous splendor and hyperbolic statements of masculine physique are not the focus of Ní Dhomhnaill's attention. She presents an enlarged and unfolded reflection of Medb's "peppery overgrown elf." Her Cú Chulainn is "A fhir bhig, dhoicht, dhorcha ... / ná tabharfadh an oiread sin sásaimh do mhná" (112, "Small dark rigid man ... / who'd satisfy no woman," 113). Although Cú Chulainn of the Ulster cycle has sex with an impressive number of women, the poet chooses to emphasize his impotence and to degrade him to the level of a contemporary condition, thus completely changing the conceptual register of the national epic and making the situation comically familiar.

Such dislocation of the mythically assigned roles also takes place in Ní Dhomhnaill's representation of Medb. Ferdia's brief remark in the saga—"You're a strong tongue, Medb" (171)—is expanded into the queen's passionate declaration of war on all the men of Ireland. In general, the technique of sound-tracking the otherwise verbally reserved female figures of the *Táin* is strategic for Ní Dhomhnaill's transgressive reinscriptions. Even the titles of the Morrigán poems contain the sememes of speaking, for the Goddess' supernatural power of prognostication is supplemented by the power of speech. Besides, the approach to Medb in the *Táin* provides an antipodal frame of reference for that to Cú Chulainn in terms of the opposition between lofty and base; while he is always heroically splendid, she is several times depicted "making water on the floor of the tent" (177). In the following passage, Medb's humiliation in the presence of her foe, Cú Chulainn, and her lover, Fergus, precedes the humiliation of her whole campaign:

> So Fergus took over the shelter of shields at the rear of the men of Ireland and Medb relieved herself. It dug three great channels, each big enough to take a household. The place is called Fual Medba,

> Medb's Foul Place, ever since. Cúchlainn found her like this, but he
> held his hand. He wouldn't strike her from behind....
> Medb said to Fergus:
> "We have had shame and shambles here today, Fergus."
> "We followed the rump of a misguiding woman," Fergus said. "It is
> the usual thing for a herd led by a mare to be strayed and
> destroyed." (250–51)

Ní Dhomhnaill is often said to turn things on their heads, which describes her procedures of representation much better than the no-less-often and concurrently-mentioned "deconstruction,"[184] because it implies an ongoing carnival, with its inversion of hierarchies and power structures, switching the positions of "high" and "low" and making them slide into each other, and misbalancing an established order. The carnivalesque virtuosity of leaps, performed by the poet, matches those of the Hag of the Mill in her contest with the mad Suibhne. Like the Hag, Ní Dhomhnaill does not yield to her mythic adversaries. By positioning her militaristic Celtic women in amplified spaces and thus assigning Cú Chulainn a peripheral role, she takes revenge on the canonized hero.

Cú Chulainn's neurotic male anxiety also forms a contrastive juxtaposition to the descriptions of the Morrigán. The Goddess' self-representation emphasizes her fertility and assertive sexuality that ultimately impairs the hero: "ríon álainn, mar phósae phinc ar chrann" (122, "a queen like a tree be-garlanded," 123). This portrayal both accentuates the Morrigán's power over time when she can constantly move backward and forward, being both a beauty and a hideous hag, and creates an expressive tension by applying floral imagery to a sinister and destructive war-goddess. Simultaneously, her description becomes an element of another dichotomy generated by the Goddess' proliferating personae when the doubles turn into symmetrical opposites, representing the Morrigán's loving and revenging selves: the Great Queen, a pink flower;

---

[184] See, for example, Bríona Nic Dhiarmada, "Going For It—And Succeeding," *Irish Literary Supplement* 12, no. 2 (1993): 3; Patricia Boyle Haberstroh, *Women Creating Women: Contemporary Irish Women Poets* (Syracuse: Syracuse University Press, 1996), 194.

versus the Badhbh, the black and pitiless whore. Here Ní Dhomhnaill also plays on a notorious ancient Virgin/Whore dichotomy, which has acquired a high profile in the arsenal of rigid binaries instrumental in constructing the female subject within and by patriarchal cultural and psychic structures. An ironic mimicking of the traditional patriarchal split signifying both fear of and attraction to the feminine provides yet another example when the poet subversively appropriates certain masculinist strategies of representation. The depiction of the Badhbh through the Morrigán's eyes is built upon the image found in the Great Queen's obscure prophetic remarks from the *Táin*. Ní Dhomhnaill accumulates all mythic aspects of the Badhbh, the vulture, and delineates the Great Queen's discourse in two blocks. The first one focuses on the Badhbh and encompasses her morbid and sinister features, which are asserted through syntagmatic repetition:

> Is í an bhadhb í,
> ar foluain os cionn an tslua.
> Priocann sí na súile
> as na leanaí sa chliabhán.
> Is í an scréachán í,
> éan búistéara ... (124)

> She is the hooded crow
> hovering over the crowd.
> She picks the eyes
> from kids in cots.
> She is the screecher,
> the butcher-bird ... (123, 125)

Both parallel constructions begin with the copula followed by "í," which again closes the line and establishes the pattern: "Is í ... í." The next fragment, the predicament for Cú Chulainn, presents the same structural technique. The repetition "beidh do chuid fola" ("your blood will be"), "beidh do chuid feola" ("your flesh will be") consists of minimal grammatical units. The fragment is also fused by alliterative design, formed by the rhymed "fola," "feola," "fuara." They simultaneously build a deadly, bloodlusting string: blood, flesh, cold. The image of the haematomaniac butcher-bird semantically anticipates a consistently bloody carnage in the progression of the poem; brutality that rips the surfaces of the flesh and destroys the organic integrity of the body becomes the signifier of the divinity of terror. In the presence of the Badhbh, the monstrous double, violence unequivocally becomes an instrument of the Morrigán's desire; the slippage from the erotic to the combatant, sadistic femininity has now been completed. The gaze that in the *Táin* is usually directed onto the ferocious spectacle staged by the hero is reverted. Cú Chulainn who usually shreds his immediate victims—Etarcomol split in two from head to toe with a sword; Nad Crantail pierced by a spear, beheaded, and cleaved into four pieces; Mand shattered to fragments against a rock[185]— now, deglamorized, is gazed upon in the theatre of reciprocal violence:

> beidh do chuid fola
> ina logaibh faoi do chosa;
> beidh do chuid feola
> ar crochadh
> ina spólaí fuara
> ó chruacha stíl ... (124)

> your blood will be in pools
> under your feet
> your flesh
> will hang
> in cold joints
> from meat hooks ... (125)

The literal dismembering of Cú Chulainn parallels Ní Dhomhnaill's textual strategies: she proceeds by severing and dissecting the regnant forms of discourse to create a new assemblage and to observe a result. It is not accidental that the instrument of the hero's torture is the polysemantic "stíl"; it is not only a "hook" (used in translation), a familiar paraphernalia of butchery, but also "style," a word that codifies authority and is feared

---

[185] Jeremy Lowe, "Contagious Violence and the Spectacle of Death in *Táin Bó Cúailnge*," in *Language and Tradition in Ireland: Continuities and Displacements*, ed. Maria Tymoczko and Colin Ireland (Amherst and Boston: University of Massachusetts Press, 2003), 92–93.

as possessing its own autonomous power, including the power to kill an iconic opponent and to liberate herself from the strictures of epic tradition. Style is the factor that determines the modes of exposition and transformation in Ní Dhomhnaill's discourse, which is invaded by arms-bearing women and terrifying battle phantoms.

Cú Chulainn's link with the Badhbh, who represents chaos and death and whose name connotes rage, fury, and violence,[186] is close. Like the hero who single-handedly opposes and destroys scores of enemies, the red-mouthed Badhbh of the *Táin* kills and terrifies; at her night cry, "a hundred warriors died of fright" (239). Both are where death is, the Badhbh calling from among the corpses of those fallen at Cú Chulainn's sword. Descriptions of Cú Chulainn's heroic deeds in the *Táin* often employ the image of this spirit of destruction. For example, a metaphoric parallel with the battle-goddess as the supreme manifestation of rage intensifies the expressiveness of the account of Cú Chulainn's famous warp-spasm: "Malignant mists and spurts of fire—the torches of the Badb—flickered red in vaporous clouds that rose boiling above his head, so fierce was his fury" (150, 153). As in the saga—where, after Cú Chulainn's last battle, it is a crow or raven, the Badhbh, who sits on his shoulder to denote that he is dead—she phantasmically appears on Cú Chulainn's shoulder in the final lines of Ní Dhomhnaill's poem to celebrate the Morrigán's triumph over the object of her obsessional affection and desire:

> mar ní ar do dhealbh
> in Ard-Oifig an Phoist amháin
> a chím í suite
> ar do ghualainn,
> a Chú Chulainn. (124)

> because it's not just on your statue
> in the G.P.O.
> I see her sitting
> on your shoulder,

---

[186] Green, *Celtic Goddesses*, 43.

Cú Chulainn. (125)

While translating tradition into her own idiosyncratic language, the poet breaks the stylistic closure of epic by alluding to another, modern fulfilled epic of the Easter Rising. Its sacrificial myth is iconographically embedded in the statue of the hero at the General Post Office in Dublin. Having become one of the symbols of the new republic, Cú Chulainn's sculpture has completed the process of a profound museization of Gaelic military masculine ethos. The speaker's fury is a ferocious reaction against fetishized pieties and is directed against their material embodiment in the monument to transhistorical masculinity. Ní Dhomhnaill's Morrigán-Badhbh prophesies death of the symbol.

Ní Dhomhnaill, to counterbalance the transhistorical construct of masculinity, uses mythological material as building blocks for her personal myths of womanhood. The poet scrutinizes Celtic myths and dissects them, selecting some details and enlarging them, erasing negativity inherent in master myths, providing shocking explanations, and leaving the rest under the turned-over magnifying glass. All the details used by Ní Dhomhnaill are there in canonical texts, but she subtracts the epic constants and substitutes marginal images, phrases, sometimes only implications, which she develops according to her revisionary strategies. She opens up the closed structure of ancient myths by inserting, modifying, and contaminating them, creating a precedent for further reworkings. The traditional male fear of women turns into Cú Chulainn's neurosis in the face of female autonomy. Ní Dhomhnaill's "translated" myth reflects on his vacillating impotence rather than on his canonical omnipotent, invariant identity. Both this fear and neurosis are counterpoised to no less powerful female fear of men's violence, but Ní Dhomhnaill does not stop at the zero point of fear; she challenges it by taking an offensive, not a defensive stand. Her femininity is ready to make incursions. She effectively dismantles the ideal of masculinity as a stable signifier by revealing its reliance on fictions of supremacy. The poet disables prescriptive models of hypervirility through parody and pastiche, with their subversive potential. In her interpretation of mythic symbols of masculinity, Ní Dhomhnaill infects the stability of myth with the germs of process by locating it both in an inconclusive present and an "absolute past," and by constantly leaping back and forth from the pagan darkness to routine details of contemporaneity. She thus creates a serio-comical field in which the past, projected onto the present, and the present, superimposed onto the past, merge into an ambiguous and amorphous spatiotemporality. By intertwining the masculinity myth of the past with the male myth of the present, she disrupts the closed epic structure with its unchanging hero and turns Cú Chulainn into a modern degenerate.

In the process of Ní Dhomhnaill's demystification and demythologization, a vociferous, avenging, and defiant Goddess of female sovereignty appears. Ní Dhomhnaill uses myth as a scheme for woman/man relations and comes up with a strikingly evocative feminine imagery, which acquires archetypal dimensions nourished by torrential undercurrents of oral tradition against a conventional monomyth of transhistorical masculinity based on a male paragon. Alongside the vehemently outspoken nightmarish Phantom Queen and regal Medb, Ní Dhomhnaill's cycle implicitly invokes another specter—Fedelm Banfhile, the prophetess and poet at Medb's court. The revival of all these tangible specters by the writer signifies the return to what she sees as one of the distinctive signs of contemporary Irish-language women's writing: "get[ting] back to what we were going on about before we were interrupted by the male side of the psyche that caused Christianity and witch-burning. We are going back to where the Sybil was interrupted in mid-sentence by the invasions."[187]

---

[187] Nuala Ní Dhomhnaill, "Nuala Ní Dhomhnaill: Interviewed by Lucy McDiarmid and Michael J. Durkan," in *Writing Irish: Selected Interviews with Irish Writers from the* Irish Literary Supplement, ed. James P. Myers, Jr. (Syracuse: Syracuse University Press, 1999), 111. Some feminist scholars suggest that among the "archetypes" that make up the female psyche, sibyl is "woman who gives birth to poetry and art" (M. Wandor, ed., *On Gender and Writing* [London, Boston, Melbourne, and Henley: Pandora Press, 1983], 67).

III *Trompe-l'oeil* Sexualities:

The Erotics of Ukrainianness in Oksana Zabuzhko, Yuri Pokalchuk, Les Poderviansky and Yuri Vynnychuk

In 2004 the prestigious Ukrainian press Kal'variia published the translation *Сповідь киянина еротомана* (*The Confession of a Kyivan Erotomaniac*) written originally in French by an anonymous Ukrainian author in 1912. The book is surrounded by an aura of literary mystification not uncommon for erotic literature, its title and confessional style evoking the spirit of Henry Spencer Ashbee (1834–1900), the unflagging compiler of *Index Librorum Prohibitorum* (1877), leading authority on pornography in Victorian Britain, and the alleged author of *My Secret Life* (The Sex Diary of a Victorian Gentleman) (1871) that has long provoked fierce literary debate.[188] The authorship of *Сповідь* (*The Confession*) has been hypothetically ascribed to either one of Lesia Ukrainka's brothers or to Ahatanhel Krymsky (1871–1942),[189] an eminent Ukrainian Orientalist, belletrist, linguist, expert in over thirty languages, literary scholar, folklorist, and translator. *Сповідь* (*The Confession*) was sent, as a letter, to Havelock Ellis (1859–1939), the pioneer of sexology who challenged Victorian aversion to public discussions of sexuality; it appeared in 1926 in *Mercure de France* and was recommended as an "erotic masterpiece" to Vladimir Nabokov (1899–1977) by a then exceptionally influential Edmund Wilson (1895–1972), thus becoming yet another prototext for the psy-

---

[188] Ian Gibson, *The Erotomaniac: The Secret Life of Henry Spencer Ashbee* (Cambridge, Massachusetts: Da Capo, 2001).

[189] Ivan Luchuk, "Sumburni prypushchennia (pisliaslovo redaktora)," afterword to *Spovid' kyianyna erotomana,* by Anonim (L'viv: Kal'variia, 2004), 140–41.

chologically volatile world of the obsessive attraction to a nymphet figure in *Lolita* (1955).[190]

Сповідь киянина еротомана (The Confession of a Kyivan Eroto-maniac) typified a veritable explosion of exploratory writing about sex in all its exotic manifestations throughout Europe at the turn of the twentieth century. However, this project of transforming sex into text stands alone against the Ukrainian literary landscape since the emergence of a Ukrainian erotic tradition was interrupted by the foundation of the Soviet state, characterized by the unswerving repression of the sexual and the persistent promotion of the ideological "kenosis" as one of the fundamental principles of the officially sanctioned socialist realist literature. Before the break-up of the Soviet Union, works concerned with sexuality were practically absent in Ukraine. Taboo in the official socialist realist canon, they were also excluded from dissident literary production, which was primarily preoccupied with political issues. As far back as in the first decades of the twentieth century, when Ukraine was experiencing a short outburst of a cultural revival that turned into "Executed Renaissance" in the 1930s, Volodymyr Vynnychenko (1880–1951), a prominent statesman and author of electrifying modernist prose, was accused of writing "pornography" because of his affirmation of sexuality that was incompatible with the prevailing ascetic revolutionary ideal. He was among those literati who were breaking the code of self-censorship adopted by Soviet revolutionary writers in general. Because of his opposition to mainstream ideology, Vynnychenko—the first and last Ukrainian "pornographer" of the Soviet era—emigrated and settled in France, a rare gift of fortune because Ukrainian literature was virtually wiped out by Stalinist repressions.

The postindependence period in Ukraine has become a time of liberation from different forms of totalitarian and colonial oppression, including the systematized social repression of the body in the sterilized Soviet society, in which the domains of "pleasure" were prescribed and

---

[190] Kazbiek Biektursunov, "'Blachevnyi' kinets'," introduction to *Spovid' kyianyna erotomana*, by Anonim (L'viv: Kal'variia, 2004), 4–5.

thoroughly sanitized by the state. With the body eliminated from the picture for the benefit of the soul for a lengthy period of time, Ukrainians seem to subscribe to the definition of a "spiritual" nation. In an ongoing postindependence debate about Ukrainian national identity, matters of the flesh do not score too highly. In *Теорія українського кохання (Theory of Ukrainian Love)* (2002), Mykola Tomenko deliberates on ethnopsychological and sociocultural traditions of Ukrainianness and juxtaposes them to the expansion of mass culture that "is destroying cultural values and ethics of human relationships."[191] He continues arguing that "Ukrainians have never been cynics; that is why today's 'erotization' of nation through mass culture either from the East or from the West is not only antipolitical or antiaesthetic: it is—unnatural."[192]

Whether one likes it or not, "unnatural erotization" exists. The discovery and investigation of the formerly untrodden ambivalent terrains of desiring bodies are being represented in a wide range of contemporary literary practices that are breaking political, social, and cultural injunctions to silence on the issues of sexuality. Being both one of the constitutive components of such works and the medium that most vociferously advocates free and diverse sexual self-expression, erotic literature questions the postulates of social structures that support and encourage negative attitudes to any form of sexuality. It releases repressed experiences and desires, which can be instrumental in overcoming the consequences of oppressive orders that neutralized and codified the body in the iconographic terms of a desexed socialist realism, in forging a new sexual identity utterly nonexistent under the Soviet hygienic moral code, and in disrupting the continuum of the inherited authoritarian tradition. By way of example, a depressingly monotonous stream of "positive" characters in the Soviet literature whose libido was channeled exclusively into the construction of communism has profoundly eroded any comfortable sense of the body in the sphere of representations that constitute social

---

[191] Mykola Tomenko, *Teoriia ukraïns'koho kokhannia* (Kyïv: Mizhnarodnyi turyzm, 2002), 11.

[192] Ibid.

identity. Furthermore, as Homi Bhabha points out, when it is theorized in postcolonial terms, the "body is always simultaneously (if conflictually) inscribed in both the economy of pleasure and desire and the economy of discourse, domination and power."[193]

Oksana Zabuzhko, the "Ukrainian Sylvia Plath" and the most controversial contemporary Ukrainian writer so far, has opened a Pandora's Box of dormant psychosexual and erotic explorations by her *Польові дослідження з українського сексу* (*Field Research in Ukrainian Sex*) (1996).[194] Her book became the first postindependence national bestseller and was translated into a number of European languages. The contradictory reception of Zabuzhko's novel, generated by the insulted virtue of (post)Soviet neopuritans, can be described as a miniature copy of the notoriety once surrounding D. H. Lawrence's (1885–1930) *Lady Chatterley's Lover* (1928), yet the intellectual immaturity of her attackers and the absence of laws and regulations on the basis of which the author could have been charged with pornography and obscenity saved her work from being removed from bookstore and library shelves. *Польові дослідження* (*Field Research*) is the first explicitly erotic work in Ukrainian literature written by a woman. Zabuzhko's search for the power of self-articulation by positioning herself as an autonomous subject of erotic desire is presented through a fictionalized account of a real-life affair that blurs the line between the genres of novel and life-writing by its sophisticated manipulation of reality into fiction; in addition, the text destabilizes the distinction between high and popular culture. Zabuzhko's erotica provides a much needed opportunity for the rethinking, or rather (re)inventing, of Ukrainian female sexual identity, but it is also a discourse on what Freud calls "common unhappiness,"[195] the experience that informs women's writings and lives at large. In one of her interviews, Zabuzhko

---

[193] Homi K. Bhabha. *The Location of Culture* (London and New York: Routledge, 1994), 96.

[194] Oksana Zabuzhko, *Pol'ovi doslidzhennia z ukraïns'koho seksu* (Kyïv: Zhoda, 1996); hereafter cited parenthetically in the text.

[195] R. D. Hinshelwood, "Psychoanalysis as Natural Philosophy," *Philosophy, Psychiatry, and Psychology* 12, no. 4 (2005): 325.

speaks about the complete identification of her Ukrainian women readers aged twenty-five to sixty with her heroine and concludes: "[I]t suddenly appears that you somewhat mystically apply sound not to your own words but to those of many thousands of specific living beings who suffered and largely remained silent, as if they did not exist at all: all that is not expressed in words very quickly sinks into oblivion. By giving voice to something, you allow it to exist."[196] Thus, her character's personal psychodrama represents the wider societal scheme of repressive control imposed through discipline and punishment.

Zabuzhko's novel explores sadomasochistic intrigue, with all the accompanying nuances in understanding of sexual identity, bodily pleasure, and the relationship of violence to subjectivity and society in the late twentieth century. By representing pain in her sexual quest journey, Zabuzhko retaliates against the century-old view that masochism is natural to women.[197] Yet her protagonist appears to reenact obsessively the masochism in which Soviet society has been schooled so well by the authoritarian state. The system oriented toward absolute control over the bodies of its subjects, which was established through the political technologies of victimization, successfully implemented the attitude of submissiveness toward authority. Paradoxically, under the Soviet regime, the

---

[196] Oksana Zabuzhko, "Where There Are No Knights, a Robber Baron Will Turn Up," *Den'*, www.day.kiev.ua/DIGEST/1999/28/culture/cul-1.htm (accessed November 23, 2005).

[197] This nineteenth-century myth, theoretically substantiated by Freud's concept of "feminine masochism" and developed by a number of his successors into the straightforward assertion of women's biological predisposition to masochistic behavior, has been instrumental in homogenizing women into a category and assigning them invariant social functions. By rationalizing and "medicalizing" the prevailing sexual division of social roles and the supporting myths of women's passivity in social and sexual relations, the psychiatric profession has been promoting the existing models of sexuality, gender, and power. In this framework, masochism has become a central ideological construct in the production of a feminine stereotype that provides a zone where conflicting male fantasies and phobias are evicted—a site for pleasure and anxiety. See John K. Noyes, *The Mastery of Submission: Inventions of Masochism* (Ithaca and London: Cornell University Press, 1997), 16–17.

whole country had engaged in masochistic activities for decades, as if having signed an implicit social contract based on the Deleuzian definition of masochism, according to which the rights of one party and the obligations of the other are neither disputed nor subject to revisions;[198] moreover, the most profound characteristic of this social "agreement" is that "slavery [had been] instituted within a contractual relation."[199] In the sphere of gender, the trampled male ego tried to compensate for its impotency in relation to the prevailing power structures by abusing, denigrating, and subjugating women. *Польові дослідження з українського сексу* (*Field Research in Ukrainian Sex*) reveals the mechanisms by which cultural models of domination and subordination are shaped and projected onto heterosexual gender roles. The novel also presents a pattern both of the sexually codified violence to which many women are exposed and of the victimization they seem to accept. Zabuzhko's text is instrumental in understanding "how domination is anchored in the hearts of the dominated," to use Jessica Benjamin's expression,[200] and why being a woman—especially in Ukraine, as Zabuzhko's character emphasizes—automatically fixes positional roles. By delineating women along the gender axis, male-supremacist culture consigns them to submission and acquiescence to brutality. The author represents woman's dependency in quasi-sexualized terms, through the implied missionary position that equates her to the passive receptivity of the soil:

> Із цією блядською *залежністю*, закладеною в тіло, як бомба сповільненої дії, з несамостійністю цією, з потребою перетоплюватись на вогку, хляпаву глину, втовчену в поверхню землі.... (18)

> With this fucking *dependency* deposited in the body like a delayed-action bomb, with this nonindependence, with this need to melt into

---

[198] See Gilles Deleuze, "Coldness and Cruelty," in his *Masochism*, trans. Jean McNeil (New York: Zone Books, 1991), 91–93.

[199] Gilles Deleuze, *Desert Islands and Other Texts: 1953–1974*, ed. David Lapoujade, trans. Michael Taormina (New York: Semiotext[e], 2004), 134.

[200] Jessica Benjamin, *The Bonds of Love: Psychoanalysis, Feminism, and the Problem of Domination* (New York: Pantheon Books, 1988), 5.

a damp, splattering clay pounded into the surface of the earth....

Zabuzhko sees the roots of women's subjugation not only in her society's misogyny but also in men's double subservience under colonial and totalitarian rule, which emasculates them and thus subsumes the colonized into already existing gender relations. Under these conditions, the authoritarian oppressive practices are redirected against women, exactly duplicating both the colonizers' practices and the colonial scenario of mastery and submission. The protagonist places her own compliance with her lover's violence and with their abusive relationship in the context of sociocultural experiences collectively shared by that particular stratum of women who identify themselves with Ukrainian subalternity, not with the ideologically concocted and zealously promoted "Soviet people" into which all constitutive nations of the USSR were methodically homogenized:

> [Н]ас ростили мужики, обйобані як-тільки-можна з усіх кінців ... потім такі самі мужики нас трахали, і ... в обох випадках вони робили з нами те, що інші, чужі мужики робили з ними[.] І ... ми приймали й любили їх такими, як вони є, бо не прийняти їх— означало б стати по стороні тих, чужих[.] ... [Є]диний наш вибір, отже, був і залишається—межи жертвою і катом: між небуттям і буттям-яке-вбиває[.] (140)

> [W]e were brought up by guys who were fucked in every way from all sides ... later we were screwed by the same kind of guys, and ... in both cases they did to us the same thing that the others, the *foreign* guys, did to them [.] And ... we accepted them and loved them as they are, for not accepting them would mean taking the side of the others, the foreign ones[.] ... [T]hus the only choice we had and still have is between the victim and the torturer: between nonbeing and being-that-kills[.]

While retrospectively wandering through the hell of the Soviet reality at the end of the 1970s and the beginning of the 1980s, Zabuzhko almost consistently processes the brutal regulatory tools of the state apparatus, targeted at an inevitable subjection, through human bodily experiences. She highlights the confluence and continuity between the political, homosocial, and forced homoerotic orders and conceives them through the pervasive male sexual fear of being abused and used like a woman, pathology deemed more dangerous than femininity itself in patriarchal cultures. Indicative of the distinct homophobic attitudes in society and baring a pronounced derogatory label, the idea of femininity-in-masculinity is thus perceived as the final negation of a man's social and political identity.

Zabuzhko's protagonist, though, does not invariably occupy one and the same position in the pain-seeking scenario. She shifts subject-object relations, thus destabilizing them, and moves freely along the "submission-mastery" axis. She alternates between a laughing witch-dominatrix and a sexual slave at the other end of the "whip." The narrator's body is bruised and scarred by the male's desire for power, yet she remains a strong woman and is seen by her partner as a violator of his male sovereignty, resulting in what sexologists call psychogenic impotence.[201] It is ironic that the heroine encounters neither a virile knight nor an epiclike hero-dissident, but an almost metaphysically impotent contemporary Ukrainian man. According to the psychoanalytical canon, her artist-lover's identity is defined by the phallic and heterosexual economy of lack both on the psychological and physical, performative level, since he experiences a metaphorical form of castration. Simultaneously, he suffers the castration trauma that is characteristic of the dispersed and dislocated subjectivities of the colonized.

The eroticism emanated by the protagonist is perceived by her lover as threatening and destructive because his maleness cannot accept it. For him, the source of her intimidating female essence lies in her genitalia; hence, he attempts to maintain his domination by repeated frenzied assaults on her vagina during their quasi-gynecological erotic games. He sees the vagina as a devouring vortex and a locus of fecundity that exists and functions separately from the rest of the body, as well as a contending counterpart to his reproductive organ and thus subject to

---

[201] See, for example, Joshua A. Bodie, William W. Beeman, and Manoj Monga, "Psychogenic Erectile Dysfunction," *The International Journal of Psychiatry in Medicine* 33, no. 3 (2003): 273–93.

castration. However, the psychological shape-shifting of Zabuzhko's heroine and her transformation from an enduring object of offensive desires into a witch figure, which results in the reversal of the power dynamic, align her with traditional castrating females.[202] By portraying the protagonist, who acts out her yearnings through swings between aggression and passivity, pain and pleasure, and domination and submission, the author desexualizes men and resexualizes women.

The novel's minimalist plot provides a strategically limited space for Zabuzhko's narrative of desire in which desire is obstructed, drained, and left unfulfilled. The bond that links desire to pain and numbness is made explicit by the writer. In the aftermath of her love affair, the protagonist is left in a trancelike indifference, as if pain and fixation always end in emptying out of self. Her hollowed body turns into the human canvas for the inscriptions of a brutal, power-obsessed artist:

> [Л]итки розцяцьковано, як мапу, архіпелагом різнотонних, червонястих і брунатних, лускатих і злущених плям—шрами, порізи, опіки, навіч представлена історія дев'ятимісячної (атож, дев'ятимісячної!!!) mad love, із якої вийшла—правдива madness. (14)

> [C]alves ornamented like a map, with an archipelago of multihued, reddish and brown, scaly and shelled blots—scars, cuts, burns, a visual history of the nine-month-long (yes, nine-month-long!!!) mad love that turned into true madness.

A sadistic draftsman, the male artist produces his graph of dominance-seeking masculinity in which violence becomes the other face of power. His is the desire pushed to the extreme that rips apart the communion between the lovers and exposes, as Georges Bataille contends in his discussion of Sade, "the true violent nature of eroticism."[203]

---

202 On witchcraft, fear of castration, and psychogenic impotence, see Edward Bever, "Witchcraft Fears and Psychosocial Factors in Disease," *Journal of Interdisciplinary History* 30, no. 4 (2000): 573–90.

203 Georges Bataille, *Erotism: Death and Sensuality*, trans. Mary Dalwood (San Francisco: City Lights, 1986), 167.

Having inherited the multilayered legacy that encompasses masochistic neuroticism of Soviet "injustice collectors,"[204] self-effacement of a canonical socialist realist hero in the name of communism, and a cult of suffering in the nineteenth-century literary tradition, Zabuzhko substantially infuses erotogenic masochistic practices with moral masochism. Being often concomitant with the desire to fabricate a different cultural order, moral masochism provides a drive for change. This drive, which acknowledges intensity, tensions, and contradictions of desire, channels Zabuzhko's text against repressive constructions of human subjects and of their gender and social relations. Her representation of erotic subjectivity invades the discursive territory previously officiated by neutered, sexless male practitioners of socialist realism, who allowed women into their pantheon of unattainable virtues exclusively as satellite characters—reliable comrades, faithful friends, and chaste wives—to support assertive phallocentric masculine integrity.

Yuri Pokalchuk's sexual adventures and fantasies are played out on the opposite end of the spectrum from Zabuzhko's liberated female subjectivity. The strategies these authors employ in rethinking and rewriting the body could not be more different. Pokalchuk, an established writer and translator from many European languages, has engaged in writing Ukrainian foundational pornographic fiction by turning the private body into the public spectacle. His project aims at filling one of the numerous gaping holes in the Ukrainian literary process, thus expanding its operational area, as well as the functional field of the Ukrainian language, and contributing to the viability of both. The piquant subject matter of his collection of short stories, *Те, що на споді* (*What Lies Beneath*) (1998),[205] has been inspired by political desire that is enhanced by a missionary drive to attract the largely russified Ukrainian reader to literature written in Ukrainian. This brings to mind another prominent writer of

---

[204] Daniel Rancour-Laferriere, *The Slave Soul of Russia: Moral Masochism and the Cult of Suffering* (New York and London: New York University Press, 1995), 2.
[205] Iurii Pokal'chuk, *Te, shcho na spodi* (L'viv: Kal'variia, 1998); hereafter cited parenthetically in the text.

the Ukrainian "Executed Renaissance," Mykola Khvylovy (1899–1933), who reportedly once remarked that he would be confident in the survival of the Ukrainian language if it were to be spoken by presidents and prostitutes. As if venturing to enforce the implementation of Khyvolovy's widely cited injunctive, a group of Ukrainian writers (including Pokalchuk) organized a public action, "Ukrainian books—for Ukrainian whores," to popularize Ukrainian-language literature by distributing their books to the priestesses of Ukrainian sexland on one of the highways leading to Kyiv on March 7, 2007.[206] Jokes aside, I should mention in passing that Pokalchuk has succeeded in breaking through language barriers; his collection, like Zabuzhko's novel, has been enjoying popularity among readers with various language preferences. In addition to his linguopolitical preoccupations, the author's ongoing project is to experiment with pushing and manipulating the boundaries of the permissible in sexual representation.[207]

Although in one of his interviews Pokalchuk claims that all his depictions of eroticism are based on his own sexual experiences,[208] *Te, що на споді* (*What Lies Beneath*) is apparently well-informed by current operational definitions of pornography and tends to draw, to a noticeable degree, on the conventional compensatory male power fantasies and misogynist myths characteristic of the genre. The collection includes most of the hottest pornographic scenarios: conflation of rape with seduction, ano-rectal eroticism, group sex, incest, castration, prostitution, homoeroticism, and gang-banging. Sex scenes, however, do not completely subsume human relationships, for the author provides psychological motivations for his characters' actions. In "Зло" ("Evil"), the police hunt for a

---

[206] "Pys'mennyky rozdavaly knyzhky poviiam na Okruzhnii u Kyievi," *Hazeta po-ukraïns'ky*, March 9, 2007, http://www.gpu.ua/index.php?&id=153164 (accessed March 19, 2007).

[207] *Te, shcho na spodi* was followed by *Ozernyi viter* (Ivano-Frankivs'k: Lileia-NV, 2002), *Shablia i strila* (Kharkiv: Folio, 2003), and *Zaboroneni ihry* (Kharkiv: Folio, 2005), to name a few.

[208] Ol'ha Stanchak, "Blits-interv'iu z Iuriiem Pokal'chukom," *Dzyga: Literatura*, http://dzyga.com.ua/interv/pocalchuk.htm (accessed March 13, 2007).

young girl because she has been transmitting venereal disease to men and boys she picks up along the highway. Driven to insanity, she runs away from home after being raped by her father, lives in the meadow, and has indiscriminate sex with strangers in exchange for food. This bleak story has two focalizers, the girl herself who is in a perpetual state of numbness, and a young doctor in whose arms she ends her frenzied flight at the denouement. In another story, "Молитва" ("The Prayer"), a woman is paralyzed with fear when attacked in her own apartment by a teenager who threatens to shoot her if she does not have sex with him while being filmed. Before leaving, the boy introduces himself as the son of the woman's lover. He is trying to prevent the ultimate collapse of his family, which has been drifting apart because of his father's illicit love affair, by getting discrediting pictures that, as he hopes, will induce his father to give up his extramarital relationship. Pokalchuk's pornoproduction also involves darker aspects of past and present, as in "Кінець" ("The End"), which narrates the protagonist's sexual maturation through numerous erotic exercises. In the conclusion, the protagonist is sent by the author to die violently as a member of the Ukrainian student resistance battalion, which attempted to block the 1918 Bolshevik advance on the capital at Kruty, a railroad station northeast of Kyiv, and whose captured fighters were castrated by the Russians before execution. While not all of Pokalchuk's sexual encounters are entirely deprived of commitment, affection, understanding, passion, or even love ("З других рук"— "Secondhand"), the function of all his narratives remains the same: to provide as many opportunities as possible for the sexual act to take place. His stories manifest the ideology of pornography outlined by Angela Carter in her discussion of the Sadeian woman:

> There is no room here for tension or the unexpected. We know what is going to happen; this is why we are reading the book. Characterisation is necessarily limited by the formal necessity for the actors to fuck as frequently and as ingeniously as possible. But they do not do so because they are continually consumed by desire; the free expression of desire is as alien to pornography as it is to marriage. In pornography, both men and women fuck because to fuck is their

raison d'etre. It is their life work.[209]

Те, що на споді (*What Lies Beneath*) is lavishly adorned by erotica in visual art. The book includes, for example, reproductions of works by Michelangelo (1475–1564) and Caravaggio (1571?–1610), exposing homoerotic desire, evidently to provide illustration for the only story that deals with gay subject matter. Interestingly enough, in this particular piece, suggestively titled "Блакитне сонце" ("Azure Sun") ("azure" is a Ukrainian slang term for "gay"), Pokalchuk's regime of representation switches to understatements and avoidance of frank descriptions of sex as opposed to those stories that depict heterosexual relations. His gallery of visual enticement stretches chronologically to include Eric Fischel's (b. 1948) *Bad Boy* (1981), a painting of an adolescent boy voyeuristically viewing a woman's (his mother's) genitalia and naked body up close, which is said to have made the artist's career. This one is probably allocated to a story in which Pokalchuk ambitiously rewrites Sophocles's *Oedipus Rex*. However, if in Fischel's painting the perversion is implied in the voyeuristic transaction, the story actually narrates the incestuous relationship in shocking and superfluous detail. "Едіп народився в Дрогобичі" ("Oedipus Was Born in Drohobych")—almost like the 1866 Leopold von Sacher-Masoch's (1836–1895) *Der Don Juan von Kolomea* (*Don Juan of Kolomyia*)—attaches itself to a well-known intertext and thus to an "archetypal" human condition. The story reads as an attempt at liberation either of repressed desires or from the chains of oedipal categories in Freudian theory. Similarly, in "Юність Дон-Жуана" ("Don Juan's Youth"), Pokalchuk employs yet another celebrated character recurring in various European literatures for nearly three centuries: Don Juan. In addition to an extensive network of precursor texts, the name also evokes an association with a medical condition, satyriasis, also

---

[209] Angela Carter, *The Sadeian Woman and the Ideology of Pornography* (New York: Pantheon Books, 1978), 13.

known as the Don Juan syndrome, an excessive, uncontrolled sexual activity by a man with little or no emotional involvement.[210]

Throughout history and across different cultural traditions, writers, artists, poets, and philosophers have been looking for explications of an opaque "riddle of femininity." As if in a search of the clue to this mystery, Pokalchuk, in a number of stories, chooses a woman-centered type of sexual representation ("Мадам"—"Madam," "Яка я є..."— "The Way I Am...," "Треба" — "Must," "Те, що на споді" — "What Lies Beneath"). Women become here the directors of the sexual scene and use men to gratify their desires. Although in this Pokalchuk appears to reverse the sociosexual conditions conventionally experienced by men and thus to question the male-defined eroticism of power, he falls into the pattern seen in many other masculinist discourses that explicitly draw the equation between "woman" and "sex" and fix its invariant meaning. The writer conceptualizes the once enigmatic woman in a concise formula that does not imply any uncertainty about the feminine because, for him, the ultimate desire of every woman is to be laid. By means of such a frank pornographic orientation, Pokalchuk writes his *Bildungsroman* of sexuality that turns into, to some extent, a phallic declaration of potency and power. It frequently seems as though the repeated descriptions of sex are aimed at acting out the author's fantasies of sexual domination, some of them being profoundly suppressed adolescent erotic dreams.

Although some of Pokalchuk's male protagonists are teenagers, inexperienced virgins at the point of departure in their sexual adventures, they perfectly comply with prevailing porn scripts of erectility and verticality. Pokalchuk's women are always responding ecstatically and orgasmically to multiple fucking. The apotheosis of Pokalchuk's resourcefulness reveals itself in the following account of what could be loosely termed lovemaking. Here the mechanistic assemblage of woman's sexual insatiability and her adolescent partners' utilization of varied

---

[210] "Satyriasis," in *Human Sexuality: An Encyclopedia*, ed. Vern L. Bullough and Bonnie Bullough (New York and London: Garland, 1994).

sexual practices (vaginal, anal, and oral concomitantly) borders on the grotesque:

[В]она лежала на ... [Славкові] із стрижнем у задньому проході.... Костик задер її ноги на свої плечі і обережно увійшов у її піхву, і тепер вона застогнала уже голосно від нових неочікуваних і незнаних досі відчуттів; обидва стрижні у ній рухались синхронно, навіть більше—зараз рухалась вона між обома стрижнями, тепер вчуваючи велетенську насолоду від обох зразу в собі ... і коли вона відчула ... [Євгенів] стрижень у себе на вустах, а потім у роті, а потім на язиці, вже спраглий, сильний, бажаючий ... вони вже всі хотіли вибухнути і рухались зараз, як єдиний дивний людський механізм, як машина, якої ще не довинайшло людство і яка могла б давати особистості найповніше задоволення. (242)

[S]he was lying on ... [Slavko] with his penis in her anus.... Kostyk lifted her legs up onto his shoulders and carefully entered her vagina, and then she groaned loudly because of the new, unexpected, and previously unexperienced sensations; both penises were moving synchronically inside her, even more—now she was moving between both penises feeling gigantic pleasure from both of them inside her ... and when she felt ... [Ievhen's] penis on her lips, and then in her mouth, and then on her tongue, thirsty, strong, desirous ... they all wanted to explode already and were now moving like a single human mechanism, like a machine, that humankind has not yet invented and which might have given an individual the fullest pleasure.

It is worthwhile mentioning that almost all of Pokalchuk's descriptions are focused on women—moreover, women in their thirties who initiate coitus with male teenagers. This is the rite of passage into manhood and the establishment of a masculine sexual identity designed by the author that ultimately undermines his assertion of male sexual mastery by explicitly revealing its infantile basis.

Another promoter of the genre, Les Poderviansky, whose collection of plays *Герой нашого часу* (*Hero of Our Time*) (2000)[211] has been wittily termed "pornoethnography,"[212] is known even to those who have no

---

[211] Les' Poderv'ians'kyi, *Heroi nashoho chasu* (L'viv: Kal'variia, 2000); hereafter cited parenthetically in the text.

[212] Vadym Trinchii, "Pro pornoetnohrafiiu," *Krytyka*, May 2001, no. 5: 24.

idea about or interest in Ukrainian literature. A visual artist and stage designer, Poderviansky has become a cult literary bad-boy in Kyiv as the author of short plays that have been circulated in audio recordings among mass listeners for almost ten years. The fact that his works are made into musical remixes points towards Poderviansky's growing popularity. Moreover, the publication of *Герой нашого часу* (*Hero of Our Time*), by the highly fastidious Kal'variia publishing house, demonstrates Poderviansky's acceptance into the Ukrainian literary mainstream. Although in his preface to the collection, Ihor Lapinsky heralds Poderviansky as a prophet who has reflected the "apocalyptic faithlessness" of the time, Lapinsky also recommends that the reader place the book on a "secret shelf" alongside pornographic magazines and videos.[213]

Poderviansky's plays are extremely disturbing not only because of their violence—unmotivated murders, gluttony, alcoholism, defecation, fights, indiscriminate and unrestricted screwing—but also because of their aggressively obscene language, which is based on three strictly tabooed words associated with copulation. The most shocking aspect of this linguistic choice is that this is a kind of language spoken by a considerable stratum of the population in Ukraine. This "sociolect" has its own name, *surzhyk*, and is a mixture of Ukrainian and Russian whose intermediateness bears sociocultural characteristics of an undereducated, uncultured, boorish, and vulgar populace. *Surzhyk* has become a proper linguistic medium for the product of the most revolting socio-political experiment carried out by the Soviet regime—hybridized Soviet people—to reflect the derangement and idiocies of Soviet life. In addition, *surzhyk* turns out to be equally adequate to represent an impotent and powerless individual in the face of the new order's absurdity.

Constructed from Soviet myths, Poderviansky's plays adopt their main themes and ideas blended in bizarre, macabre scenarios; these themes include: revolutionary romanticism, fraternity among Soviet na-

---

[213] Ihor Lapins'kyi, "Sho neiasno? Vidvaha, nasnaha i zvytiaha Lesia Poderv'ians'koho," introduction to *Heroi nashoho chasu*, by Les' Poderv'ians'kyi (L'viv: Kal'variia, 2000), 9.

tions, Young Pioneer childhood, Communist ideology, military and patriotic upbringing, strong family, and associations of artists and writers.[214] However, it is socialist realism and its canon that are placed under the dramatist's merciless scrutiny. Poderviansky is modulating a corpus of works, produced by the Soviet school of writing, that was used as sociological material to mold the political mythology of the authoritarian state, as well as those from Russian prerevolutionary literature that constituted an integral part of school curriculum, being thoroughly screened and ideologically sanctioned. The title of Poderviansky's collection, for example, replicates the title of Mikhail Lermontov's (1814–1841) canonical work published in 1840. One of the plays, *Павлік Морозов* (*Pavlik Morozov*), supplemented with the subtitle "An Epic Tragedy," draws on an officially designated martyr figure of the period of Stalin's forceful, genocidal collectivization in the agricultural sector in the 1930s. The historical Pavlik Morozov (1918–1932) was killed, in Siberia, by his kulak[215] grandfather for informing on his father to Stalin's secret police; Pavlik's commendable "political vigilance" (a key moment in Soviet propaganda) caused his father's arrest, conviction, and execution. Having been elevated to the status of a heroic symbol, he was forced upon young pioneers as a role model exemplifying the duty of law-abiding Soviet citizens to become informants even at the expense of family ties.

Poderviansky populates his "tragedy" with other real and fictional characters (133–134).[216] The name of Pavlik's mother, who is described as looking like a symbolic Motherland figure in Soviet propaganda posters, is Pelaheia Nylivna. This mother evokes the title character from Maxim Gorky's (1868–1936) *Мать* (*Mother*) (1906), a novel set in 1905 during the first Russian revolution and featuring a religious woman who is converted to revolutionary ideals after her son's arrest as a political ac-

---

[214] Volodymyr Dibrova, "Prynts Hamlet Khams'koho povitu," *Krytyka*, May 2001, no. 5: 26.

[215] Many, if not most, kulaks resisted the Soviet collectivization campaign.

[216] Subsequent references to character descriptions will be to the indicated pages, for they include the cast of characters.

tivist. Furthermore, Pavel Vlasov, Pelaheia Nylivna's illegitimate son and Pavlik's half-brother, the degenerate apelike antagonist in Poderviansky's play, alludes to the revolutionary protagonist in *Мать* (*Mother*). In addition, it was Gorky, the much celebrated spokesman for proletarian culture under Stalin's regime and the first head of the Writers' Union, who formulated the restrictive principles of socialist realism that became the doctrine for future generations of Soviet writers.

Poderviansky's cast of characters also includes a blind prophet in Apollo's temple, Mykola Ostrovsky, who instructs his followers in spiritual refinement and divine matters. Here Poderviansky summons Nikolai (Mykola) Ostrovsky (1904–1936), another legendary figure in Soviet history. After having served in the Red Cavalry during the Civil War (1919–1922), Ostrovsky acted as a Red commissar enthusiastically responding to the call of the Communist Party to participate in the epochal construction of a new society. Wounded several times, affected by typhus and polyarthritis that resulted in paralysis and blindness, he wrote an autobiographical novel, *Как закалялась сталь* (*How the Steel was Tempered*), for which he was awarded the Order of Lenin in 1935. This book was included into the Soviet literary canon and studied at schools. Mythologized as a paradigm of self-sacrifice, Ostrovsky became just another clichéd item in the propaganda discourse. Poderviansky places his prophet into a crystal coffin hung from the ceiling of the Apollo temple in the middle of the Siberian taiga, on the marshes. Architecturally the temple resembles a wooden shed on chicken legs, reminiscent both of Russian folk tales and of *Руслан и Людмила* (*Ruslan and Liudmilla*) (1820) by Aleksandr Pushkin (1799–1837), the founder of modern Russian literature whose oeuvre was reductively interpreted for the instructional needs of the "class-conscious" Soviet educational system. The crystal coffin is also borrowed from Pushkin's poem wherein it is used for a beautiful sleeping princess to lie awaiting the arrival of a prince.

In addition, the play features general Vlasov—Pelaheia Nylivna's lover, Pavel Vlasov's father, and Canaris's secret agent. The text here draws on the historical general Andrei Vlasov (1900–1946), a Red Army officer who collaborated with the Germans during World War II, formed the Russian Liberation Army which fought against the Stalinist regime, was tried and executed in 1946, and became an emblematic traitor. There are also two characters in absentia: Canaris, chief of the Abwehr in the Third Reich—the double of Admiral Wilhelm Canaris (1887–1945), chief of the Abwehr and the hidden hand of the resistance in the Wehrmacht; and Zeus, a heavenly "leader and teacher" (a standard metonymic reference to both Lenin and Stalin). Alionushka and Ivanushka, from a Russian fairy tale, both appear as well, denoting here the monstrous subconscious. Furthermore, the traditionally meek Alionushka is featured as a mermaid cross-pollinated with a vampire.

The "mythological" layer of the play is represented by Menopause, a messenger of the Gods; Sphinx, a winged, clawed monster with breasts and cunt; Bitch and Whore, bloodthirsty chimerae, goddesses of shit, flies, and menstruation; and Minerva's owl, which is turned into a huge fat bird, Filin (eagle-owl), general Vlasov's agent. The supporting cast consists of pioneers, kulaks, fascists, whores, apparitions, devils, dragons, and gorgons.

The scene is set in a Siberian taiga during World War II, a favorite time frame of Soviet literature that tirelessly draws its inspiration from the "Great Patriotic War" to romanticize and lacquer it in heroic discourse. The atmosphere of the play is also supercharged with artificially staged "hunts" in Soviet history—for spies of the hostile bourgeois world as external evil agents and for "enemies of the people" as internal ones. Everybody in the play is drinking, whoring, and fighting. Pavlik, a *Hitlerjugend*-looking hero, murders his father, mother, and the Sphinx; and fucks the whores, the goddesses, Alionushka, and a white lamb, Ivanushka. In the final combat with his King-Kong-shaped half-brother, Pavlik strikes a fatal blow but is tragically squashed by his rival's heavy corpse, which falls on him. The death of the hero is hysterically lamented by Filin, echoing the famous battlefield scene in Shakespeare's *Richard III* (1597).

In his absurdist play, Poderviansky, by tearing down the happy façade that camouflaged violence against individuals in the name of communism, juxtaposes his anti-utopian nightmare to a utopian fantasy created by Soviet authors. Each play in the collection similarly rotates around the same type of absurdities, phobias, and crazed and senseless brutalities. Pornography is probably seen by Poderviansky as the most adequate mechanism to reflect on the calamitous aftermath of Soviet rule. His is exceedingly masculinist discourse; its phallocentrism is made absolute through the dissolution of any, even the most vague, standards of decency. Obscenity comprises the body of Poderviansky's language, and his characters live in and through this obscene language, which predetermines and structures their thinking and being. In his review of *Герой нашого часу* (*Hero of Our Time*), Vadym Trinchi mentions that Poderviansky's collection could have been called *Life of the Genitals*.[217] If the male reproductive organ could have gained a certain physical and intellectual autonomy, it would have acted as Poderviansky's characters do. In his comediography of violence, the phallus *par excellence* invariably becomes the hero of our time.

Not unlike Poderviansky, Yuri Vynnychuk—"one of the groundbreakers of the erotic genre in Ukrainian literature,"[218] termed for his creative productivity as its "symbolic phallus" by Andri Bodnar,[219] and the first editor of the erotic magazine *Гульвіса* (*Lovelace*) published in Lviv in the 1990s—also partakes in far-reaching intertextual games, albeit in a very different manner. Vynnychuk consistently displays creative and whimsical anarchy by juggling different conventions, genres, canons, and cultural codes, new and old alike. Having been turned into a space for engaging in a dialogic relationship with a number of texts—literary, cine-

---

[217] Vadym Trinchii, "Pro pornoetnohrafiiu," 26.

[218] "Iurii Vynnychuk," *Potiah 76: Tsentral'no-ievropeis'kyi literaturnyi chasopys*, 2002, no. 1: 131.

[219] Andrii Bodnar, "Zamist' peredmovy," introduction to *Mal'va Landa,* by Iurii Vynnychuk (L'viv: Piramida, 2004), 5.

matic and historical—his *Житіє гаремноє* (*Life in the Harem*) (1996)[220] demythologizes and demystifies one of the Ukrainian cultural icons of ideal womanhood through its hybridization with the conventional Orientalist fantasies of Western libertine pornography. Vynnychuk fabricates a pseudoautobiographical manuscript of a historical figure—Roxolana—Nastia Lisovska (1505–1558), the most cherished concubine of Süleyman the Magnificent who legally married the sultan and became the first really powerful woman in the Ottoman dynasty. In fact, it is the rise of the political power of Roxolana "that many historians (Westerners and Turks alike) pinpoint as the beginning of the decline of the Ottoman Empire."[221]

Roxolana was captured by the Ottoman vassals during their slave raid into Ukraine in 1520 and donated to the imperial harem by a nobleman who had bought her at a slave market and was greatly impressed by her knowledge of Greek and Latin.[222] Her story has nourished the imaginations of Ukrainian writers, composers, and artists, who have been, throughout the last century, busily creating their male cult of an eminent Hurrem Sultan.[223] The escalation of the Roxolana myth, which

---

[220] Iurii Vynnychuk, *Zhytiie haremnoie* (L'viv: Piramida, 1996); hereafter cited parenthetically in the text. Vynnychuk has also authored a labyrinthine *Mal'va Landa* (L'viv: Piramida, 2004) saturated with grotesque eroticism, and *Vesniani ihry v osinnikh sadakh* (L'viv: Piramida, 2005), in which Vynnychuk claims to have turned all the women he loved into literature.

[221] Filiz Turhan, *The Other Empire: British Romantic Writings about the Ottoman Empire* (New York and London: Routledge, 2003), 51. A more recent publication by Galina Yermolenko counterbalances this negative attitude towards Roxolana by introducing an East European perspective featuring her as a national symbol. See her "Roxolana: 'The Greatest Empress of the East,'" *The Muslim World* 95, no. 2 (2005): 231–48.

[222] Serhii Makhun, "Slaves in the Sublime Porte: Slavic Factor at the Court of Suleiman I," *Den'*, http:// www.day.kiev.ua/DIGEST/2002/01/culture/cu14.htm) (accessed November 23, 2005).

[223] Her life has also inspired a number of Western narratives. Among earlier works, she was portrayed as one of the characters in William D'Avenant's (1606–1668) *Siege of Rhodes* (1656, part 2, 1659), Fulke Graville's (1554–1628) *Mustapha* (1603), and Roger Boyle's (1621–1679) *Mustapha* (1668); and referred to by Francis Bacon (1561–1626) in his "Of Empire" (*Essays*, 1597–1625).

turned into virtual "Roxolanomania,"[224] arrived at a new turn of the spiral with the twenty-six-part TV "serial monster" (1995–1996). Based, in the best case scenario, on five pages of a fifty-year-old factual material,[225] this soap opera has summed up the efforts of literary Roxolaniads to produce a bizarre crossbreed of romantic sexualized patriotism and establish a conspicuous Roxolana stereotype.[226]

As Zabuzhko observes, none of these works focused on Nastia Lisovska's versatile and truly Renaissance personality as an outstanding diplomat, *intrigante*, benefactor, and reformist comparable to her younger contemporary, Catherine de Medici (1519–1589). Instead, the authors were hypnotized by Süleyman and Roxolana's relationship and thus romantically fetishized Roxolana as an object of imperial desire. Such a symbolic role assigned to their female compatriot implicitly involves, among other things, the colonizer–colonized dichotomy. Zabuzhko argues that the fact that Roxolana's status as a love slave could generate the surge of patriotic feelings points towards Ukrainian males' accep-

---

[224] Oleksandr Halenko, "Vytivky ukraïns'koho oriientalizmu," *Krytyka*, April 1999, no. 4: 12.

[225] Ibid., 13.

[226] For example, one of the businesses in Ukraine that deals with marriage, dating, and escort is called *Roxolana Marriage and Travel*. Its services are featured on different websites advertising "Beautiful Ladies from Sevastopol, Crimea," evidently aimed at foreign consumers as the language of the sites is English:
Foreign Women Megasite <www.foreignwomenmegasite.com/links/link1.html>;
Mail Order Brides <www.bridesbymail.com/mob/europe.html>;
Foreign Brides < www.alldatinglinks.com/mailore.html>;
Date-World < www.date-world.com/> (all accessed 14 March 2007).
What adds a sardonic twist to this enterprise is that during the Süleymanic period (1520–1566), which was the golden age of the Ottoman Empire, embracing vast territory and diverse variety of peoples as the result of its successful military campaigns, Ukraine became a donor of concubines for Turkish harems. In addition, one of the largest slave markets of the fifteenth and sixteenth centuries and on, which provided odalisques for harems in the Sublime Porte, was located in Caffa (now Feodosiia) in the Crimea. Of course, the idea of trafficking is probably not the one that the agency intended to highlight; Roxolana most likely figures here as an exemplum of a success story and illustration of the natural charms and attractions Ukraine can offer in terms of specific human resources.

tance of their own subservience in relationship to the Russian Empire.[227] Ukrainian male mythmakers, both past and present, seem to identify with Roxolana, thus implicitly conceding to the conventional colonial strategy of effeminization—when colonizing men apply feminine qualities to colonized males in order to delegitimize, discredit, and disempower them. Since the cult of masculinity traditionally rationalized imperial rule by equating an aggressive, muscular, chivalric model of manliness with racial, national, cultural, and moral superiority, masculinity has become a "tropological site" on which, as Revathi Krishnaswamy writes elsewhere, "many uneven and contradictory axes of domination and subordination in colonial society are simultaneously constituted and contested."[228] It was not only the colonizers who propagated the notion of effeteness, resting the entire structure of colonial homosociality on the ideologeme of effeminacy, but also the Ukrainian elite that internalized such colonial representations, thereby providing a fertile ground for discursive practices that display power in gendered and sexualized terms.

This comprises, in part, Vynnychuk's frame of reference for *Житіє гаремноє* (*Life in the Harem*). Using Roxolana, who has been admitted to the Ukrainian national pantheon of heroes, in the harem setting that she truly enjoys, Vynnychuk plays with the cult of Ukrainian cultural symbols. *Житіє* (*Life*), which the author considers his "most brutal" book,[229] provides yet another highly peculiar page of his "imaginary history" of Ukraine. In one of his interviews, Vynnychuk recalls how he decided to turn this project into literary mystification. Prior to the publication of the novel in installments in the now defunct Lviv newspaper *Post-поступ* (*Post-postup*), an article about the discovery of Roxolana's diary, which provoked an ensuing public scandal around the "immoral" subject matter of the recovered manuscript, appeared. Soiuz Ukraïnok (The Ukrainian

---

[227] Zabuzhko, *Khroniky vid Fortinbrasa,* 168.

[228] Revathi Krishnaswamy, *Effeminism: The Economy of Colonial Desire* (Ann Arbor: University of Michigan Press, 1998), 8.

[229] Vadym Dyshkant, "Ukraïns'ki pys'mennyky ne zhyvut' z literatury," *Den'*, November 4, 2004, http://www.day.kiev.ua/290619?idsource=126816&mainlang=ukr (accessed March 14, 2007).

Women Union) wrote an open letter to Vynnychuk, printed in the daily *Молодь України* (*Youth of Ukraine*), in which they demanded the immediate termination of the publication of the diary. The enraged patriots argued that the dissemination of the discovery is detrimental to Roxolana's illustrious image, and they supported their adamant claim by numerous quotations that seemed to state that Roxolana's sole mission in the harem was to enlighten the sultan about Ukraine.[230]

Interestingly, this is not Vynnychuk's first project aimed at disorienting publishers, readers, and, by extension, the system. He fabricated an epic, *Плач над градом Кия* (*Lament over the City of Kyi*) (1984), supposedly written by a fictitious Irish monk, Rianhabar, who allegedly survived the siege and pillage of Kyiv by Batu Khan's (?–1255) Mongol-Tatar armies in 1240. Vynnychuk's "translation" from Gaelic was published in a then reputable literary newspaper, *Літературна Україна* (*Literary Ukraine*), and in the no less highly regarded journal, *Жовтень* (*October*, 1984, no. 9),[231] and was referred to in scholarly publications and in *Українська літературна енциклопедія* (*The Ukrainian Literary Encyclopedia*).[232] Vynnychuk's Macphersonian undertaking signified an intellectual revolt against the suffocating atmosphere of Soviet cultural dogma, an exquisite aesthetic gesture of evasively political dissent.

While writing his similarly subversive version of Roxolana's life, Vynnychuk clearly articulates and develops those aspects of Roxolana's career that apparently captivated his predecessors and contemporaries, but which were carefully self-censored and suppressed. The author amplifies the sexual overtones of the previous intertexts to produce an erotic manual and thus transgresses a "sacred boundary" of quality literature and its moral stance. In his attempt to provoke the reader to ponder how

---

[230] Iurii Vynnychuk, "Pro vse tse tiazhko rozkazaty," *Potiah 76: Tsentral'no-ievropeis'kyi literaturnyi chasopys*, no. 4, http://www.potyah76.org.ua/potyah/?t=28 (accessed March 16, 2007).

[231] Ibid.

[232] R. I. Dotsenko, "Irlands'ka literatura," in *Ukraïns'ka literaturna entsyklopediia*, vol. 2, ed. I. O. Dzeverin et al. (Kyïv: Ukraïns'ka radians'ka entsyklopediia im. M. P. Bazhana, 1990), 332.

best to speak of lust and desire beyond cliché, he makes the idiom of "high" porn even higher because his language is opulently stylized through transpositions of an obsolete Ukrainian lexis that simulates the authenticity of the sixteenth-century text. At the beginning of the memoir, Roxolana explains:

> Читала юж-єм писанія о коханню од грекинь списані, од сарацинок також, іно нігде не чула, жеби русинка тоє писала. Прето будучи в зуполной пам'яті і цілому розумі, сим хочу прислугу вчинити для всіх, которії в коханню знаходять радість і втіху, ажеби надалі то єще кунштовній справовали і не гляділи на тоє спросно (себто не вбачали розпусту). (6)

> I have read writings about love transcribed from Greek women and also from Saracen women, but never have I heard about a Ruthenian female writing such things. That is why, with my memory sound and my reason integral, I want to do a favor for all those who find joy and delight in love, so that later on they refine lovemaking and not look at it askance (that is regard it as licentiousness).

By featuring Roxolana as the first Ukrainian grand dame of sexual liberation, Vynnychuk, in passing, mimics numerous feminist projects of the discovery and reconstruction of women's literary tradition, further empowering his narrator through the discussion of taboo subjects. Roxolana's story becomes both an erotic confession of her personal experiences and a set of instructions in lovemaking for public use, utilizing the conventions of *Bahname*, the Turkish sixteenth-century erotic guide made popular in Europe in the nineteenth century alongside the Indian *Kama Sutra* and the Arabic *The Perfumed Garden*.

Having laid the scene in the Imperial Harem of Süleyman the Magnificent, the writer does not attempt at its representation as the locus of power in the Ottoman Empire, with an extremely organized system of administration and hierarchy; instead, he turns it into a lascivious sexual playground in which subordination is broken, and concubines, bored to death, delight in lesbianism and indulge in erotic games with eunuchs. Vynnychuk enacts sexuality as a ritual with a highly elaborate code in the place that has become one of the biggest mystifications of Orientalism, which mirrored Western psychosexual needs and provided the space on which to project fantasies of illicit eroticism. Rana Kabbani writes while analyzing English translations of Oriental texts: "The great Seraglio, so deeply entrenched in the European imagination, arrested the perception of even the most gifted scholars. Its shadow fell heavily on the landscape they traveled through, so that they hardly saw anything at all of the details before them."[233] In fact, however, as Leslie P. Peirce contends in an examination of major myths about the Ottoman Empire, sex was not the fundamental dynamic of the harem, which was ruled rather by family politics.[234] Peirce continues that, according to the "more astute and well informed of European observers[,] ... the imperial harem was more like a nunnery in its hierarchical organization and the enforced chastity of the great majority of its members."[235]

While playing with one of the most pervasive myths of the West, with the harem as its central symbol, Vynnychuk's fake memoir draws on the nineteenth-century pornographic convention in the manner of *The Lustful Turk* (1828) and other "obscene novels obtainable at the seedier bookstalls of Paris, with their moustache-twirling Sultans and cowering slave-girls."[236] For example, in *The Seducing Cardinal's Amours* (1830) and *Scenes in the Seraglio* (between 1820 and 1830), the imaginary harem as the "garden of delight" is featured as a staple concept, and the confessional letter is used as a narrative strategy.[237] Likewise, Vynnychuk adopts this mode of representation that allows him to portray his character as both subject and object of erotic desire. In doing this, he

---

[233] Rana Kabbani, *Europe's Myth of Orient: Devise and Rule* (London: Macmillan, 1986), 66.

[234] Leslie P. Peirce, *The Imperial Harem: Women and Sovereignty in the Ottoman Empire* (New York and Oxford: Oxford University Press, 1993), 3.

[235] Ibid., 6.

[236] Margaret Atwood, *Alias Grace* (Toronto: McClelland and Stewart, 1999), 442.

[237] Lisa Z. Sigel, *Governing Pleasures: Pornography and Social Change in England, 1815–1914* (New Brunswick, New Jersey, and London: Rutgers University Press, 2005), 42.

imports the Western tradition, which Ukraine has "missed," together with sexual revolution and other matters related to the body.

In addition to the Western Orientalist intertextual dimension in Vynnychuk's literary counterfeit, a Ukrainian one also exists. This one is linked to Krymsky, whose extensive scholarly output on the Orient contains two histories of Turkey—one published in 1910 (vol. 2)–1916 (vol. 1) in Moscow; the other, in 1924 in Kyiv. Krymsky's studies of the Ottoman Empire under Süleyman's reign embrace a Slavic and particularly Ukrainian element that addresses, among other issues, the role of Roxolana in Turkish history. Krymsky's attitude is ambivalent, or rather antipathetic, towards this historical figure who combines a powerful mind and charisma with ruthlessness towards her political adversaries. The scholar's unprejudiced representation of his famous countrywoman runs counter to the already established reverential portrayals of Hurrem Sultan by his contemporaries.[238] Moreover, Krymsky's histories of the East, characterized by an interdisciplinary approach and vast range of topics, also include an inquiry into erotic and pornographic Oriental literary traditions, as well as into sexual practices and customs. According to Solomiia Pavlychko, Krymsky's "*History of Turkey* abounds with references to sexual mores of sultans' courts, janissaries, and so on. Krymsky became interested in Eastern sexuality long before it became a separate subject of research in Western scholarship."[239] It is notable that his choice of focusing on issues associated with sexuality—in the best case perceived as marginal, in the worst case labeled bourgeois and obscene—is quite unconventional, even unthinkable, in light of the class-oriented bastardized Marxist methodology as the only analytical tool admissible in the Soviet Union. Most likely, his interest in eroticism has come into play as a factor in speculations regarding his possible authorship of the 1912 anonymous erotomaniac narrative.

---

[238] Solomia Pavlychko, *Natsionalizm, seksual'nist', oriientalizm: Skladnyi svit Ahatanhela Kryms'koho* (Kyïv: Osnovy, 2000), 178.

[239] Ibid., 180.

By weaving an intricate canvas out of numerous literary and historical texts, Vynnychuk seems also to pick up unconsciously the line of literary erotomaniac mystifications in the mode of *Сповідь киянина еротомана* (*The Confession of a Kyivan Erotomaniac*). To appreciate his radical intertextuality, with its circularity of reference, one should be familiar with its descriptive systems, themes, social mythologies and histories, and with other texts. However, the reader who does not have this background and whose horizon of expectations is clear will still enjoy the universally recognizable codes, stylistic charm, irony, and eccentric nuances in Vynnychuk's dynamic prose.

Although the texts under consideration here are so different, all chart the Ukrainian social, political, cultural, and sexual body through the infusion and conceptual displacement of pornographic discourse whose function is expanded, making it in part a means of shock therapy. By conducting her "field research in Ukrainian sex," Zabuzhko maps a liminal territory of Ukrainian sexuality to create her own corporeal cartography. Through her protagonist, who experiences erotic and spiritual catharsis, the writer engages in the project of cognitive liberation from the received tradition. Unlike Zabuzhko's body inscape delineated by the immediacy of her erotic becomings, Pokalchuk's challenge to culturally enforced regimes of gender and sexuality does not extend much farther than his literary and political project of producing national pornography; as such, the book does its work, for at some moments it stirs, titillates, and gives rise to frissons of sexual pleasure while still remaining a fantasy of sexuality and sexual liberation that has yet to come of age. Diversely, Vynnychuk's playful pastiche, in which he joins a male harem of Roxolana's admirers, is a deviant postcolonial endeavor wherein everything is inverted with postmodern zest and gusto. While reading, misreading, reassembling, and misinterpreting the system of hereditary and learned texts, rules, and figures in the corpus, Vynnychuk self-consciously lets the machinery show, thus demonstrating the fictitious and constructivist nature of any discourse, including the fanatically professed "objectivity" of socialist realism. In contrast, Poderviansky's pornographic characters are creatures of brutal sexualized reality drawn on the paragons of socialist realist textual productions. His revisionist impulses are directed against this canon, which features imperious and spellbinding Major Texts. Unlike the works of Zabuzhko, Pokalchuk, and Vynnychuk, Poderviansky's violent, satirical, absurdist plays do not represent an iconoclastic break from the Soviet epoch and from socialist realism as its ideological medium. Instead, they signify the degeneration of both.

IV   Zooming the Island In and Out:

Exploratory Desire in Nuala Ní Dhomhnaill, Paul Muldoon, Seamus Heaney, Richard Murphy, Michael Longley, Ciaran Carson and John Montague

In an ambivalent Irish cultural matrix, with its multilayered psycho-historical and sociocultural patterns deposited in literature, the *topos* of the island is underlaid with multiple connotations: it reflects Irish insular psychology; it is the point of destination in numerous seafaring quest narratives; it figures as one of the key symbols of Celtic mythology; and it has been reduplicated in Irish literary heritage since ancient times, making poetry analogous to sailing. The poets have been navigating incessantly along the channels of Irish psychohistory to this place of origin—the territory set apart and insulated from the rest of space—whose internal consistency allows it to attain the existential status of a world and is instrumental in making it a site of auto-reflexivity. In his "Desert Islands," Deleuze emphasizes the essence of the island as "imaginary and not actual, mythological and not geographical."[240] It is the movement of imagination that makes the island a prototype of the collective psyche, a place for return, reconstitution, and re-creation: "The geographical dynamism of the island (island as rupture with the continent, and island as an eruption from the deep) is taken up in the mythical dynamism of mankind on the deserted island (a derived rupture and an original rebeginning)."[241] Although defined as an island, this is rather a nonplace, a *heterotopos* that is more an idea about space than any actual place,[242] an elusive

---

[240] Deleuze, *Desert Islands*, 12.

[241] Ibid., 98.

[242] Benjamin Genocchio, "Discourse, Discontinuity, Difference: The Question of 'Other' Spaces," in *Postmodern Cities and Spaces*, ed. Sophie Watson and Katherine Gibson (Cambridge, Massachusetts: Blackwell, 1995), 42–43.

spatial continuum and a marker of the desire for "beyond." This transient space, unattainable though imaginable, charted by the routes of multiple voyages captures a convoluted nexus of imagination, ideology, and power; moreover, in the postcolonial context, interrogating representations of place and space is crucial for the production of cultural and political identity.

Through a discussion of the *topos* of the island as the stage for, and articulation of, manifold desires, I intend to examine here the ways in which this ideologeme is employed, reformulated, and transformed in different poetic registers by a number of authors while they are surveying the desiring-territories of Irish literary tradition. Although I gravitate towards cross-gender dynamics in these products of both deliberate and unconscious intertextuality by reading Nuala Ní Dhomhnaill's work against a number of texts authored by men, I have no intention either to demonstrate the remarkable qualities of her poetry at the expense of male writers, nor to interpret a rather loosely and conventionally established dichotomy of female/male as that of positive/negative. In addition, Ní Dhomhnaill's concern with the Irish language, which she considers to be her fated medium,[243] allows for an investigation into what Kiberd calls "the depth of the [Irish] political unconscious."[244] While Ní Dhomhnaill's identificatory modality—"in what language *I* is expressed, and *I am* expressed"[245]—undoubtedly challenges the centrality of the colonially imposed language and encompasses a vast network of imaginary projections (historical, cultural, and symbolic), the male English-language poets under consideration represent yet another phase in the perpetual "Translating Ireland" project, initiated by the Revival, as a way of bringing it into being.[246] Incidentally, all of them, with the exception of Richard Murphy—Paul Muldoon, Seamus Heaney, Ciaran Carson, Michael Longley, and

---

[243] Ní Dhomhnaill, "Why I Choose to Write in Irish," 3.

[244] Kiberd, *Inventing Ireland*, 615.

[245] Jacques Derrida, *Monolingualism of the Other; or, The Prosthesis of Origin*, trans. Patrick Mensah (Stanford, California: Stanford University Press, 1998), 28.

[246] See, for example, Cronin's *Translating Ireland* and Kiberd's *Inventing Ireland*.

John Montague—might have developed a symbiotic relationship with Ní Dhomhnaill's poetry as they are among contributing translators to the bilingual edition of her work, *Pharaoh's Daughter* (1990).

In Ní Dhomhnaill's "Immram" ("The Voyage") cycle, the island emerges as a magnetic locus for imagination. A site without any actual locality, it appears at diverse geographical areas that change from day to day: near the Great Blasket, in the Indian Ocean, southwest of Slea Head, in South Dakota, Nevada, Wyoming, or the docks of Galway. The poet thus creates a multidimensional space further amplified by the conflation of fantasy and hallucinatory visions with the external, "objective" world, as well as by the blending of mythic wondrous voyages with distinctly recognizable signs of the present. For example, she arranges an exhibition of a nonexistent island at the Heritage Center and sends a crew of anthropologists to explore the ghostly apparition and to arrive at a unanimous conclusion that it is radioactive.[247] In addition, in a poem that provides a fabulous Isle of Speaking Birds from Máele Dúin's mythic wonderings with a modern counterpart—a shop window piled with stuffed birds—Ni Dhomhnaill's speaker writes a postcard home complaining about unreasonably priced Otherworldly merchandise (*AC,* 94–95).

The poet's phantom landforms materialize and disappear like ancient voices calling one to embark on a quest journey to places unknown and unknowable, as in "An Bhreasaíl" ("Hy-Breasil"):

> Cloisim tú
> ag glaoch orm
> san oíche
>
> ag rá liom teacht
> go dtí do oileán
> draíochta. (*AC,* 76)
>
> I hear you call
> out to me

---

[247] Nuala Ní Dhomhnaill, *The Astrakhan Cloak,* trans. Paul Muldoon (Winston-Salem, North Carolina: Wake Forest University Press, 1993), 84–87; hereafter cited parenthetically in the text as *AC.*

> in the night
>
> asking me to come
> to the Isle
> of Enchantment. (*AC*, 77)

Ní Dhomhnaill further unfolds a mysterious island into the *heterotopology* of a nowhere land. She transforms the pagan Irish paradise into a fluid and luring site that unties the fixity and immobility of space by becoming even more intangible than its literary precursors—a mere sound. This mystic place of dreams, however, consistently reappeared on old maps. The legend says that a patient watcher looking to the West from the extreme west point of Ireland can catch a sight of it during sunset. Some seafarers thought they had located the island and "called the land they found 'Brazil.'"[248]

Likewise, Paul Muldoon's "Immram" and "Immrama" draw on an old saga about Máele Dúin's great voyage among the Blessed Islands featuring the hero's "spiritual quest" and psychological development.[249] However, unlike Ní Dhomhnaill, in whose poetry mythic and contemporary elements are cross-pollinated, Muldoon appropriates the mythic structure and overwrites it with alternative narratives and meanings. He once remarked that the Irish literary tradition is characterized by its "valorization of obliquity and tangeniality" and its concomitant "disregard for the line between sense and nonsense" and "linear narrative."[250] Muldoon himself exemplifies these features in his reassessment of the ancient space in postmodern terms, depicting "voyages that are in any

---

[248] Charles Squire, *The Mythology of the British Islands: An Introduction to Celtic Myth, Legend, Poetry, and Romance* (London: Blackie and Son, 1905), 133.

[249] Joseph Falaky Nagy, *Conversing with Angels and Ancients: Literary Myths of Medieval Ireland* (Ithaca and London: Cornell University Press, 1997), 284.

[250] Quoted by Andrew J. Auge, "To Send a Shiver through Unitel: Imperial Philosophy and the Resistant Word of Paul Muldoon's 'Madoc—A Mystery,'" *Contemporary Literature* 46, no. 4 (2005): 636.

way linear."[251] In the interchange of incessant paradoxes, constant movements between bluntness and evasion and inventive use of language, the speaker of "Immrama" "trails" his father's spirit, with geographical precision, from "the mud-walled cabin" in Ireland to "almost" Argentina.[252] The father of Muldoon's minimalist epic nonetheless ends up, quite ironically but yet consistently with the other legend, in Brazil, as if accidentally "discovering" it and falling in-between the cracks of myth. The author thus disrupts the sociospatial order and decontextualizes coherent mythical, personal, and political narratives.[253]

In "The Disappearing Island," Seamus Heaney also utilizes the traditional discourse of marvelous voyages to the threshold of the Promised Land, a Christianized version of the Blessed Isles of the West, while infusing it with a poetic form of a vision. The speaker of Haney's arid allegory, St Brendan the Navigator, beholds the island capsize, casting everything into the sea:

> The island broke beneath us like a wave.
>
> The land sustaining us seemed to hold firm
> Only when we embraced it *in extremis*.
> All I believe that happened there was vision.[254]

Heaney's flight into the metaphysical is structured on the opposition and fusion of drift and solidity, with its intense relationship of land and water, reality and fantasy; and on an intricate interplay between metaphor and *realia*, in which a "real thing" vanishes, making a place for the exchange between one metaphor and another.[255] The island depicted in the poem could also be Ireland, or Station Island, or the island of the Self. Heaney

---

[251] Steven D. Putzel, "Fluid Disjunction in Paul Muldoon's 'Immram' and 'The More a Man Has the More a Man Wants,'" *Papers on Language and Literature* 32, no. 1 (1996): 90.

[252] Paul Muldoon, *Why Brownlee Left* (London and Boston: Faber, 1980), 23.

[253] Christopher T. Malone, "Writing Home: Spatial Allegories in the Poetry of Seamus Heaney and Paul Muldoon," *ELH: English Literary History* 67, no. 4 (2000): 1084.

[254] Seamus Heaney. *The Haw Lantern* (New York: Farrar Straus Girous, 1987), 51.

[255] Kiberd, *Inventing Ireland*, 598.

dissolves his original landscape by descending into cultural origins below Ireland's topography so pervasive in the elaborate lore of place of his earlier work. Daniel Tobin suggests that in this poem—and this statement can be applied to the other poets under discussion here—the horizons of "consciousness are no longer identified with the geographical horizons. Rather, geography itself reflects an internal state of consciousness.... Things are no longer founded on their own shapes but by a surrounding emptiness that nearly makes them otherworldly."[256]

Richard Murphy's "Sailing to an Island" represents yet another facet of iconoclastic practices in rethinking and reformulating traditional forms and vocabularies. Murphy historicizes geography by populating it with specters of the past and the Cleggan islanders of the present:

> We point all day for our chosen island,
> Clare, with its crags purpled by legend:
> There under castles the hot O'Malley's,
> Daughters of Granuaile, the pirate queen
> Who boarded a Turk with blunderbuss,
> Comb read hair and assemble cattle.[257]

Murphy's island is a space onto which he superimposes a set of cultural, conceptual, and spatial frameworks. His summoning of the ghost of the defiant Granuaile, an adventurous historical figure immortalized in an impressive array of legends, provides the poem with an additional discursive slant. The daughter of the great seafaring clan of the O'Malley's of Clare, Granuaile challenged imperial authority by defending Irish rights and customs and harassing Elizabethan overlords of Ireland. Having been granted, by Elizabeth herself, the charter that gave her *carte blanche* to sail the Western Seas,[258] Granuaile transgressed the female restrictions on mobility by sailing her own fleet and became in part an

---

[256] Daniel Tobin, *Passage to the Centre: Imagination and the Sacred in the Poetry by Seamus Heaney* (Kentucky: University Press of Kentucky, 1999), 219.

[257] Richard Murphy, *New Selected Poems* (London and Boston: Faber, 1989), 3; hereafter cited parenthetically in the text.

[258] Caitlín and John Matthews, *British and Irish Mythology: An Encyclopaedia of Myth and Legend* (London: Diamond, 1988), 86.

emblematic successor of powerful Celtic goddesses and warrior queens. Having been acknowledged by English cartographers and administrators as one of the "leaders of sixteenth-century Ireland, as valid as any of her male peers,"[259] this free-floating female agent provides a nostalgic oppositional backdrop for the mundane lives of her heiresses whose images, nevertheless, have an elegiac ring. Granuaile is the bygone glorious past whose spirit is irreversibly severed from the present, and Murphy's is the quest voyage for the myth of a "shrewd and brutal swordswoman" (3).

In Murphy's reading of the *topos*, the island turns into a symbolic site of violent femininity and an arena for desire to capture its phantasms. In other rearticulations of this poetic trope, however, the desire is often structured, channeled, manipulated, and territorialized into sexuality through the translation of the landform in the ocean into a woman's body—one of the Ur-metaphors which is rooted in the originary etiological myths[260] and has quite predictably evolved into a pseudogeographic locus for the enactment of desire. The ritualized repetitive pattern of the imaginary morphology of specifically gender-coded islands thus becomes instrumental in establishing the invariable parameters of cultural meanings, which secure the workings of certain symbolic orders within the heterosexual matrix. In this respect, normative heterosexuality crafts a corporeal contour that vacillates between the materiality of the land and the female body and the imaginary. In addition, the stratification of the "natural" (feminine island) and "social" (masculine navigator) based on the tired dyadic differentiation of "sexes" and their spheres of influence reinforces the conventional scenario in which, according to Judith Butler, "the social unilaterally acts on the natural and invests it with its param-

---

[259] Ann Chambers, *Granuaile: The Life and Time of Grace O'Malley c. 1530–1603* (Dublin: Wolfhound Press, 1998), 151. Chambers refers to a new map of Ireland published several years after Granuaile's visit to the court of Elizabeth, "where her name figures prominently among the listed Irish chieftains—the only woman included" (ibid).

[260] Darby Lewes, *Nudes From Nowhere: Utopian Sexual Landscapes* (Lanham, Boulder, New York, and Oxford: Rowman and Littlefield, 2000), 3.

eters and its meanings."[261] However, though seemingly fixed and restricted by the imposed spatial and discursive boundaries, this body
tends to move beyond its own limits and constraints.

Thus, among specific usages of female bodies, as territories in the
symbolic production of Western culture, gendering an uncharted landscape as feminine and equating woman with untrodden desiring-zones
have undiminishable surplus value. While focusing on the forms of en-
coding of male desire in European literature, within various historical and
geographical frameworks, Klaus Theweleit emphasizes that as long as
the "body of woman continues to serve as a territory of desire in place of
the body of the earth, which is withheld, there is no need for historical
images to die away."[262] In the case of Ireland, where the collective psychological paradigm has been determined to a considerable extent by a
traumatic sense of history, the land traditionally allegorized as a woman
is "laden with a history and mythology of invasion, dispossession, planta-
tion, famine, eviction, land wars, emigration, and rural depopulation."[263]
Referring to the Irish literary tradition, Kiberd states that the "age-old
notion of the land as female" contributed to a conventional representation
of women as arenas of contest and conquest languishingly awaiting sal-
vation by a "gallant national saviour."[264]

Ciaran Carson's "The Insular Celts" provides an archetypal template of Celtic sensibility that emblematizes the earth's body as the body
of infinite womanhood. Carson's first "cartographers"—the poet's oeuvre
in general reveals his longstanding fascination with maps[265]—establish
their patterns of iconography of the Irish landscape by constructing a

---

[261]   Judith Butler, *Bodies That Matter: On the Discursive Limits of 'Sex'* (New York
      and London: Routledge, 1993), 4.
[262]   Klaus Theweleit, *Male Fantasies: Women, Floods, Bodies, History*, trans. Ste-
      phen Conway in collaboration with Erica Carter and Chris Turner, vol. 1 (Minnea-
      polis: University of Minnesota Press, 1987), 359.
[263]   Nash, "Remapping the Body/Land," 244.
[264]   Kiberd, *Inventing Ireland*, 362.
[265]   David Wheatley, "'The Blank Mouth': Secrecy, Shibboleths, and Silence in North-
      ern Irish Poetry," *Journal of Modern Literature* 25, no. 1 (2001): 10–11.

sexual space superimposed on the land, which becomes a double-valanced site for acquisition, subordination, and settlement. His metaphorization of femininity, in which female body/land turns into the surface for male inscriptions, becomes the condition of men's historical and cultural production:

> To hard hills of stone they will give
> The words for breast; to meadowland,
> The soft gutturals of rivers,
>
> Tongues of water; to firm plains, flesh,
> As one day we will discover
> Their way of living, in their death.[266]

The body of the feminized island traversed by relentless mapmakers, converting its curved spaces into flat charts, is allotted thus to the place both of a body outside discourse and of the site for the production and operation of power. As Elizabeth Grosz maintains, "[t]he appropriation of the right to a place or space is correlative with men's seizure of the right to define and utilize a spatiality that reflects their own self-representations."[267] Carson's colonizers of Ireland name the land into being by installing topography at a prelinguistic site, in the act of symbolic appropriation that is "inseparable from the seizure of the land itself."[268]

As opposed to Carson's almost benevolent acting upon the bodyscape, Heaney's "Act of Union" shifts into the domain of blatant politics, where the Anglo-Irish relations are represented in terms both of a gendered island and of a sexual act:

> Your back is a firm line of eastern coast
> And arms and legs are thrown
> Beyond your gradual hills. I caress

---

[266] Ciaran Carson, "The Insular Celts," in *Contemporary Irish Poetry*, ed. Anthony Bradley (Berkeley: University of California Press, 1988), 396.

[267] Elizabeth Grosz, "Women, *Chora*, Dwelling," in *Postmodern Cities and Spaces*, ed. Sophie Watson and Katherine Gibson (Cambridge, Massachusetts: Blackwell, 1995), 55.

[268] Geoff King, *Mapping Reality: An Exploration of Cultural Cartographies* (New York: St. Martin's Press, 1996), 28.

> The heaving province where our past has grown.
> I am the tall kingdom over your shoulder
> That you would neither cajole nor ignore.[269]

Female "bogland"—an allusion to one of Heaney's complex and ambivalent feminine key-symbols that has "bottomless" connotations—is helplessly prostrated, limbs far apart, with no role except enforced submission, under the gaze and in the possession of the aggressive, warriorlike masculinity inflicting pain that is like pulsating explosions within a mined territory, "rending," "battering," "burst[ing]." Besides the pain of childbirth, the description contains a more sexually violent variant of interpretation, that of rape, penetration, ejaculation. Here, space is conceived in terms of colonization and domination.

The connections among conquest, colonization, and rape, and the employment of a traditional Irish poetic trope of the rape of the female land, by the male aggressor,[270] are made even more explicit in Heaney's poem "Ocean's Love to Ireland":

> The ruined maid complains in Irish
> Ocean has scattered her dream of fleets,
> The Spanish prince has spilled his gold
>
> And failed her ... (47)

This "possessed and repossessed" body/island becomes an object of a double assault to exterior malefactors and benefactors. The anthropomorphic, feminized, and sexualized territory/land is either exposed to a male gaze or subjected to intrusion.[271] In both poems, Heaney seems to accept the definition of Ireland as essentially feminine, in which femininity

---

[269] Seamus Heaney, *North* (London: Faber, 1975), 49; hereafter cited parenthetically in the text.

[270] Steven Matthews, *Irish Poetry: Politics, History, Negotiation. The Evolving Debate, 1969 to the Present* (London: Macmillan, 1997), 119.

[271] Karen Marguerite Moloney offers an unconventional approach to Heaney's oeuvre (including "Ocean's Love to Ireland") by reading it in the framework of the *Feis* of Tara ("marriage of sovereignty"). Moloney emphasizes the poet's reverence for archetypal femininity and interprets it as an emblem of hope for Ireland. See her *Seamus Heaney and the Emblems of Hope* (Columbia: University of Missouri Press, 2007), 72-88.

is linked with subordination to the "masculine" colonizer, an "imperially / Male" (49) speaker with his assertively active lexicon and syntax, that reflects a widely spread colonial strategy to implement the structures of external authority, basing them on gender asymmetry. In fact, while deliberating on the genesis of his poetry, Heaney compares the process of creating a poem with a "somnambulist encounter between masculine will and intelligence and feminine clusters of image and emotion. I suppose the feminine element for me involves the matter of Ireland, and the masculine strain is drawn from the involvement with English literature."[272] Heaney's "Act of Union" and "Ocean's Love to Ireland" seem to draw self-consciously on this culturally internalized traditional gender distinction.

The tendency to employ generic plot and imagery in an exploration of the morphology of body/island is explicit in Ní Dhomhnaill's "Oileán" ("Island") and Michael Longley's "Galapagos." Both poets use a corporeal island as a ready-made framework, by projecting open spaces of the body onto a natural landscape; both invent their bodyscapes to undertake metaphoric mappings of the regions of desire; both present a map-like body view.

The lexical arrangement of Ní Dhomhnaill's "Oileán" ("Island") fluctuates within a lexico-semantic field of fluidity. The recurrent image of water incorporates time and space and functions both as a marker of the text's coherence and as the nucleus of its structure. In this the poet draws on the tradition in which water is regenerative—essential for life, fertility, and healing in the Celtic religion[273]—and on the depth and mystery of water as the supreme symbol of the feminine in Irish mythology. "Oileán" ("Island") begins with a panoramic view of the body in the great ocean exposed to the author's cartographic eye. The poem is structured on an antithetic principle that incorporates a single theme: the lover— "fuarán" ("a cooling drink"), "deoch slánaithe" ("a healing drink"); the

---

[272] Seamus Heaney, *Preoccupations: Selected Prose 1968–78* (London: Faber, 1980), 34.

[273] Green, *Dictionary of Celtic Myth*, 223–24.

poetic persona—"i lár mo bheirfin" ("when I was burning"), "sa bhfiabhras" ("when I was feverish").[274] Contrasting pairs create a rich and contradictory spectrum of sensual perceptions that run like an electric charge between two opposite poles, delineated along a bipolar semantic axis, providing an exchange of pleasure as inexhaustible as nature. Ní Dhomhnaill consistently exploits water imagery in her vista, fusing natural and human shapes to create a refracting aquatic surface for sunlight. Simultaneously, accumulated water imagery works to dissolve the solidities of conventional imagistic constructions.

The opening lines of the three initial stanzas form the following structural pattern:

"Oileán is ea do chorp" ("Your body an island")

(stanza I);

"Toibreacha fíoruisce iad t'uisí" ("Your forehead a springwell")

(stanza II);

"Tá do dhá shúil / mar locha sléibhe" ("Your eyes / are mountain lakes") (stanza III).

Parallel constructions shape a "pictorial" part of the poem, traditionally romantic in its visual mode. It is static due to its lexical composition; nouns and adjectives preponderate over verbs. Much in its poetical arsenal—trite epithets and metaphors in the manner of established clichéd images—is appropriated from male poetry.

In Longley's "Galapagos," the woman/island correlation may be considered a double allusion in which both elements are interpreted by each other as in the surrealist game of *l'une dans l'autre*. This interchangeability of woman and land is characteristic of many of Longley's exquisite amorous poems. As Peter McDonald writes, "[t]he processes involved in 'nature-' and 'love-' poetry are very similar in Longley, each

---

[274] Ní Dhomhnaill, *Selected Poems / Rogha Dánta*, 70, 71; hereafter cited parenthetically in the text as *RD*.

necessitating a reverential exploration of new territory."[275] "Galapagos" adds yet another modification to an impressive volume of male poetic production, cited and analyzed by Theweleit, as if supporting the scholar's statement that "in all European literature (and literature influenced by it), desire, if it flows at all, flows in a certain sense through women. In some way or other, it always flows in relation to the image of woman. (It is far rarer for it to flow aimlessly....)"[276]

Both Ní Dhomhnaill and Longley's spatial definitions are based on a cinematic representation of the island; but while Ní Dhomhnaill's is a panoramic shot permeated with images of fluidity, Longley's is a tracking one that narrates the body in a fragmentary fashion. "Galapagos" also starts descriptively, but more dynamically, by introducing the verb "scattered" in the first line. The word is loaded with energy and leads the verse straight into its subject:

> Now you are scattered into islands
> Breasts, belly, knees, the mouth of Venus,
> Each a Galapagos of the mind ...[277]

Longley's voyager-lover, who celebrates his intellect as he pays tribute to a body/island that is his to investigate and discover, accentuates conventional symbols of female sexuality. His landscape-as-woman metaphor seductively invites one to explore geographical and sexual frontiers within a particular body range—from neck to upper thighs. Such representational strategies are ironically confronted in Kathy Prendergast's *Body Map Series* (1983), in which she also revisits the golden age of imperial masculinity. The artist evokes the great age of British Empire engaged in redrawing the world map by providing her images with annotations in the manner of Victorian maps and diagrams. As Catherine Nash writes: "The breasts are labelled as volcanic mountains, the abdo-

---

[275] Peter McDonald, "Michael Longley's Homes," in *The Chosen Ground: Essays on the Contemporary Poetry of Northern Ireland*, ed. Neil Corcoran (Bridgend: Seren; Chester Springs: Dufour, 1992), 74.

[276] Theweleit, *Male Fantasies*, 272

[277] Michael Longley, *Poems 1963–1983* (Edinburgh: Salamander; Dublin: Gallery, 1985), 69.

men as desert, the navel as crater. The map of this body in *Enclosed Worlds in Open Spaces* is flanked by cross sections of the volcanic mountains/breasts, the desert/abdomen, and a tableland above the pubic area marked as a mountain range."[278] Unlike Ní Dhomhnaill, who opposes such surveying techniques in representing the female body by romanticizing her personal geography, thereby concerning herself with forehead, eyes, and eyelashes, Longley appears to comply with the convention that promotes body-charting techniques restricted to erotogenic zones; he seems to apply mapping that is determined in advance. He observes fragmented, disunited parts of the female body available for male penetration and knowledge. His selectively designed corporeal cartogram resembles in a way medieval portolan charts, used to map small areas for navigation purposes. Longley's representational strategy of fragmentation, however, is double-edged and may provoke a completely opposite interpretation, according to which disjuncture becomes an act of resistance to the conventional practices of totalizing woman. Commenting on such a discursive politics, Mary Ann Caws, for instance, points out that "being partial prevents our being seen as homogeneous, and thus acts against the exclusion or appropriation of 'all of us,' all our mind and body, since we are seen only in part."[279] In this respect, Longley's feminized island, or rather islandized woman, becomes a destabilizing, decentered place—a gendered *heterotopos* of the Other.

Although magnetized by the exotic world of Galapagos, Longley's speaker remains a scientist, classifying and categorizing as part of his rationalizing project. Under his taxonomic eye, a kind of prehistoric life of instincts emerges: the tortoise, which tends to live almost eternally; the iguana, with stable, unshifting eyes; and the night-dwelling lemur. Natural, organic species inhabiting this feminized landscape emphasize its in-

---

[278] Nash, "Remapping the Body/Land," 231.

[279] Mary Ann Caws, "Ladies Shot and Painted: Female Embodiment in Surreal Art," in *The Female Body in Western Culture: Contemporary Perspectives*, ed. Susan Rubin Suleiman (Cambridge, Massachusetts, and London: Harvard University Press, 1985), 272.

stinctiveness, unconsciousness, and sensuality completely divided from the mental or spiritual. All are weird, "peculiar"; everything is in slow motion, almost immovable, unalterable, and time seems to have stood still. This wild, oscillated, insular world is invaded by a male protagonist, a scientist, whose mind is ready to explore the/a female realm, explicitly emphasizing the binary mapping of the masculine, progress-oriented civilization and the feminized, natural, unhistorical world.

The idea of a triumphant male intellect is intensified by the reference to the *Beagle*, the English frigate of the nineteenth century on which Charles Darwin (1809–1882) carried out his naturalist research. This was done at a time when male explorers and navigators studied, described, and classified—and thus acquired control over—unknown and portentous places, frequently associated with the fecundity of both aboriginal flora and women. The poem's title too evokes the immediate association with Darwin, since his name has become inseparable from the Galapagos Islands, whose harsh contours sheltered strange creatures that appeared nowhere else. It is also worth mentioning that Darwin's expedition to the Galapagos, one of the most significant voyages in scientific exploration that remains the nineteenth century's most unsettling legacy, fundamentally changing the world's vision about life, provided much experiential evidence that fuelled his later theorizing.

Darwinism, and especially *The Descent of Man* (1871), was also instrumental in clearly reinstating the view that civilization was driven by masculine reason and energy, demonstrating the physical, mental, and moral superiority of male over female to support the assumptions that were deeply ingrained in the social thought of the tradition.[280] Longley's scientist is very much like an inquisitive Victorian gentleman, a focal point in the evolution of the species: under the mythic sails of evolutionary theory, he embarks on an exploratory quest voyage constrained by the limits of phallogocentric cultural mappings. Furthermore, the Darwinian

---

[280] Sandra Siegel, "Literature and Degeneration: The Representation of 'Decadence,'" in *Degeneration: The Dark Side of Progress*, ed. J. Edward Chamberlin and Sander L. Gilman (New York: Columbia University Press, 1985), 205–206.

allusion provides some disturbing implications for Longley's compart-
mentalization of the female body. Darwin personifies nature as female in
an implicitly violent manner through his imagery of wedging and wedges
mutilating anthropomorphic land, which is charged with brutality and is
"shockingly sadistic."[281] The poem also resorts to generally accepted use
of gender in the discourse of discovery.

Both Longley's visual surveillance of island/woman—with desire as
surveying instrument, implying latent violence suggested by metaphoric
dismemberment—and Heaney's discourse of the perpetrator of violence,
differ from Ní Dhomhnaill's anthropomorphic island, which is not specifically gendered. Her deterritorialization of sexuality erodes an established
grid and nullifies the binarism of masculine and feminine. Her island
somehow becomes an island of a manly woman and of a womanly man,
to paraphrase James Joyce. It is essentially androgynous, if compared to
the explicit gender roles in her other poems, those addressed to a man,
wherein she is very frank in emphasizing male virility. She thus ensures
herself the freedom to trespass on assumed gender norms, casting a
seductive spell of uncertainty and warping fixed gendered subject-object
positions.

The ambivalence of Ní Dhomhnaill's corporeal landform invites a
disparate play of interpretations. Patricia Boyle Haberstroh, for example,
insists that the poem "describes a man's body" and sees it as Ní Dhomhnaill's homage to the "male muse."[282] If this assumption is developed
further, the poet assigns her female speaker the privilege of the gaze
through gender role reversal. In this she seems to appropriate elaborately constructed masculinist literary *somatopias*, in which for centuries,
as Darby Lewes argues, "women were represented as a bewildering
variety of topographical forms: islands, peninsulas, even entire conti-

---

[281] Gillian Beer, *Darwin's Plots: Evolutionary Narrative in Darwin, George Eliot and
Nineteenth-Century Fiction* (Cambridge: Cambridge University Press, 2000), 71–
72.

[282] Haberstroh, *Women Creating Women*, 186.

nents,"[283] traditionally acting out the conflict between masculinized culture and feminized nature. On a less gender-oriented note, one may also assume that the island described in "Oileán" ("Island") is Inis na mBró or An Fear Marbh (The Dead Man), which looks like a man in repose and is one of the Blasket Islands situated off Ireland's southwest coast. This implication would evoke traditional journeys to the wondrous Isles of the West in Irish legend and myth, as well as places quintessentially Irish. This interpretation pulls yet another string of associations. The famed Blasket islands, located at the end of the world, were beloved of generations of poets for whom they represented the politically potent vision of Gaelic and free Ireland and were perceived to be a "Homeric Gaelic fount of simplicity and rugged human endurance."[284]

Deborah McWilliams Consalvo's interpretation based on John Montague's eroticized translation runs counter to the previous one, for she views the island as female.[285] In fact, if read intertextually within European tradition, the poem clearly contains a plethora of transmigrating images conventionally correlated in male poetry with female body as a stage for desire: woman-in-the-water, woman as a cooling stream, woman as a fountain from which man drinks, vagina as wave, love as a sea voyage.[286] In addition, Ní Dhomhnaill's serene, almost puritanically chaste depiction is disturbed by the metaphor of ploughing, which is recurrent in her poetry and is associated with the male perspective. The latter opens up yet another possibility of reading the poem as a poetic gender cross-dressing, with all its textual simulacra and parodic implications similar to the ones in "Amhrán An Fhir Óig" ("Young Man's Song") (*RD*, 80–81). Both this self-referential intertextuality and the dialogue the

---

[283] Lewes, *Nudes From Nowhere*, 15.

[284] Kevin Toolis, "The Only Gaels in the World," *Guardian Unlimited*, March 19, 2000, http://books.guardian.co.uk/reviews/history/0,,148306,00.html (accessed March 29, 2007)—a review of Cole Moreton's *Hungry for Home: Leaving the Blaskets: A Journey from the Edge of Ireland* (New York: Penguin, 2001).

[285] Deborah McWilliams Consalvo, "The Lingual Ideal in the Poetry of Nuala Ní Dhomhnaill," *Éire-Ireland* 30, no. 2 (1995): 151.

[286] Theweleit, *Male Fantasies*, 283.

poet thus engages in with the canon—past and present; Irish, British and European—clearly point out her postcolonial, postmodern, and feminist textual strategies of rewriting.

Although I consider Ní Dhomhnaill's somatopic metaphor to be essentially androgynous, gendering it as female does not necessarily mean that the traveler sailing the white bronze boat and the island have to be cast on the binary opposition of sexes. Ní Dhomhnaill's evocative power, kaleidoscopic affluence of meaning, and carnivalesque shape-shifting of poetic voices may elicit the suggestion that the poem implies homoerotic desire in that both the speaker and the island are female. This ambiguity in gender fluidity leaves the definite and fixed character of such constructs as sex and gender and of subject-object relations in suspense, as in another Ní Dhomhnaill poem, "Leaba Shíoda"—"Labysheedy (The Silken Bed)" (*RD*, 154–157). A double of "Oílean" in terms of its rhetorical and formal elements, this work, according to some critics, is one of Ní Dhomhnaill's "most beautiful and accomplished love poems [that] has been described as a classic among lesbian poems worldwide."[287] From this perspective, all the water imagery of "Oílean" mentioned above as consistent with male canonical representations may acquire diametrically opposite connotations, relating the whole semantic field of liquidity to exclusively feminine experiences. While theorizing lesbian sexuality, Judith Rooth, for example, writes that the female body, "whose morphology, perceived as myriad and diverse, configures an excessive uncountability that parallels the theoretical ungraspability of the liquid and provides a pretext for the originary fragmentation of polymorphous erotogeneity seen as characterizing feminine sexuality."[288]

Another turn of the "feminine" spiral in the above mentioned McWilliams Consalvo's argument also links Ní Dhomhnaill's island to the representation of the fecundity of the Irish land. This reading would equate the island with Ireland-as-body and thus associate the poem with a tradi-

---

[287] Nic Dhiarmada, "Tradition and the Female Voice," 391.

[288] Judith Rooth, *A Lure of Knowledge: Lesbian Sexuality and Theory* (New York: Columbia University Press, 1991), 124.

tional symbolic representation of the country as female. Moreover, in one of her interviews, Ní Dhomhnaill speaks about her multiple muses and concludes:

> The greatest muse in Ireland is the country—Éire, again seen as a woman, and the whole sovereignty of Ireland. That's what lies deepest in our hearts here in Ireland. There has been an ongoing love affair between people and the land and the land and the people here for millennia. And we have lavished our imaginations on it until we have projected on to it the depths of our own psyches.[289]

Is that where Ní Dhomhnaill is coming from in "Oileán" ("Island")? Interestingly, in the same interview, the poet also says, "But the muse doesn't have to be either male or female,"[290] as if defying any urge to dichotomies and producing the androgynous vision of the emblematic source of inspiration whose gender boundaries are as permeable and ambiguous as the body of her island.

The motif of a traveler or navigator, reminiscent of numerous voyage motifs in the Irish literary tradition, is also elaborately expressed in "Oileán" ("Island"). However, if for Longley the traveler is a scientist, even on his way to the islands of enchantment, Ní Dhomhnaill's poetic persona romantically sails a white bronze boat under "na seolta boga bána / bogóideacha" (*RD,* 70, "the soft white / billowing sails," *RD,* 71). White sails here may allude to a victorious journey in the folktale of Céatach, Son of King Cor from Ireland; hoisted on his return from Greece, the white sails should signal to his wife that he is alive whilst black sails should signify his death.[291] White sails, with a red touch of love and passion, would move the bronze boat of the explorer-lover, its dynamics being enhanced by a graphic, spiral movement achieved through a manipulation of the word "cleite" ("feather"), which slips and spins from one line

---

[289] Rebecca E. Wilson, "Nuala Ní Dhomhnaill," in *Sleeping with Monsters: Conversations with Scottish and Irish Women Poets,* ed. Gillean Somerville-Arjat and Rebecca Wilson (Edinburgh: Polygon, 1990), 153.

[290] Ibid.

[291] Sean O'Sullivan, ed. and trans., *Folktales of Ireland* (Chicago: University of Chicago Press, 1966), 48–49.

to the other, occupying different positions to emphasize the aural quality
of words:

> gan barr*chleite* amach uirthi
> ná bun*chleite* isteach uirthi
> ach aon *chleite* amháin
> droimeann dearg
> ag déanamh ceoil ... (*RD*, 70; my italics)

> not a feather out of place on it
> but one feather
> red feather with white back
> making music
> to my self on board ... (*RD*, 71)

The speaker will navigate under the billowing sails of Irish folkloric imagery, for Ní Dhomhnaill's description of the boat reproduces almost verbatim the recurrent passage from the legend "Art, King of Leinster," thus
making the poem a collage of assorted images and textual blocks from
the oral tradition. The passage, iterated three times in the legend, reads:
"He hoisted his soft bulging sails, there wasn't a top feather turning in or
out in his delightful beautiful one-legged, slender, smooth vessel, from
stern to stern, except one brown, white-backed, red feather on the top of
the highest mast, where it made music, sport, and mischief for the hero
on board."[292] Ní Dhomhnaill's subversive analytic mimicry allows her to
"quote" freely from different sources and to sail across the grids established by different cultural cartographies, constantly trying on the voices
and masks of the canonical repertoires. Besides, a compressed repetition of the island image at the end, which completes the frame initiated
by the opening line of the verse, brings to the surface the associations
with both *aisling* and *immram*, as if supplementing the mystic island of
"An Bhreasaíl" ("Hy-Breasil") with body.

Essential differences between the textual dynamics, strategies,
image production, and semantic valences in Ní Dhomhnaill and male
authors become particularly visible in the English translation of "Oileán"

---

[292] Ibid., 99, 101, 107.

by Montague. His "Island" demonstrates how and to what degree Ní Dhomhnaill's poem is deterritorialized in the process of its decoding, re-coding, interpretation, and "refraction" in the target cultural and linguistic system. I would also like to explain at the outset that at no stage in my analysis do I question Montague's superior qualities and poetic idiosyn-crasies, yet the overall strategy of his beautiful poetic maneuvers con-sists in a total stylistic and semantic reaccentuation and intensification of the original. Montague's interpretative transcription tends to lead to an additional asymmetry between the source (Irish) and the target (English) text, which exists on its own anyway, inherent in the interface of Irish and Anglo-Irish traditions.

Although, in some cases, Montague follows the original quite close-ly, his lexico-semantic and stylistic transformations influence the poem as a whole, creating a highly sexualized image of the body/island. That view is established in the initial stanza by the insertion of "nude," with all its erotic associations:

> Your nude body is an island
> asprawl on the ocean bed. How
> beautiful your limbs, spread-
> eagled under seagull's wings.[293]

By modifying Ní Dhomhnaill's corporeal island with this particular attri-bute, Montague seems to emphasize conventionalized regimes that rep-resent woman's body laid flat for exposure: nudity, as opposed to naked-ness, is always, according to John Berger, placed on display, and that display is always for the male spectator.[294] The body on display acknowl-edged openly as the object of desire is to a considerable extent excluded from the erotics of exchange and becomes a site for narrating the sexu-ality of an active masculine lover. The lexical addition in translation pulls the whole set of elaborations into this particular erotic key. Consequently,

---

[293] Nuala Ní Dhomhnaill, *Pharaoh's Daughter*, revised edition, trans. Ciaran Carson et al. (Winston-Salem, North Carolina: Wake Forest University Press, 1993), 41; hereafter cited parenthetically in the text as *PhD*.

[294] John Berger, *Ways of Seeing* (London: Pelican, 1972), 54.

"mara móire" ("of great ocean") becomes "ocean bed," to culminate in an impressive mirrorlike image of "spread-eagled" under "seagulls' wings," like a bird in flight and its shadow, one male, one female. The introduction of an eagle V-shape in Montague's translation—consistent with other female triangles and great V's ceaselessly duplicated in Western culture—makes the erotic even more explicit. All this is correlated to the original: "Tá do ghéaga spréite ar bhraillín / gléigeal os farraige faoileán" (*PhD,* 40, "Your limbs are spread on a bright sheet / over a sea of gulls"). Montague's erotic voyage logically ends in the climactical last stanza undercutting the ambiguity of Ní Dhomhnaill's poem:

> Montague's version
>
> ... thrust
> through foaming seas
> and come beside you
> where you lie back,
> wistful, emerald,
> islanded. (*PhD,* 41, 43)
>
> Original
>
> ... threabhfainn
> trí fharraigí arda
> is thiocfainn chughat
> mar a luíonn tú
> uaigneach, iathghlas,
> oileánach. (*PhD,* 40, 42)
>
> Interlinear
>
> I would plough
> through high seas
> and I would come to you
> where/as you lie
> lonely, emerald,
> islandlike.

As opposed to Mantague, who bases his representation on the manifestly divisive logic of two extremes—"thrusting" masculinity and passively awaiting femininity, the original creates a zone where the distinction is obscured.

The analogous economy of translation can also be found when the fluidity of blood and honey in Ní Dhomhnaill—"tá íochtar fola orthu is uachtar meala" (*PhD,* 40, "mix of blood and honey")—is replaced by "deeps of blood, honey crests" (*PhD,* 41), with distinct opposition of depth and surface, liquidity and firmness, in Montague's translation. The polysemantic "crest," absent in the original, involves a change in paradigmatic view over the image. This transformation is sustained further with the insertion of extremely expressive metaphoric epithets: "A cooling fountain you furnish / in the furious, sweltering heat" (*PhD,* 41), while the original reads: "Thabharfaidís fuarán dom / i lár mo bheirfin" (*PhD,* 40, "Could give me a cool drink / should I be burning"). A well becomes a fountain with a visible upward motion through the surface, its vertical thrust eliminating the touch of Otherworldliness in Ní Dhomhnaill's image.[295] The procedure of stressing the opposites unbalances the text, shifting its lexical, semantic, and stylistic weight and introducing new imagistic dimensions. In general, the translator overaccentuates the binary logic of the poem, inserting contrastable planes of his own.

Montague's erotization is emphasized by Robert Welch as a shortcoming in an otherwise "elegant and well-crafted" translation. Having quoted the last stanza, Welch continues that, unfortunately, here translation interferes "with the intelligence and awareness of the original, in that the sexual note, which is inserted, distracts from the beautiful manoeuvre the poem is making. Nuala, in the poem, is translating Mangan ("Dark Rosaleen") back into the Irish of Bardic poetry ("iathghlas, oileánach"), something the (male?) sexuality of the translation omits."[296]

---

[295] Since wells involve underground sources, they were perceived by the Celts as a "means of communicating with the underworld, as a link between the upper and lower worlds" (Green, *Dictionary of Celtic Myth,* 224).

[296] Robert Welch, "Translation as Tribute," *Poetry Ireland Review* 34 (1992): 129. James Clarence Mangan's ballad "Dark Rosaleen," referred to by Welch, is a reworking of a folk song that combines political allegory "with frank sexual imagery," which has been "diluted and etherealized" in Mangan (C. L. Innes, *Woman and Nation in Irish Literature and Society, 1880–1935* [Athens, Georgia: University of Georgia Press, 1993], 21).

Throughout the target text, Montague's insertion of a sexual note by means of the development of erotic images of male desire consistently disturbs the original and seems to reinscribe the traditional representations Ní Dhomhnaill in fact eschews. Her "Oileán" may be read as an expurgated "translation" of male narratives into her own voice, for she "translates" into Irish all that has been translated out of it. Montague "translates" it back into male stereotypes.[297] What was meant to be opposed arrives at its point of departure in translation. The implied proto-model and the translator's sexual sensibility are superimposed, thus multiplying male eroticism at least twofold by means of conventional male representation. The translator concretizes the potently polyvalent source text by verbalizing its hypothetic implications and limiting the poetic perception by one suggested invariant reading.

It must be acknowledged that Montague's interpretation of "Oileán" is remarkably appealing. McWilliams Consalvo, for example, refers to it in her "The Lingual Ideal in the Poetry of Nuala Ní Dhomhnaill" to demonstrate appreciatively how his version, as opposed to Hartnett's translation, captures "explicitly the eroticism of the poet's description."[298] (It is worthwhile mentioning here that the degree of adequacy of Hartnett's target text is high). It seems that the line between the translation and the original text disappears, and the former starts dominating the latter, when McWilliams Consalvo writes that Montague's translation "illustrates not

---

[297] In one of her interviews, Ní Dhomhnaill uses Montague's "Island" to illustrate the difference in how male and female poets translate her work, thus bringing forward the idea of the gendered nature of translation: "In the poem 'Oiléan' ('Island'), the last verse begins 'If I had a boat.' This is written in the conditional and very much an aspiration. However, in the first translation of this poem by John Montague, he wrote 'And I have a little boat.' I pointed out to him that it was not the present tense, but the conditional. I experienced this as a genuine difference between the male and the female, where John had the ontological security to say 'And I have' in a way that I don't. But after having pointed it out, he said 'Fine'! But I found it really interesting that that was the automatic and unconscious choice that he made" ("Travelling through Liminal Spaces: An Interview with Nuala Ní Dhomhnaill by Loretta Qwarnström," *Nordic Irish Studies* 3, no. 1 [2004]: 65).

[298] McWilliams Consalvo, "The Lingual Ideal," 151.

only an act of human copulation but, more significantly, the act of physical penetration."[299] Finally, the target text becomes privileged over the original, and Ní Dhomhnaill is completely absorbed by Montague in McWilliams Consalvo's statement that "Ní Dhomhnaill couples *images of ejaculation (the 'thrust through foaming seas')* [my italics] with those of the earth-mother cavity ... to represent Irish fertility."[300] Montague has apparently provided here interpretative orientations insuring the dominance of masculine image-making procedures.

In discussing Montague's divergences from the source text, I am far from the concept of translation as a mechanical transplantation of the original into another literary system that excludes interpretative transfer and is based on the hypersemanticity of transmission. It is only natural that Montague, with his distinctly personal voice, cannot efface his own poetic self to become a mere vessel for the original's transcription. However, without trying to impose a restricting demand of a formal closeness of translation to the source language text as the only criterion of its excellence, I suggest that the intrusiveness of translational interventions should be minimized. In the consistent raids on the original, the line between freedom of creative interpretation and violence against the author can be easily crossed. A high degree of mutation might, in the extreme, turn into mutilation and "colonize" the original completely. The intrusive (or abusive) intertextual dynamic between the author and the translator ultimately affects what Michel Foucault calls the author-function,[301] and here it is not only Ní Dhomhnaill as a unique poetic voice who is in question, but the author as a social construct, with various types of attachments—political, ideological, cultural.

While meticulously delineating trajectories along which she moves charting the map of her personal landscape, associating landscape and identity in her literary and symbolic appropriation of place, and incor-

---

[299] Ibid.

[300] Ibid.

[301] Michel Foucault, "What Is an Author?" in *The Foucault Reader*, ed. Paul Rabinow (New York: Pantheon Books, 1984), 108–113.

porating various aspects of literary tradition and cultural history, Ní Dhomhnaill, in several poems—such as "Amhrán An Fhir Óig" ("Young Man's Song") and "Masculus Giganticus Hibernicus" (*RD,* 80–81; 78–79)—loots freely from dominant poetic discourses. As if ricocheting the Montaguesque representational tactic, she reflects on the male perception of the female body as an open space, an uncultivated virgin land that has to be courted and deflowered, and of the male as an explorer, tiller, disturber, and aggressor. However, her self-representational equation of body with land/island reaches far beyond the conventional poetic definitions of women as the passive and silent embodiments of matter when her vision of corporeal island is translated into a dream image in "Cailleah" ("Hag"). Once the repressive forces of conscious control are relaxed, allowing the content of the unconscious to rise to the surface, the speaker's formative memory, incorporated into a massive landform, breaks out of its confinement. She regresses to a suprahumanized landscape onto which she projects herself and with which she identifies:

> Taibhríodh dom gur mé an talamh,
> gur mé paróiste Fionntrá
> ar a fhaid is ar a leithead,
> soir, siar. Faoi mar a shíneann sí. (*PhD*, 134)

> Once I dreamt I was the earth,
> the parish of Ventry its length and breadth,
> east and west, as far as it runs … (*PhD*, 135)

The dream abolishes conventional time and space, presenting the Self distorted and magnified. The speaker's vista blends natural and human shapes, place names, and parts of her body. Ní Dhomhnaill's somnambulist cartographer charts her parish-of-Ventry-of-her-childhood-as-body map, sinking into predictive visions of dream quests and searches for omens from legend and myth. The speaker's daughter is also drawn into the dream and becomes her mother's double—a mirror through which the speaker's twilight state of consciousness, evoking the invisible, externalizes itself, though in a horrific form. In this Ní Dhomhnaill blends dream, reality, myth, childhood, and a child both literally and metaphorically. While at the beginning the body is desexualized and emotionally neutral, eventually it acquires distinct feminine parameters that are terrifying and threatening. A mountain, heaving like a giantess with swaying breasts, who tries to gobble up the speaker's daughter, reminds us of Celtic folk tales about cannibalistic ogresses consuming baby flesh. Here, a confusion of the fields of representation, imaginary–real–symbolic, takes place. The dream world supplies the unconscious energy whose capricious volatility breaks through in the "awakening" stanza:

> Bhí an taibhreamh chomh beo
> nuair a dhúisíos ar maidin
> gur fhéachas síos féachaint an raibh,
> de sheans, mo dhá chois fliuch. (*PhD*, 134)

> That dream was so real
> That when I woke next morning
> I glanced down to see if, perchance,
> my feet were still wet. (*PhD*, 135)

The reality is presented in a surrealistically chimerical form of broken associations. It is difficult to say whether the speaker's dream contaminates reality or vice versa; the borderline between them is vague.

Ní Dhomhnaill's dream, possessing a multiple figurativeness, invites various interpretations. It may be read as a body-text which establishes the relationship between the Irish mind and body and tries to negotiate it because, as Cheryl Herr writes, "in tradition as well as in colonial and postcolonial Ireland, the body has frequently been associated representationally with danger...."[302] Perhaps, however, the body may become a near-Gothic exaggeration, or it may appropriate a popular mode of representation in literary tradition, or it may evoke primordial images of collective unconsciousness. The title is also suggestive as "cailleach" ("hag") relates the poem to numerous significant hags of Irish mythology and folklore, primarily to the *Cailleach Bherri*, the Hag of Berre, shaper and guardian of the earth, a giantess performing a geo-tectonic function. Then come ambivalent, multifaceted hags who undergo

---

[302] Herr, "The Erotics of Irishness," 6–7.

metamorphosis like a hideous hag from an origin-myth about Niall, where she is transformed into a beautiful woman who declares that she is Sovereignty. Terrible war-goddesses, recurrent in Ní Dhomhnaill's poems, also change their image from that of a mature woman to: a beautiful young girl; or a hideous old hag; or, of course, Kathleen Ní Houlihan; or a *spéar bhean*, an *aisling* sky woman, appearing in one of her emanations as a hag.

In her interview with Rebecca E. Wilson, Ní Dhomhnaill elaborates on the idea of negative femininity represented by the hag, which she calls "Hag Energy," the quality that has not been eradicated from the Irish collective consciousness, as it has in most cultures.[303] It is the *cailleach*, a shiftable hag, who is Ní Dhomhnaill's female muse. This invariably ugly female spirit, inhabiting every road intersection in Ireland, nourishes Dhomhnaill's poetic resources and is a medium in her "response[s] to the unspeakable." Her hag energy is something "that destroys you, creates psychic dismemberment literally, sends teeth and hands and legs flying all over the place."[304] Ní Dhomhnaill's hag figure uncomfortably intrudes into the terrain of conventional ideas and representations of a sublime emblematic muse that has been inspiring poets for centuries.

While retextualizing male models of imagery, Ní Dhomhnaill undertakes a voyage, challenging prefabricated female identities, to accumulate and differentiate her poetic territory. Her quest narrative is opposed to Longley's traditional discourse of the explorer, characterized by the scientist's need for information, who sexually charts the land; to Heaney's enactment of political and colonial suppression and subordination in sexual terms; and to the map-making practices of Carson's Celtic discoverers, who achieve dominion over the land by being granted the privilege of naming. In her utilizing of woman-as-island metaphor, with its whole anthropocentric entourage, Ní Dhomhnaill operates within the framework of a "minoritarian," peripheral tradition, whereas male poets tend to accept majoritarian codes, by adopting what Said calls the "great

---

[303] Wilson, "Nuala Ní Dhomhnaill," 154.
[304] Ibid., 153.

topoi of colonial culture,"[305] the quest and conquest voyages, and by assuming the authority of European observer, scientist, traveler, and explorer.

For both Ní Dhomhnaill and male authors there is the final destination of their journeys: the other's territory. The tradition of depicting Ireland as a woman and as a female body may be explained by the fact that when chaos and destruction threaten, it is natural, as Deleuze and Guattari point out, to "draw an inflatable, portable territory," to put the territory on one's own body and territorialize it.[306] A succession of invasions and the final colonization of Ireland developed this defensive stratagem in the form of a desired body. The essentialized female body, the body of the other, becomes a rationale through which male identity—be it sexual, cultural, or national—is defined. Opposed to this politics of representation, Ní Dhomhnaill's anthropomorphic and geomorphic configurations challenge gender-bound power dynamic.

The works under discussion here represent writing from a range of cultural and political perspectives and across poetic generations. All are offshoots of different mappings, allowing for a proliferation of possible interpretations created by shrouded references to various aspects of Gaelic culture and Irish history. The authors invent their islands by examining the shared territory that underlies Irish poetry. They employ inherited imagistic systems and linguistic patterns, conventional poetic genres, a wide range of associated commonplaces that have been operative for centuries, as well as myth and folklore. As Richard Kearney observes examining the contemporary role of myth, each culture "needs to go on telling stories, inventing and reinventing its mythic imaginary, until it brings history home to itself."[307] The writers' exploratory discourses, in which traditional passageways have become fused with new ideologies, reorder the continuum of tradition, keep mythological narratives in dialogue with

---

[305] Said, *Culture and Imperialism*, 30.

[306] Deleuze and Guattari, *A Thousand Plateaus*, 320.

[307] Richard Kearney, *Postnationalist Ireland: Politics, Culture, Philosophy* (London and New York: Routledge, 1997), 121.

history, and recast the symbolic horizons of the island, reconfiguring its boundaries and surfaces.

While navigating the discursive territory surrounding the *topos*, Ní Dhomhnaill charts the liminal and pluridimensional spaces to enact the pursuit for female desire; Heaney departs from the violence of Irish history into the visionary unknown; Murphy provides a parable for his travel between two cultural formations; Muldoon creates his personal originary myth with ever-confusing and propagating lineages; Carson meticulously fills in the spaces on imaginary maps; Longley surveys the contours of woman-as-landform who/which is unspeakably other; and Montague's "performative" translation puts Ní Dhomhnaill's original in motion and, as Paul de Man writes elsewhere, gives it the "movement of fragmentation, a wandering of errance, a kind of permanent exile."[308] All these poets re-articulate the meaning of the long-established trope, which to a considerable degree conditions the groping character of their texts' insights, and awaken desire in diverse forms—intellectual, geopolitical, cultural, historical, colonial, amorous, and sexual. By employing this *topos*, with its transmigrating themes and rhetorico-ideological conventions, these poets revisit the spaces already traversed and draw their own demarcation lines on existing cultural maps, thus renegotiating their borders.

---

[308] Quoted by Homi Bhabha, *The Location of Culture*, 326.

V   Through the Dark Lens of *Woyzeck* and *Lenz*:

Violence and Postcolonial Schizophrenia in John Banville and Yuri Izdryk

Written at the twilight of Romanticism, when the political energies for progressive reform in largely monarchical and repressive Europe were still fermenting to be unleashed during the revolutions that swept across the continent in 1848,[309] Georg Büchner's (1813–1837) work has been attracting and impacting generations of scholars, writers, composers, theatre directors, and filmmakers. Ever-shifting critical responses to Büchner represent him as a proto-Marxist revolutionary, a writer completely outside *Zeitgeist*, an exponent of reflective pessimism, a programmatic fatalist, a forerunner of nineteenth-century naturalism, and a herald of twentieth-century expressionism.[310] Such a variance of readings points towards Büchner's evasiveness, which defies any attempts to categorize him. His "expressive extremity," paradoxical materialism, and "physiological vision unprecedented in literature" make his oeuvre a mesmeric foreshadowing of the "scabrous violence of modernity,"[311] reflecting the sensibilities of what Jean François Lyotard defines as one of the facets of postmodern sensibility: "The nineteenth and twentieth centuries have given us as much terror as we can take…. Under the general demand for slackening and for appeasement, we can hear the mutterings of the desire for a

---

[309] See Sperber's *The European Revolutions*, 105–116.

[310] On the history of criticism of *Woyzeck*, see David Richards, *Georg Büchner's Woyzeck* (Rochester, New York: Cadmen House, 2001).

[311] George Steiner, "Büchner Lives On," *Timesonline. TLS: Times Literary Supplement*, December 13, 2006, http://www.tls.timesonline.co.uk/article/0,,25341-250 1658,00.html (accessed April 1, 2007).

return of terror, for the realization of the fantasy to seize reality."[312] It is noteworthy that Büchner's "second coming"[313] coincides with the aftermath of an unparalleled historical crisis and the redrawing of the political map in post–World War I Europe. An Austrian composer, Alban Berg (1885–1935), who started working on his *Wozzeck* in 1914, on the eve of the disintegration of the Austro-Hungarian Empire, and completed his opera after its collapse (1921), "translated" Büchner's *Woyzeck* into a different artistic medium using an experimental, unsettling, and dissonant language of atonal music to represent the chaotic soul of its protagonist, thus opening up possibilities for future radical forms of intertextual practices.

In the process of the twentieth-century transcultural transformations and transmissions of his work, Büchner can also be seen as a precursor for the contemporary writers exploring postcolonial convoluted spaces, inhibited by wanderers, who are overwhelmed with fears of inarticulacy, powerlessness, displacement, and dissolution, and whose spatial and identitarian confusion causes a state of psychic disorganization. They comprehend the world as an anamorhosic painting whose perspective is inaccessible and whose broken "space ... is, before being rectified, the space of the schizophrenic."[314] The theme of schizophrenia or madness persistently marks postcolonial fictions. Schizophrenia has been used as a trope for exile, being featured among such migratory concepts as hybridity, nomadism, and dislocation. It has also been employed as a "common enough motif in most postcolonial writing" to represent the mental

---

[312] Jean François Lyotard, *The Postmodern Condition: A Report on Knowledge*, trans. Geoff Bennington and Brian Massumi (Minneapolis: University of Minnesota Press, 1984), 81–82.

[313] Sander L. Gilman, for instance, writes: "Forgotten by the end of the century except as the dead brother of the much more famous materialist philosopher Ludwig Büchner, he [Büchner] was resurrected at the beginning of the twentieth century as one of the 'moderns'" ("Büchner and Madness: Schizophrenia in Georg Büchner's *Lenz* and *Woyzeck*," *Bulletin of the History of Medicine* 74, no. 1 [2000]: 165).

[314] Sabine Melchior-Bonnet, *The Mirror: A History*, trans. Katharina H. Jewett (New York and London: Routledge, 2001), 239.

state of the subject, who is unable to negotiate between premodern traditions and the ideological impact of Western modernity[315] and postmodernity. In addition, schizophrenia has been featured on the colonizer's end
of the spectrum, both in novels and nonfictional narratives, as the retri-
bution for those who cross the boundaries and integrate within alien
spaces or people—the "colonised land seduces European men into madness,"[316] as Ania Loomba puts it.

This chapter inquires into the "mad intertextuality"[317] among John
Banville's *The Book of Evidence* (1989),[318] Yuri Izdryk's *Воццек* (*Wozzeck*) (1997),[319] and their "dark" precursor texts by Georg Büchner.
Büchner's last unfinished play, *Woyzeck* (1836, published 1879, staged
1913), has become, since its author's death, one of the most intensely
debated texts in German literature regarding the arrangement, for reading and performance, of the fragments left in drafts, with various sequences of scenes. An Ur-Brechtian *Woyzeck* depicts the tragic disintegration of a poor soldier who descends into an uncontrollable rage,
madness, and murder and is based on the case of Johann Christian
Woyzeck, who killed his mistress and was publicly executed in Leipzig in
1824. Büchner's novella *Lenz* (1835) is itself a fragment, with the title
assigned to it by Büchner's posthumous editors. It is a metafictional narrative about the *Sturm und Drang* author Jakob Michael Reinhold Lenz
(1751–1792)—whose wretched life was surrounded by a "vivid, partially
legendary aura in the radical and clinical circles" frequented by Büchner

---

[315] Ian Almond, "Rogues of Modernity: Picaresque Variations in the Postcolonial
Genre of the Enlightenment Missionary," *Orbis Litterarum* 61, no. 2 (2006): 97.

[316] Ania Loomba, *Colonialism/Postcolonialism*, 2nd ed. (London and New York:
Routledge, 2005), 117.

[317] Monika Kaup, *Mad Intertextuality: Madness in Twentieth-Century Women's
Writing* (Trier: WVT, 1993).

[318] John Banville, *The Book of Evidence* (London: Picador, 1998); hereafter cited
parenthetically in the text.

[319] Izdryk, *Votstsek* (Ivano-Frankivs'k: Lileia-NV, 1997); hereafter cited parenthetically in the text.

in Strasburg[320]—that focuses on the protagonist's fractured consciousness and incurable disorder of the soul.

The ghosting of the nineteenth-century artist figure and the transpositions of the drama of acute social deprivation into *Künstlerroman* by both Irish and Ukrainian writers are not confined to the precursors' surface structure. There are some markers of direct indebtedness to, for example, *Woyzeck*—"the name of the main character, his condition of psychological distress, the importance of jealousy within his emotional repertoire, and the motif of the loss of the beloved"[321]—in Izdryk, and the actual murder case, the same psychological disturbance, rivalry, and more ambivalent losses of no less ambivalent beloveds in Banville. Still, both contemporary authors reach deeper levels by grasping what is essential in Büchner. As Deleuze and Guattari suggest, Büchner never tries to seek a foundation in accordance with a methodical, pedagogical, initiatory, and symbolic conception; rather, he has his own way of traversing textual space, proceeding from the middle and through the middle: "*Between* things does not designate a localized relation going from one thing to the other and back again, but a perpendicular direction, a transversal movement that sweeps one and the other way, a stream without beginning or end that undermines its banks and picks up speed in the middle."[322] Likewise, Izdryk and Banville subject their novels to various erosions and conflicting trajectories, flows, and motions. Their texts seem to be exposed to a violent current that, as metaphorically described in the chapter titled "The Great Water" in Izdryk's novel, sweeps away everything in its way "миттєво змінюючи ландшафт, утворюючи кручі та урвища на своїх сомнамбулічних і рухливих берегах" (39, "altering the landscape in an instant, shaping cliffs and precipices at its som-

---

[320] Steiner, "Büchner Lives On."

[321] Marko Pavlyshyn, "Wozzeck IV," introduction to *Wozzeck*, by Izdryk (Edmonton and Toronto: Canadian Institute of Ukrainian Studies Press, 2006), xiv.

[322] Deleuze and Guattari, *A Thousand Plateaus*, 25.

nambulistic and shifting banks").[323] Izdryk and Banville's narrative vectors stretch in multiple directions, creating an intricate rhizome in which the authors maneuver between things, establishing a logic of the "and," neglecting the foundations, and alleviating endings and beginnings. The processes of diffusion and transformation of earlier existing narratives at work here advance through the fragmentation of textual, individual and social bodies, thus contesting narratives of individual, social and natural unity, homogeneity, and totality.

In *The Book of Evidence* and *Воццек* (*Wozzeck*), society is dehumanizing and dehumanized, both hostile and incomprehensible for Freddie Montgomery and Wozzeck, who lose in an intellectual and emotional clash with a violent and senseless world. Both twentieth-century works reveal a disturbing link between culture, perception, and violence. This violence resembles a termitelike formation that sprawls around: it is the violence of the chaotic world which is redirected by the protagonists onto their respective victims; it is the societal violence of incarceration administered upon Freddie and Wozzeck; it is the violence of exclusion; it is the protagonists' latent violence towards their memory; it is the violence against multiple precursor texts, dissected and reassembled, as well as the violence of confinement by these other texts; and it is the violence of the protagonists' desires. Except for the harsh signs of contemporaneity, with its numerous crises and disorientations, there is also something primordial and disturbing about Freddie and Wozzeck's violent acts. The strangeness and uncanniness of their violence appear both to precede and transcend what Girard formulates in his theory of the threshold beyond which sacrificial violence is transmuted into culture, thus ensuring social coexistence: "It is only at this point that the vicious circle of reciprocal violence, wholly destructive in nature, is replaced by the

---

[323] Izdryk, *Wozzeck*, trans. Marko Pavlyshyn (Edmonton and Toronto: Canadian Institute of Ukrainian Studies Press, 2006), 41; hereafter cited parenthetically in the text.

vicious circle of ritual violence, creative and protective in nature."[324] According to Girard, violence, which is simultaneously an instrument, object, and all-inclusive subject of desire, becomes the only focus of literature and criticism and their "ultimate referent." He argues that "violence, in every cultural order, is always the true *subject* of every ritual or institutional structure."[325]

Both *The Book of Evidence* and *Воццек* (*Wozzeck*) are centered on an artist figure; both represent what Joseph McMinn calls fictions about fiction;[326] both explore the anxieties and pathologies of the male psyche. Büchner's chilling exploration of madness springs from the author's extensive reading of contemporary psychiatric texts that reveals his fascination with psychopathology as a medical student.[327] In fact, in his examinations of Lenz's psychotic world from within and Woyzeck's external manifestations of insanity, Büchner formulated a psychopathological syndrome of schizophrenia long before the term was introduced into circulation at the beginning of the twentieth century by Eugen Bleuler (1857–1939), one of the most influential psychiatrists of his time.[328] While Büchner's representation of schizophrenic consciousness operates within the area of the nineteenth-century clinical psychology, Banville and Izdryk expose what Michel Foucault defines as a condition of postmodernity that "makes schizophrenia possible, not because its events render it inhuman and abstract, but because our culture reads the world in such a

---

[324] René Girard, "From Mimetic Desire to the Monstrous Double," trans. Patrick Gregory, in *Mimesis, Masochism, and Mime: The Politics of Theatricality in Contemporary French Thought*, ed. Timothy Murray (Ann Arbor: University of Michigan Press, 1997), 88.

[325] René Girard, *Things Hidden since the Foundation of the World*, trans. Stephen Bann and Michael Metteer (London: Athlone Press, 1987), 210.

[326] Joseph McMinn, *John Banville: A Critical Study* (Dublin: Gill and Macmillan, 1991), 110.

[327] On Büchner's medical education, see J. L. Crighton, "Anatomy and Subversion: 150th Anniversary of Georg Büchner's Death," *British Medical Journal* 294 (1987): 489–91.

[328] Gilman, "Büchner and Madness," 166.

way that man himself cannot recognize himself him in it."[329] Incidentally, Izdryk once mentioned in an interview that he sees Wozzeck as an exercise in "psychotherapy"[330] and claimed to be experientially familiar with life in a psychiatric ward.[331] Banville and Izdryk's schizoanalyses[332] vacillate within the field of contemporary theories of narratology and intertextuality[333] as their characters struggle to narrate themselves with frenzied verbosity.

The narrative takes the form of a prison-memoir that relates Freddie Montgomery's life and crime in *The Book of Evidence*, and a mental hospital patient's recollections of the fifty-two-day- and fifty-one-night-long love rites that drive him to insanity in *Воццек* (*Wozzeck*). Reasonable prisoners of their own madness, framed, as is their nineteenth-century antecedent, by a claustrophobic, institutional space of societal confinement and surveillance, they are incessantly inventing, reinventing, revisiting, and fantasizing multiple pasts that are twisted into a Moebius strip, a single-sided figure with no inside or outside to its endless surface. Their insomniac realms are structured and manipulated by imagination

---

[329] Michel Foucault, *Mental Illness and Psychology*, trans. Alan Sheridan (Berkeley, Los Angeles, and London: University of California Press, 1987), 84.

[330] Liubko Deresh, "Kollazhnykh del master," *Stolichnyie novosti*, May 18–24, 2004, http://www.cn.com.ua/N309/culture/personage/personage.html (accessed April 9, 2007).

[331] Anatolii Ul'ianov, "Izdryk rezhet liudei," *Proza*, April 22, 2004, http://www.proza.com.ua/peoples/izdryk_rezhet_ljudej_2161.shtml (accessed April 9, 2007).

[332] I use Deleuze and Guattari's concept of schizoanalysis, which "treats the unconscious as an acentered system," a rhizome (*A Thousand Plateaus*, 18), as opposed to centripetal ideas of identity and psyche.

[333] The importance of intertextuality in postmodern practices is discussed by Graham Allen in *Intertextuality* (London and New York: Routledge, 2000), 174–208. Françoise Canon-Roger, for example, examines a wide range of intertextual connections of Banville's novel with visual art, literature, historical annals, and mythology in "John Banville's *Imagines* in 'The Book of Evidence,'" *European Journal of English Studies* 4, no. 1 (2000): 25–38. The 2002 edition of Izdryk's *Votstsek* includes extensive commentaries on "internal [intertextual] encyclopaedia" to the novel by Volodymyr Ieshkiliev. See his "Votstsekurhiia bet: Komentari do 'vnutrishn'oï entsyklopediï' romanu Izdryka 'Votstsek,'" in Izdryk, *Votstsek & Votstsekurhiia* (L'viv: Kal'variia, 2002), 150–83.

and oblique possessions in which violence comes and goes, thus both separating and uniting the protagonists' disparate personalities. Both Freddie and Wozzeck's solipsistic narrative exploits reveal their fragmented selves with schizophrenic versatility and eloquence. As Homi Bhabha emphasizes in his discussion of Frederick Jameson's "Secondary Elaborations," it is the schizoid subject that "articulates, with the greatest intensity, the disjunction of time and being that characterizes the social syntax of the postmodern condition."[334] Both confessions represent what might be termed as counternarratives to master psychiatric discourses. In this respect, these contemporary characters converge with Büchner's protagonist Woyzeck, for whom the distinction between self and non-self, man and nature, inside and outside is completely eroded and no longer has any meaning. Woyzeck "sees" and "hears" different things and also "thinks" and "feels" about them, thus sinking into delirious senses and hallucinatory thoughts:

> When nature's out, that's—when nature's out. When the world gets so dark you have to feel your way round it with your hands, till you think it's coming apart like a spider's web. When there's something there, yet there's nothing; and everything's dark but there's still this redness in the west like the glow of a huge furnace. When—(*Moves in starts as he tries to think it out.*) When— ... The toadstool, Doctor, it's all in the toadstool. Have you noticed how they grow in patterns on the ground? If only someb'dy could read them.[335]

As in the cases of Freddie and Wozzeck, doctors, by providing the diagnosis of madness, grant a social sanction to immolate the character's sanity to desire. Here different aspects of Woyzeck's psyche are telescoped together, and fears emerge from behind the curtain. For him, words and objects become significations divorced from any meaningful equivalence. They stand out as symbols of some silent, menacing mystery. Driven mad through self-destructive internalization of oppression, regimental sadism, medical experimentation, and his sweetheart's infi-

---

[334] Bhabha, *The Location of Culture*, 307.
[335] Georg Büchner, *Woyzeck*, trans. John Mackendrick (London: Methuen, 1979), 14–15.

delity, Woyzeck, the delusional "reader" of the bizarre patterns formed by toadstools, sets out on his voyage of intensity, with an ultimate destination—murder.

The Book of Evidence is also based on a sensational case, the actual murder of an innocent woman by Malcolm Macarthur in 1982 in Dublin. His senseless, bloody, unpremeditated, and unmotivated crime shocked the public, and the whole affair was described as "grotesque, unbelievable, bizarre and unprecedented."[336] Like Büchner, Banville externalizes Freddie's violence—Freddie abducts a woman who incidentally gets in his way while he is stealing the Dutch portrait that has become an object of his obsessive desire and eventually beats her to death with a hammer. In the murder scene, Freddie registers his actions with the minute details of a detached observer:

> I pushed her away from me and swung the hammer in a wide, backhand sweep. The force of the blow flung her against the door, and her head struck the window, and a fine thread of blood ran out of her nostril and across her cheek. There was blood on the window, too, a fan-shaped spray of tiny drops. She closed her eyes and turned her face away from me, making a low, guttural noise at the back of her throat. She put a hand up to her head just as I was swinging at her again, and when the blow landed on her temple, her fingers were in the way, and I heard one of them crack, and I winced, and almost apologised. Oh! She said, and suddenly, as if everything inside her collapsed, she slithered down the seat on to the floor.
> (114)

The description foregrounds the relationship between the victim and victimizer enclosed in the disabling space of the car. What makes the situation paradoxical, however, is that Freddie seems to speak essentially the language of the victim as if giving voice to her experience. This paradox can be explained through Deleuze's ideas, which he derives from Bataille's analysis of Sade. Deleuze states that only "the victim can describe torture; the torturer necessarily uses the hypocritical language

---

[336] Joseph McMinn, *The Supreme Fictions of John Banville* (Manchester and New York: Manchester University Press, 1999), 101–102.

of established order and power."[337] Freddie's account of the assault is not exactly about power play but about his crumbled ethical and moral values, about his existential condition, which sends him into a free fall that manifests itself in his attempt to explain the reasons for his transgression: "I killed her because I could" (198). Freddie's degeneration of morality causes his dissolution as the subject. His perceptions occur as if through a veil, and it is difficult to say what is seen, imagined, or hallucinated in Freddie's narrative.

The slaughter of Josie Bell, who is caught up in the frantic interchange of Freddie's other and self, acts as the aesthetic technique of convulsion, revealing the fearful double, Bunter, in the manner inaugurated by German Romanticism that used the theme of a double to express the "divisions of subjectivity and the exacerbation of desires in the face of which the real world slowly lost its significance and its credibility."[338] By recovering the repressed other, who is a hidden murderer and a criminal, the protagonist struggles, on the one hand, to isolate evil from what he considers, "in a fundamentally narcissistic manner,"[339] to be his real self and, thus, aestheticizes the origin of his violence. On the other hand, he conjures Bunter in order to explain himself, though without getting closer to the understanding of his situation, and is, in the end, haunted by himself. Simultaneously, Freddie's separation of his violence from its origin suggests his madness. Girard argues in his study on the reciprocity of mimetic relationships, which is displayed by doubles, "If the madman sees double, it is because he is too close to the truth."[340] From this point of view, Freddie is a seer of his "true" self, but this discovery is problematized by the almost incessant histrionics in which he engages. The schizophrenic diversity of roles and images tried on, assigned, and performed either by him or others points in the direction of psychosis. How-

---

[337] Deleuze, "Coldness and Cruelty," 17.

[338] Melchior-Bonnet, *The Mirror*, 264.

[339] Rüdiger Imhof, *John Banville: A Critical Introduction* (Dublin: Wolfhound Press, 1997), 185.

[340] Girard, *Things Hidden*, 302.

ever, Banville, in one of his interviews, emphasizes that Freddie is "a perfectly sane human being," and his invention of Bunter does not mean a personality split:

> That's just Freddie making an excuse. Nobody would take that seriously. There is no other self—it's him. There is no other self —indeed there is no self, period! There are an infinite number of "Bunters" we're composed of in the way that a rainbow is composed of a huge number of particles of light and water. We're made of light and liquid too, but the rainbow is a very beautiful thing to look at. Far more beautiful than human beings.[341]

Banville seems to regard personality as an endless interplay of different surfaces that deem the idea of the Self senseless and obsolete. This is very much like the proliferating comings of Wozzeck's apparitions, which are simultaneously selves and others, once more exposing an ambiguous dynamic in the relationship with a pervasive double that can take on either a singular form or can be multiple and plural. At the same time, in both characters the performative aspect of identity is aggressively pushed to the extreme, turning them into the source of production and displacement in their own Living Theatre.[342]

Prior to the quoted passage, Banville's conversation highlights another important tenet in the discussion of Freddie—the idea that violence is produced exclusively by the most dangerous of creatures, the human being, and is not characteristic of any other species. In this light, Bunter is an invented accomplice who helps Freddie disguise the agency of his violence, as if once again supporting Girard's statement that history re-

---

[341] Rudolf Freiburg and Jan Schnitker, eds., *"Do you consider yourself a postmodern author?": Interviews with Contemporary English Writers* (Münster: LIT, 1999), 29.

[342] Of the subject formation in theatricality and performance, Josette Féral says: "Performance is the absence of meaning.... Performance does not aim at a meaning, but rather makes meaning insofar as it works right in those extremely blurred junctures out of which the subject eventually emerges. And performance conscripts this subject both as a constituted subject and as a social subject in order to dislocate and demystify it" ("Performance and Theatricality: The Subject Demystified," trans. Terese Lyons, in *Mimesis, Masochism, and Mime: The Politics of Theatricality in Contemporary French Thought*, ed. Timothy Murray [Ann Arbor: University of Michigan Press, 1997], 292).

veals the human origin of violence and that the mystified double is itself the product of violence.[343] In addition to the existential interplay of doubles, by conjuring Bunter, Freddie takes revenge against the gang of amateur psychologists whom he mocks and defies, offering the most clichéd psychiatric version to relieve himself of responsibility for his crime. Moreover, by constructing his narrative in a quasi-clinical register, he assumes yet another role—that of a doctor-patient.[344] Further, on a broader cultural scale, the transit from primary to alter ego reflects one of the signs of the time: an ongoing preoccupation with the markers of unstable identities—disconcerting Doubles, Doppelgängers, multiple personalities that stem from moments of crisis and uncertainty and, as Hillel Schwartz explains, from societal fears, discontinuities, and disjunctions "most acute at the ends of centuries."[345]

Freddie is engaged in a disruption of manifold surfaces—his cultured, sophisticated self is torn apart by the eruption of Bunter, his alter ego, a sadistic monster for whom violence becomes a device for liberation. Notwithstanding the nightmares of double agency, Freddie feels really free for the first time in his life. Yet Bunter is another façade, a wild joker thrown into the game. The narrator's fascination with the surface of things is reflected in his enthrallment with the Dutch portrait, which becomes instrumental in triggering Josie Bell's murder. The woman in the anonymous seventeenth-century Dutch painting stands for the instigator of the crime and as an emblem of all women in Freddie's life. It is noteworthy that such a natural and conventional object of desire as women is substituted for Freddie by an artifact. Transmuting desires and objects of the world into mental operations and losing all contact with the real be-

---

[343] Girard, *Violence and the Sacred*, 162–163.

[344] Thus, Freddie's is a narrative with an "alternating" speaking subject. In such fluxes, according to Guattari, it becomes irrelevant who is speaking—"a doctor, a patient, an untreated patient, a present, a past, or future patient" (*Chaosophy*, ed. Sylvère Lotringer [New York: Semiotext(e), 1995], 98); and Freddie seems to embrace most of these roles.

[345] Hillel Schwartz, *The Culture of the Copy: Striking Likeness, Unreasonable Facsimiles* (New York: Zone Books, 1996), 81.

come symptomatic of his conception of women in general and of his confusion between art and life.[346] He often sees women as figures in art, and it is difficult to say whether this viewpoint represents the descent from the work of art to the human body or the ascent from the human body to the work of art. His imaginative perception inserts Anna Behrens into the canvases of Dutch masters and Klimt, makes his mother a Lautrec creation, and turns Daphne into an abstracted Maya.[347]

Izdryk's novel similarly structures representational snapshots in Wozzeck's memory. The narrative is comprised of "photographic" scenes in which A. becomes an arrested image and freezes into postures identifying her with a work of art. It is not accidental, perhaps, that the author sends A., after she abandons Wozzeck, to Prague to become an assistant to the world-famous Czech photographer Jan Saudek (b.1935), whose strikingly emotive, disturbingly violent, and erotically charged imagery builds into what the artist himself calls his "Theatre of Life." A. starts as the great master's model and is placed in the frame of the photograph, in which "вона оголена цілує чоловічу руку" (97, "she is nude and kissing a man's hand," 108)—a verbal facsimile of Saudek's "Deep Devotion of Veronika" (1994). (On the actual photograph, though, the model is draped in gauze with a floral design). There is a ghostly intertextual echo between Izdryk's Prague episodes and Banville's fascination with what he calls "one of the three magic capitals of the world."[348] Prague is brilliantly alchemized out of fragments of research as a setting for his novel *Kepler* (1981)[349] and reappears in a personal travelogue *Prague Pictures: Portrait of a City* (2003). Moreover, Banville's Prague also has its photographer, Josef Sudek (1896–1976), who superbly cap-

---

346 Imhof, *John Banville*, 175; McMinn, *The Supreme Fictions,* 112.

347 Banville's concern with vision and visual art is discussed at great length in Canon-Roger's "John Banville's *Imagines,*" 25–38.

348 Coilin O'Connor, "John Banville: Using Words to Paint Pictures of 'Magical' Prague," *Radio Prague*, July 30, 2006, http://www.radio.cz/en/article/81511 (accessed April 5, 2007).

349 Tim Adams, "Reality Czech," *The Observer*, September 21, 2003, http://books. guardian.co.uk/reviews/travel/0,6121,1046138,00.html (accessed April 5, 2007).

tured Prague's light and mood. It is in the magic Prague that Izdryk's A. becomes a successful photographer herself, blessed with the precise and nuanced eye and empowered by it. Eventually A. starts multiplying into various personalities—a computer graphic artist, a reporter of shocking news from the epicenter of the war in Bosnia, and a nomad resurfacing in different countries as if mastering space and time, her only point of stability being inscribed in Wozzeck's perpetual torment. However, A.'s transmutations are happening on the periphery of Wozzeck's narrative, as a mere retransmission of the rumors about her vagabond life that reach a forsaken lover.

Wozzeck is less successful in framing his women than Freddie is; A. flees Wozzeck's narrative constraints to achieve autonomy and agency. But Freddie's control of frames is not completely stable either. While his "real" women are apparently fixed into static images, the woman in the Dutch portrait seems to step out of the canvas and acquires almost human dimensions in Freddie's account of their truly "dangerous liaison" to an imaginary jury, which includes a lengthy description of the *Portrait of a Woman with Gloves*[350] and concludes with a dramatic rhetorical

---

[350] Banville thus describes the portrait: "A youngish woman in a black dress with a broad while collar, standing with her hands folded in front of her, one gloved, the other hidden except for the fingers, which are flexed, ringless. She is wearing something on her head, a cap or clasp of some sort, which holds her hair drawn tightly back from her brow. Her prominent black eyes have a faintly oriental slant. The nose is large, the lips full. She is not beautiful. In her right hand she holds a folded fan, or it might be a book. She is standing in what I take to be the lighted doorway of a room. Part of a couch can be seen, or maybe a bed, with a brocade cover. The darkness behind her is dense and yet mysteriously weightless. Her gaze is calm, inexpectant, though there is a trace of challenge, of hostility, even, in the set of her mouth. She does not want to be here, and yet cannot be elsewhere. The gold brooch that secures the wings of her wide collar is expensive and ugly" (78). While examining the role of the Dutch portrait, Canon-Roger suggests that each of its elements "can be read as a clue to the rest of the text and conversely. The inscription in a frame of a single figure gives the illusion of the simultaneous perception of a multifaceted referent. The imagination is supposed to expand from a given set of indications so as to solve the riddle" ("John Banville's *Imagines*," 31). The woman with gloves is also in the focus of attention in Anja Müller's article "'You Have Been Framed': The Function of Ekphrasis for

plea: "You have seen the picture in the papers, you know what she looks like…. Yet I put it to you, gentle connoisseurs of the jury, that even knowing all this you still know nothing, next to nothing. You do not know the fortitude and pathos of her presence…. You have not—ah no!—you have not killed for her" (78–79).

Freddie first encounters the *Woman with Gloves* unexpectedly in a golden sunset room, then holds her in his arms when he is stealing the painting, and, finally, contemplates her "asprawl" in the ditch, an image with distinct sexual undertones. The scene of their "separation" is also a moment of staging of the sight without desire, a sign of Freddie's disillusionment once an obstacle between him and the object of his infatuation has been overcome, seemingly complying with Girard's dictum that the only objects worthy of being desired are those that do not allow themselves to be possessed.[351]

The Book of Evidence offers an unconventional triangle of appropriative rivalry; an unnoticeable, mousy-grey Josie Bell becomes a surrogate rival subject who guards the painting. By obstructing Freddie's access to it, she ignites his increasingly violent desire, which becomes detached from the portrait and comes to rest upon the obstacle. Josie's asymmetrical rivalry provokes disorder and violence. In addition, there is another substitution or displacement. Freddie's initial object of desire, the portrait, which is the other's object, is discarded when it is not contested, as if there were no value to it except that emanating from another's desire. However, because things escalate to such intensity, Freddie's violence itself becomes the object of desire. Moreover, Freddie's psychosis, which drives him out of the path of reason alongside his phantom companion, causes further doublings, fragmentations, and mergers. In prison, Freddie's imagination changes Josie Bell from the obstacle into a postmortem quasi object of his desire by superimposing her photographic image onto the Dutch portrait and blending the two. The shift from

---

the Representation of Women in John Banville's Trilogy (*The Book of Evidence, Ghosts, Athena*)," *Studies in the Novel* 36, no. 2 (2004): 188–92.

[351] Girard, *Things Hidden*, 326–28.

Freddie's preferred medium of painting to photography puts an additional spin on the interplay of the real and imaginary since, as Roland Barthes writes in *Camera Lucida*, the photograph becomes a "bizarre medium, a new form of hallucination: false on the level of perception, true on the level of time: a temporal hallucination, so to speak, a modest, shared hallucination (on the one hand 'it is not there,' on the other 'but it has indeed been'): a mad image, chafted by reality."[352] The uncanniness of the photographic medium thus acts as a hallucinogenic substance conducive to the dissolution of boundaries between two women. The potential point of merger between the woman with gloves and Josie Bell, however, comes earlier in the novel when Freddie finds himself in the Behrens' Big House observing the Dutch portrait and feeling as though he has been caught in the midst of two intersecting gazes. He is under the careful, cold scrutiny of the "woman's painted stare" and of every object in the portrait; "every spot on the canvas was an eye fixed on … [him] unblinkingly" (79). Simultaneously, he finds himself under double surveillance because he is also being watched by a wide-eyed maid standing "in the open french window" (79).[353] The three are captured in a vignette, an eerie triangle surrounded by silence, with Josie turning into the woman's spectral double of sorts. The same trio is iterated in the scene when Freddie blindly staggers away with the stolen painting, the woman's eyes "staring into" his, and he senses another stare, that of the maid "standing in the open window, just as she had stood the day before, wide-eyed, with one hand raised" (110). This is the mise-en-scène where the atrocious drama begins to unfold.

---

[352] Roland Barthes, *Camera Lucida: Reflections on Photography*, trans. Richard Howard (New York: Hill and Wang, 1981), 115.

[353] Elke D'hoker offers an ethical perspective while examining this scene and draws on Emmanuel Levinas's ethical imperative in which the "face of the other—here represented in the strong gaze of the woman—challenges the self to respect the alterity of the other, to let the other live, as other" ("Portrait of the Other as a Woman with Gloves: Ethical perspectives in John Banville's *The Book of Evidence*," *Critique* 44, no. 1 [2002]: 24). D'hoker follows this line of argument, stating that the maid "places a second ethical claim on Freddie, asking him to respect her singularity and otherness" (ibid., 25).

Interestingly, the Dutch portrait evokes another of Büchner's lunatics, Woyzeck's forerunner, Lenz, who once again bespeaks the clinical genius of the writer. Büchner alternates open and closed spaces—alpine landscape and the house of the pastor, the realm of nature and the social world. It is during his walks in the mountains that Lenz finds his body connected with every element of nature: "Lenz has projected himself back to a time before the man-nature dichotomy, before all the coordinates based on this fundamental dichotomy have been laid down."[354] Having made this cosmic connection, he deterritorializes and disassociates himself from the *socius*. As Deleuze and Guattari write in their analysis of Lenz, a "schizophrenic out for a walk is a better model than a neurotic lying on the analyst's couch."[355] It is during this schizo-stroll that Lenz's feverish, delusional imagination finds a chimerical coherence between the real world and the world in art by assembling miscellaneous fragments of quickly disintegrating reality and securing them in imaginary frames of familiar art objects whose motionlessness allows for an illusionary point of stability for the protagonist. Lenz's voyeuristic eye, for example, arranges two girls in the distance into a succession of the most stunning and "intimate" paintings in the manner of the Old German School. He also wishes he were endowed with the power of Medusa's gaze so he could capture the moment of beauty forever and put it on display for everyone by petrifying the figures (a counterendeavor to Freddie's Pygmalion-like efforts to bring the *Woman with Gloves* to life by the power of his imagination). The entire setting provokes Lenz's deliberations on the transcendental nature of art, a declaration about his fascination with Dutch masters, and a highly perceptive description of his favorite Dutch painting of a woman. Moreover, Büchner's metafictional narrative about Lenz clearly evokes an additional intertextual frame of reference for both twentieth-century writers, being a precursor text to literary

---

[354] Gilles Deleuze and Félix Guattari, *Anti-Oedipus: Capitalism and Schizophrenia*, trans. Robert Hurley, Mark Seem, and Helen R. Lane (Minneapolis: University of Minnesota Press, 1983), 2.

[355] Ibid.

psychopathographies, to modify Gerhard P. Knapp's application of the term,[356] and also a showcase of schizoanalysis for which schizophrenia is "a process—the schiz—[that] serves as a point of departure as well as a point of destination."[357] While creating his portrait of the artist as a madman in progress, Büchner employs the privileged mode in representation of psychosis by interweaving Lenz's contradictory acts and experiences. He turns his character, seized by an unnamable fear, into a monomaniacal demon driven by the will to nothingness: "[H]e felt no hate, no love, no hope, a terrible void and yet a tormenting anxiety to fill it. He had *nothing*."[358]

Like Izdryk's Wozzeck, Lenz enters an indeterminate zone in which he hesitates between the inexhaustible images of the dream and evidence of reality, and in which neither day nor night and neither reality nor dream can be discerned. His is an endless slippage into madness punctuated by physical fixities and mental fixations and by madness-paced, frantic flights into the dreadful void. Büchner describes almost clinically Lenz's pathological solipsism, the division of the subject encountering his own madness: "[H]e seemed to be going blind; now it grew, the demon of insanity sat at his feet, the hopeless thought that all was but a dream gaped before him, he clung to all objects, shapes rushed past him, he pressed up against them, they were shadows, life drained from him, and his limbs were quite rigid."[359] Lenz recognizes his tragic split, his doubleness. He tries to separate his "sane" and "insane" selves; at some point, it seems as if one part of his personality is trying to save another. He

---

[356] Gerhard P. Knapp, "Lenz, (1835 [post 1839])," *The Literary Encyclopedia*, March 14, 2003, http://www.litencyc.com/php/sworks.php?rec=true&UID=10378 (accessed April 1, 2007). Knapp appropriates the term *pathography*, which was coined by Anne Hunsaker Hawkins in her studies of patients' biographical accounts of illness—*Reconstructing Illness: Studies in Pathography*, 2nd ed. (West Lafayette, Indiana: Purdue University Press, 1999)—and applies it to a wider range of works that deal with representations of pathological states.

[357] Deleuze and Guattari, *Anti-Oedipus*, xix.

[358] Georg Büchner, *Complete Works and Letters*, ed. Walter Hinderer and Henry J. Schmidt, trans. Henry J. Schmidt (New York: Continuum, 1986), 156.

[359] Ibid., 142.

throws himself into the basin of the fountain in the yard with obsessive persistence and violently causes physical pain to himself in order to restore his normal persona. This is his formula to avoid ultimate dissolution of the psychic boundaries of the Self and to cure dementia; the procedure continually recharges itself by repetition, by passing again and again through the same phases. Lenz, who is tormented by anxiety and nocturnal hallucinations and who feels claustrophobic both in interior and exterior spaces, more and more often finds himself in borderline conditions and dissociative states that twist his mind into a convoluted logic of its own. Unlike his working-class successor Woyzeck, who cannot make any sense of the world encoded in dimly ominous toadstool omens, Lenz, a refined intellectual, effortlessly reads cryptic meanings in the skies—prophetic "hieroglyphics" that are psychodramatic projections of the haunting, recapitulatory memories of the devastations he experienced because of unrequited love.

As opposed to Lenz's "therapeutic" sadistic instinct, or rather instinct for mastery, which is self-destructively turned upon the subject and thus transposed into a masochistic ritual, and to Freddie's spectacular fit of brutality, the violence in Izdryk's *Воццек* (*Wozzeck*) is latent and ambiguously released into the open. Wozzeck locks his wife and child in the basement (a fact unknown to the reader until the end of the novel) to protect them from what he sees as the cruelties and insanities of the world. The transgressively sensual violence of Wozzeck's "reality," with its macabre and erratic visions of spectralized bodies—now dissected, now impaled on his penis, now spasmodically bent in orgasm—is molded by the hidden mechanisms of psychic life, by what is both concealed and revealed in the fragments of Wozzeck's nocturnal consciousness. He tries to give form to the formless and invisible—to dreams, reveries, desires, and fears—and to speak the unspeakable and ungraspable. Wozzeck closely studies events and pulsations of innumerable shifts in persistent returns of his nightmares and apparitions, putting together an incomprehensible textual puzzle. This is a tantalizing task that often leaves him hollow and disappointed:

> Справді, що я тут у біса роблю кожного дня за цим столом, перед цією чистою карткою паперу, з цим перфектно заточеним олівцем? Якого дідька я тут роблю? Може, я вбиваю маленьких дівчаток. Я прохромлюю їх незламним кохінорівським олівцем, відрізаю їм груди, трощу зуби, перегризаю шийні хребці і довго, зі смаком, топчуся по окулярах. Я радісно мордую хлопченят. Я напихаю їхні горлянки чистими аркушами паперу потрєбітєльских форматів. Я розчленовую трупи і запихаю їх під креденс. Я промокаю плями прес-пап'є і посипаю підлогу сіллю. Я нищу всіх, хто приходить. (28)

> Indeed, what the devil do I get up to every day at this desk, in front of this clean sheet of paper and this perfectly sharpened pencil? Maybe I kill little girls. I run them through with this unbreakable Koh-i-Noor pencil, I cut off their breasts, smash their teeth, gnaw through their neck vertebrae and stamp long and lasciviously on their glasses. I delight in torturing little boys. I stuff their gullets with clean sheets of paper of handy formats. I dismember corpses and hoard them under the filing cabinet. I mop up the stains with blotting paper and strew the floor with salt. I destroy all comers. (29)

The macabre brutality of the description reappears like an echo muffled through a dream produced by "зварйован[ий] режисер" (57, "an insane director," 62) in which Wozzeck declares that the a priori indestructible characters of his nightmares irresistibly tempt him into senseless attempts "вбити, вбити, вбити, вбити" (56, "to kill, kill, kill, kill," 61), and in which he ultimately turns into a victim of his own violence. Izdryk's character, who ironically exercises this violent authorial power over Izdryk's creations, is also involved in a relationship with A. that is violent in terms of moral tortures, uncertainties, and the cruelty of Wozzeck's desired object. Wozzeck himself becomes subjected to violence at the hands of A. He breaks away from his ordinary experiences of family life to enter into a delectable bondage with A., who cannot be brought under control and becomes his invincible rival. He masochistically positions himself into the relationship of inferiority against the absolute superiority of A. Wozzeck's desires are enacted through triumphant defeat, servile mastery, and painful bliss.

It is worthwhile mentioning here that the invention of the term "masochism" itself articulates the fin-de-siècle's profound crisis concerning sexuality and violence. It has become a very "hot topic," a distinct ideological tool—"Masochism is now rebellion"[360]—and a highly popular code of sexual imagery in the closing decades of the nineteenth century. Today masochism is instrumental in redefining the problems and ideas of the age that coined the word and in articulating struggles over deep-rooted beliefs concerning gender, power, sexuality, violence, and role-playing in society. Izdryk seems to resort to representing moral and physical pain as the only remaining vehicle of communication for his character. As Deleuze explains in his "Re-Presentation of Masoch," pain and torment become instrumental in untying the pseudobond between desire and pleasure in order to let desire operate freely, thus displacing the question of suffering through the contract that remains a mystery in masochism:

> It seems to have something to do with breaking the link between desire and pleasure: pleasure interrupts desire, so that the constitution of desire as a process must ward off pleasure, repress it to infinity. The woman-torturer sends a delayed wave of pain over the masochist, who makes use of it, obviously not as a source of pleasure, but as a flow to be followed in the constitution of an uninterrupted process of desire.[361]

Izdryk's breakage operates within the framework of moral masochism, which excludes things that have reductively come to symbolize the masochistic "syndrome" perpetuated by psychoanalysis since Krafft-Ebing and Freud—fetishes, whips, leather boots, fur-clad women, and so on. Suffering, for Wozzeck, becomes a means by which desire is liberated from the familial prison, by which it is released into the open to gather speed and momentum, finding lines of escape and constructing "rhizomes" with other bodies and desires. The torments that Wozzeck un-

---

[360] David Brande, "Making Yourself a Body Without Organs: The Cartography of Pain in Kathy Acker's *Don Quixote*," *Genre* 24, no. 3 (1991): 208.
[361] Deleuze, *Essays Critical*, 53.

dergoes become the steps in his climb towards the ideal, and his masochistic "contract" with A. generates its own laws that lead directly into ritual. In "Coldness and Cruelty," Deleuze emphasizes that the masochist's obsession makes ritualistic activity essential to him since it epitomizes the world of fantasy.[362] Izdryk's symbolic order of masochism includes a set of amorous rituals stylizing archetypal rites, which are unfailingly followed by the character.

Unlike Wozzeck, who aspires towards suffering and subjection and thus assumes the role of a victim in a masochistic scenario, Freddie displays a feel for the theatrical that is enacted in a sadistic drama in which he performs the role of a persecutor. His violent act is both personal and impersonal. His preparations for the theft of the Dutch portrait strangely include purchasing a ball of twine, a roll of brown wrapping-paper, a hank of rope, and a hammer, which turn into the instruments of murder and represent a personal, though subconscious, element of his violence related to his individual tastes. This expository sight preceding the tragedy is described as a playtime during which Freddie acquires the toys to satisfy by no means Bunter but the deprived child in himself, as Freddie states in his confession. He also mentions that his visit to the store felt "as if … [he] had dreamed a prophetic dream and then forgotten it" (98). In the slaughter scene with Josie Bell as the victim, this personal element turns by reflection upon itself into the impersonal, and it is in this reflection that the monstrous exhibits itself. For Wozzeck, likewise, the movement from personal to impersonal is structured on an analogous principle when A. is transposed from flesh and blood into a dispassionate ideal. In both theatres of cruelty, however, the protagonist becomes fixated on violence inflicted either upon himself or by himself.

Wozzeck's both carnal and romantically fleshless love for A. is framed into a vision of the fragmented consciousness. The author brings various experiential layers together; they collapse into each other in the vortex of reality and mind, dream and reality, reality and fiction, past and

---

[362] Deleuze, "Coldness and Cruelty," 94.

present. Wozzeck's hypnologic experiences and parapraxes are no less real than the external, "objective" world. They extend their hold both beyond and within the diffused borders of dreams and draw into their circuit different participants, their emanations, doubles, personality-shifters, bodies, memories, and voices, either in an eruption of hypnagogic images or in the delusional readings of the world in paranoia. Miriam belongs here, an illusory, multifaceted transmogrifier in Wozzeck's world of ceaseless metamorphoses. She is either one woman with multiple personalities or several women who merge into one body: Miriam-why-I-do-not-come-with-my-own-husband, Miriam-the-Blessed-Virgin-of-the-salty-vertebra, Miriam-the-golden-throat. As opposed to A., who is associated with the sublime sphere and provokes mad passion, Miriam, a surrealistic bundle of flesh from the domains of physiology, does not arouse Wozzeck's desire. He "takes" her wearily, and she avenges him for his boredom with a tempestuous orgasm accompanied by "ряснотою ядучих міазмів, що виходять з неї разом із конвульсіями" (28, "the stream of acrid odors that passes from her with her convulsions," 29). Now she is a young witch with a pointed nose, and now her body becomes enormously exaggerated in scale; its amorphous mass fills Wozzeck's room completely and becomes an image of infinite flexibility. While Miriam easily crosses the border between his "reality" and his hallucinatory state, with its chimerical assemblages of things that are normally separate, A., always exquisitely beautiful, stays ostensibly fixed in the realm of his "sanity," an adorable model of perfection and provocateur of his madness, who appears and drifts away like a mirage. Wozzeck's dreamless sleep is not his state when he has fallen asleep but that which spins through the night and inhabits it with a startling lucidity. It is insomnia, which can fill and populate the night, and each of Wozzeck's new dreams becomes, to use Deleuze's expression, "the guardian of insomnia."[363]

Freddie is equally assailed with the bizarre and bawdy visions of his walking dreams, which put him into a trancelike condition. Some of

---

[363] Deleuze, *Essays Critical*, 130.

his nightmares are peopled by almost a stable cast of characters—Daphne, Anna Behrens, Foxy, Madge's niece, the big girl with the red neck, his mother, and the stable girl. They appear either as parts of his painfully erotic prison configurations or as the fomenters of his criminal plan; they all are filtered through an hallucinatory process in which everybody and everything lose their boundaries and enter a union in Freddie's somnambulistic perceptions. All these female bodies merge, and at the end they are subsumed by the mysterious woman in the painting: "[I]t was that Dutch figure in the picture in the garden room who hovered over the bed and gazed at me, skeptical, inquisitive, and calm" (92). In addition to dreams focused on the feminine, Freddie is also tormented by "abstract" visions, where nothing is happening and nothing is explicit. By the end, however, he is seized by full-fledged panic, and this recurring dream, which he has had all his adult life, is like a farcical, Kafkaesque trial that becomes interpreted as a sinister foreshadowing of his present condition. Not unlike Wozzeck's wanderings in the stylistically Baroque passages and decayed hallways of the grand hotels in his dream-life, Freddie's chimerical visions are sometimes set in extravagant Gothic castles, with lurking horrors, trails of slime, and shadows hanging from the walls like cobwebs, all of which are clearly designed to impress his intended audience—judges, prosecutors, and the jury.

Izdryk and Banville's intuition for "psychopathology" creates some supratextual points of conflation. There is what may be called an unconscious intertextual surge between *Воццек* (*Wozzeck*) and another novel by Banville, *Athena*. The latter's narrative is addressed to a young woman named A, who also obsesses the protagonist's romantic and erotic imagination and becomes "his principle tormentor in a cruel game of carefully prearranged misrepresentation."[364] Morrow, who is both Wozzeck and Freddie's double, is drawn, when he partakes in a sexual performance, into what might seem an eerie reenactment, with the help of A, of a certain episode of his past. Its stylized violence disturbingly iterates

---

[364] McMinn, *The Supreme Fictions*, 131.

the scene of Josie Bell's murder in *The Book of Evidence* as well as signifies the emergence of yet another connection between violence and eroticism.

As in Büchner's drama, violence in both *Воццек* (*Wozzeck*) and *The Book of Evidence* is linked to pain. The rhizomatic dispersal of the endless waves of pain paralyses the feelings and reduces everything to numbness. Both Freddie and Wozzeck repeatedly endure nauseating pain both as an immediate physical experience and as one that is mediated through a transforming consciousness. Pain, which seems to flow through subsurface spaces, negotiates the expressed and the ineffable, the othered and the selved, the imagined and the corporeal, the felt and the numb, and the dispersed and the centered. Pain obliterates the borders and boundaries between and within characters as in Izdryk's protagonist who is simultaneously "I–you–he" and is gradually dissolving into the material world:

> Ти міг розмовляти з жінкою за столиком відкритого кафе, а сам бути і тим столиком, і тією жінкою, і вимощеним бруківкою майданом, котрий виднівся з тераси, і господарем кафе, що поливає бруківку перед входом, збиваючи відстояну вранішню пилюку, і самою пилюкою або водою, а більше нічим.... (17)

> You could be talking to a woman at a table in an open-air cafe and at the same time be the table, and the woman, and the cobble-paved square that was visible from the terrace, and the owner of the cafe, who was hosing down the cobblestones at the entrance to wash away the settled morning dust, and the dust itself or the water, or nothing else.... (17)

Like Wozzeck, who painfully struggles to give substance to phantoms in his hopelessly atomized world, deprived of dichotomies and boundaries, Freddie tries to come to terms with reality and fails. Both are caught in the liminal zone between past and present, and their attempts to provide coherent narratives bridging the two fall short because of their fatal attraction to the past and confused recollections. It seems that if Freddie and Wozzeck could have found a vantage point for lateral vision, they would have made sense of chaos, but the "right" angle turns out to be ever-evasive because of the multiple versions that the past can offer. They both lose in the attempt to introduce order into their twisted, frantic private hells as if the mysterious, pervasively transmigrating design of hallucinogenic toadstools envisioned by Büchner's deranged Woyzeck has a petrifying grip on them.

Both *The Book of Evidence* and *Воццек* (*Wozzeck*) offer various points of entrance and exit into the heterogeneous, vast intertextual space. *The Book of Evidence* is structured by an elaborate system of allusions to, and quotations from, literature and visual art. While inquiring into Banville's art-trilogy, Anja Müller writes that his work "undeniably reveals an explicit awareness of postmodernist and post-structuralist theory that is sometimes displayed so ostentatiously that the narrator of the three novels, Freddie Montgomery, can be read as caricature of postmodern storyteller who despairs at his paradoxical endeavor to represent in an age that has challenged the very notion of representation...."[365] What Müller seems to overlook here is the politics of postmodernity that is at play in Banville's novel and that underwrites Freddie's "ostentatious" exercise—the role of simulacra that alienates a person from any tangible unmediated relationship with reality,[366] as well as the ideology of the writing subject (re-)(de-)constructing its self and thus resisting monological definitions.[367] Similar to Banville's disruption of linearity and disbelief in a unified subjectivity and unwavering subject position, *Воццек* (*Wozzeck*) too is synthesized by a postmodern sensibility, with its aesthetics of citation, nostalgia, undifferentiatedness, and *mise en abyme* identity of the protagonist. It is worth mentioning a somewhat "belated" character of Ukrainian postmodernism, which, according to Pavlyshyn, who sees it as a drive behind the project of decolonization, was stimulated both by transcultural trends and by the "appropriateness of the relativist, self-ironic and combinatorial qualities of the postmodern consciousness to

---

[365] Müller, "'You Have Been Framed,'" 185.
[366] See Jean Baudrillard, "Simulacra and Simulation," in his *Selected Writings*, ed. Mark Poster (Stanford, California: Stanford University Press, 1988), 166–184.
[367] On intertextuality and postcolonialism see Allen, *Intertextuality*, 166–173.

the post-Soviet condition, characterized as it was by competing values and world views, newly unstable life experiences and expectations, and the ambivalent attitudes of many to the less-than-complete demise of Soviet cultural colonialism."[368] Both contemporary writers display a tendency towards self-apprehension and self-discernment while transfiguring their protagonists' respective experiences into multilayered texts-palimpsests. The novels' postmodern stances make them marginal, infringed, final, and at the same time, open. This openness is also literal—both works form sequences: *The Book of Evidence* with *Ghosts* (1993) and *Athena* (1995), and *Воццек (Wozzeck)* with *Острів КРК (KRK Island)* (1998) and *Подвійний Леон (Double Leon)* (2000), thus retaining a self-referential intertextual dimension. Both seem to enact the whole problem of paranoia about cultural dissemination and fragmentation, or, as the Indian postcolonial theorist Leela Gandhi would call it, "postcolonial schizophrenia."

---

[368] Pavlyshyn, "Wozzeck IV," viii.

Postscript

Light vibrates in the concavity and convexity of the luminous glare on black geometrical shapes—the full and the void in a reciprocal becoming—in Taras Polataiko's (b. 1966) *Glare* series (1992–1996).[369] A phantasmal, barely perceptive *trompe-l'oeil* fold on canvas, as if measuring the depth of the exteriority, is turning into the Foucaultian doubling [*doublure*] of the outside, or being "inside the outside."[370] Polataiko captures the "additional element"[371] of Kazimir Malevich's (1878–1935) Suprematist compositions by bending the pages with the reproductions of Malevich's work to arrest the glare—an evasive depository of time and history in the radiant whiteness of the knot of light—on glossy surfaces, photographing the transformed image and painting it on canvas. He calls these works an "impossible hybrid" and the glare a "transforming agent."[372] By returning to his compatriot Malevich (the contemporary artist was born in Ukraine and relocated to Canada in the early 1990s), Polataiko delves into manifold subtexts overlaying each other. He is reclaiming, by establishing a personal genealogy, one of the aspects of the Ukrainian avant-garde movement banned during the 1930s Stalinist Terror as ideologi-

---

[369] Polataiko's *Kazimir Malevich: Suprematist Painting* (1995) on the cover of this book is one of the works from the *Glare* series.

[370] Gilles Deleuze, *Two Regimes of Madness: Texts and Interviews 1975–1995*, ed. David Lapoujade, trans. Ames Hodges and Mike Taormina (New York and Los Angeles: Semiotext[e], 2006), 256.

[371] Malevich's model of the infectious "additional element"—a new structural formative principle instrumental in turning one art system into another—consistently runs through Mark A. Cheetham's *Abstract Art Against Autonomy: Infection, Resistance, and Cure Since the 1960s* (Cambridge and New York: Cambridge University Press, 2006). See also Matthew G. Looper's "The Pathology of Painting: Tuberculosis as a Metaphor in the Art of Kazimir Malevich," *Configurations* 3, no. 1 (1995): 27–46; and E. F. Kovtun and Charlotte Douglas's "Kazimir Malevich," in the special issue on the *Russian* (my italics) avant-garde, *Art Journal* 41, no. 3 (1981): 234–41.

[372] Cheetham, *Abstract Art*, 12.

cally hostile to the state and erased from the history of art in the Soviet Union, widely accepted as "Russian" in the West, as was, and more frequently than not still is, any cultural production from "out there," behind the Iron Curtain, and unequivocally claimed by Russia after its "rehabilitation."[373] From this point of view, Polataiko's paintings become a site of ideological interaction, of resistance to cultural imperialism and kleptomania, and of negotiation of the viable continuum in Ukrainian visual art tradition. Furthermore, *Glare* is a metaphorical response to Malevich—the exponent of the "painterly unconscious" materialized in the iconic, revolutionizing *Black Square* (1915), which liberated the concept of painting from that of picturing and time and again was featured in his numerous works—in current epistemic context. It is also the exploration of multiple strata and undercurrents (on a literal level, most of Malevich's paintings have at least one old painting underneath)[374] to create a space available for conceptual mutations, explosions, abrupt associations or dissociations.

Like Idris Khan, Polataiko, with his transformative refractions of art history, seems to chase and face similar ghosts while evoking significatory powers of tradition. In an *unheimlich* interplay of unrelenting intertextuality, the work of two artists, anchored in different cultural formations, converges in their almost simultaneous reworkings of Eadweard Muybridge's (1830–1904) famous motion studies of the 1880s. Both Khan, in *Rising Series.... After Eadweard Muybridge "Human and Animal Locomotion"* (2005), and Polataiko, in *Down Time* (2005–ongoing), at-

---

[373] Among some of the most influential and innovative artists who came from Ukraine were such major figures as the Suprematist Kazimir Malevich, the Constructivist Vladimir Tatlin, the Cubist sculptor Alexander Archipenko, the Futurist David Burliuk, and the costume and set designer Alexandra Ekster. On one breakthrough project on the recovery of Ukrainian avant-garde, see *The Phenomenon of the Ukrainian Avant-Garde, 1910–1935 / Le Phenomene de l'avant-garde ukrainienne, 1910–1935 / Феномен українського авангарду, 1910–1935* (Winnipeg: Winnipeg Art Gallery, 2002).

[374] Jim Long, "Kazimir Malevich: Suprematism," *The Brooklyn Rail: Critical Perspectives on Arts, Politics, and Culture*, September 2003, http://www.thebrook lynrail.org/arts/sept03/malevich.html (accessed April 13, 2007).

tempt to unfreeze the moment of stasis and photograph the invisible while consolidating cultural symbols.[375]

This (re)constructive agency exhibited by visual art unveils the propelling thrust behind the literary texts examined here: a displacement of the representational authority of culturally fixed discourses by destabilizing any single perspective and thus producing multiple, fluid "viewing" experiences of one and the same "object." In establishing the points of conflation between and within Ukrainian and Irish literature, I navigate the area in different directions—each of them has the potential of becoming a subject for future separate inquiries—and in a contrapuntal manner to display cases of what Deleuze calls "creative symptomatology"[376] rather than venturing at a comprehensive study of the material. Yet, my analysis seems to allow for certain typology in the textual politics of Irish and Ukrainian writers. While forging their improvised traditions to invoke the unsaid and unseen of culture, these authors undertake differential temporal movements to unfurl certain historical, cultural, and literary folds: into the dark abyss of Ukrainian history—Kostenko; into the quasi-historical narratives of transhistorical masculinity in the Irish epic—Ní Dhomhnaill; into the discursive void of Ukrainian sexuality—Zabuzhko, Pokalchuk, Vynnychuk, and Poderviansky; into the originary locus of the

---

[375] Khan unfreezes time by combining the isolated moments of stationary postures in a series of Muybridge's photographs in a single image (Dyer, "Between the Lines"). Polataiko also unfreezes Muybridge by asking models to imitate the poses on the nineteenth-century pictures and photographing them with long exposures—by multiplying Muybridge's exposure time (0.17 sec) by the number of years between the past and present shots, the artist arrived at an average exposure of 22 sec. Polataiko's models are thus snapped out of time and transfixed in unbalanced poses, the "motion" being created by the tension of the body attempting stasis. Polataiko explains: "By reversing the linearity of time and direction, I addressed the conditioning of humanity by technological progress. Muybridge 'froze' his models to make them move forever as phantoms of motion pictures—an invention that irrevocably changed the way we perceive ourselves in time. I 'unfroze' his models by using technology backwards" (Personal conversation with the artist).

[376] Deleuze writes that creative symptomatology is "not just about identifying an illness, but about the world as symptom, and the artist as symptomatologist" (*Desert Islands*, 132).

Irish collective cultural unconscious—Ní Dhomhnaill, Muldoon, Heaney, Murphy, Longley, Carson, and Montague; and into the disturbed mind of fragmented schizo-subjects pulling from the past and the present—Banville and Izdryk. By intersecting multiple places, historical temporalities, and subject positions, the authors partake in the reconfiguration of their respective histories and traditions so that the irrepresentable might re-emerge from the cusp of its occlusion.[377]

Being shot through with the traces of a vast cultural network, these works supplement, through intertextual reciprocity, an established frontal point of view with a lateral one, wherein the calculated "distortion" in the represented relies on the subversion of the image, and the deconstructed similitude results in a new content.[378] The ubiquitous anamorphosic vision of the examined literary production breaks up the coherence of space and narrative, unveils hidden reality, reflects the instability of the world, and releases latent transformative energies. Both Ukrainian and Irish literatures, however, go beyond the postmodern limits of simply deconstructing existing orthodoxies into the domain of social action to devise a political strategy of empowerment and enunciation. The ongoing process of artistic and literary decolonization in Ireland and Ukraine inter-rogates the boundaries and slippages between personal, national, social, gendered, and historical disjunctions and makes all kinds of histories open for revision, rewriting, and contestation, in the course of which writ-ers are being continuously engaged in epistemic dialogues with their own tradition and colonial discourses, as well as with multicultural influxes and products of both neocolonial expansion and globalization. By means of this intertextual exchange that fosters a range of "additional elements," these authors reject multiple repressive legacies; expose, if not confront, inherited stifling paradigms, including those of gender; and dismantle im-perial as well as their own cultural and literary myths. Being palimpsests of various aspects of literary tradition and cultural history, the texts under

---

[377] David Lloyd, "Regarding Ireland in a Post-Colonial Frame," *Cultural Studies* 15, no. 1 (2001): 14.

[378] Melchior-Bonnet, *The Mirror*, 237.

consideration create, through a perpetual negotiation, an in-between space that carriers the meaning of culture. As Bhabha argues in his deliberations about such an intermediacy imbedded in the concept of dialogue rather than difference, "[i]t is in this space that we will find those words with which we can speak of Ourselves and Others. And by exploring this hybridity, this 'Third Space', we may elude the politics of polarity and emerge as the others of our selves."[379]

In the system of Bhabha's representational optics implied in the projections of the Self onto the Other and the Other onto the Self, alterity can offer new scopic regimes through which one can conceive an endurable self-image. Not dissimilar to Vynnychuk, who invents his authorial alter ego, an Irish monk Rianhabar, to behold (and record) the dark and violent episode in Ukrainian history,[380] I am also searching—in the dim, at times fractured, and mesmerizing glass of Irishness, as if trying to see through the dissemblance and duplicity of duplication—for its Ukrainian shadowy doubles, familiar and alien, embodied and disembodied, living and dead, visible but intangible—my own "additional element": to read the traces, existing and imaginary, of my own culture.

---

[379] Homi Bhabha, "Cultural Diversity and Cultural Differences," in *The Post-Colonial Studies Reader*, ed. Bill Ashcroft and Helen Tiffin (London and New York: Routledge, 1995), 209.

[380] I have deliberately disregarded here the ideologically subversive energy of Vynnychuk's enterprise, discussed in Chapter III, in order to preserve the "purity" of my argument.

Bibliography

Adams, Tim. "Reality Czech." *The Observer*, September 21, 2003. http://books.guardian.co.uk/reviews/travel/0,6121,1046138,00.html (accessed April 5, 2007).

Allen, Graham. *Intertextuality*. London and New York: Routledge, 2000.

Almond, Ian. "Rogues of Modernity: Picaresque Variations in the Postcolonial Genre of the Enlightenment Missionary." *Orbis Litterarum* 61, no. 2 (2006): 96–113.

Anderson, Nicholas. *Baroque Music: From Monteverdi to Handel*. London: Thames and Hudson, 1994.

Anonim. *Spovid' kyianyna erotomana*. Translated by Anatol' Perepadia. L'viv: Kal'variia, 2004.

Antonenko-Davydovych, Borys. "Shadows of Forgotten Days." In *Before the Storm: Soviet Ukrainian Fiction of the 1920s*, edited by George Luckyj, 247–63. Translated by Iurii Tkacz. Ann Arbor: Ardis, 1986.

Arnold, Matthew. *Lectures and Essays in Criticism*. Ann Arbor: University of Michigan Press, 1962.

Atwood, Margaret. *Alias Grace*. Toronto: McClelland and Stewart, 1999.

Auge, Andrew J. "To Send a Shiver through Unitel: Imperial Philosophy and the Resistant Word of Paul Muldoon's 'Madoc—A Mystery.'" *Contemporary Literature* 46, no. 4 (2005): 636–66.

Bakhtin, Mikhail. *The Dialogic Imagination: Four Essays*. Translated by Caryl Emerson and Michael Holquist. Austin and London: University of Texas Press, 1981.

Balabko, Oleksandr. "Lina Kostenko: 'Chasom ia—tse movchannia zadushenoï vil'noï liudyny.'" *Vechirnii Kyïv*, March 23, 2005. http://www.vechirka.kiev.ua/article.php?id_article=3461 (accessed February 11, 2007).

Banville, John. *Ghosts*. London: Secker & Warburg, 1993.

———. *Athena*. London: Secker & Warburg, 1995.

———. *The Book of Evidence*. London: Picador, 1998.

Barthes, Roland. *Camera Lucida: Reflections on Photography.* Translated by Richard Howard. New York: Hill and Wang, 1981.

Bataille, Georges. *Erotism: Death and Sensuality.* Translated by Mary Dalwood. San Francisco: City Lights, 1986.

Baudrillard, Jean. *Seduction.* Translated by Brian Singer. New York: St. Martin's Press, 1979.

———. "Simulacra and Simulation." In his *Selected Writings*, edited by Mark Poster, 166–84. Stanford, California: Stanford University Press, 1988.

Beer, Gillian. *Darwin's Plots: Evolutionary Narrative in Darwin, George Eliot and Nineteenth-Century Fiction.* Cambridge: Cambridge University Press, 2000.

Benjamin, Jessica. *The Bonds of Love: Psychoanalysis, Feminism, and the Problem of Domination.* New York: Pantheon Books, 1988.

Benjamin, Walter. *The Origin of German Tragic Drama.* Translated by John Osborne. London: NLB, 1977.

Berger, John. *Ways of Seeing.* London: Pelican, 1972.

Bever, Edward. "Witchcraft Fears and Psychosocial Factors in Disease." *Journal of Interdisciplinary History* 30, no. 4 (2000): 573–90.

Bhabha, Homi K. "DissemiNation: Time, Narrative, and the Margins of the Modern Nation." In *Nation and Narration*, edited by Homi K. Bhabha, 291–322. London and New York: Routledge, 1990.

———. "Freedom's Basis in the Indeterminate." *October* 61 (1992): 46–57.

———. "Postcolonial Authority and Postmodern Guilt." In *Cultural Studies*, edited by Lawrence Grossberg, Cary Nelson, and Paula A. Triechler, 56–68. New York: Routledge, 1992.

———. *The Location of Culture.* London and New York: Routledge, 1994.

———. "Cultural Diversity and Cultural Differences." In *The Post-Colonial Studies Reader*, edited by Bill Ashcroft and Helen Tiffin, 206–209. London and New York: Routledge, 1995.

Biektursunov, Kazbiek. "'Blachevnyi' kinets'." Introduction to *Spovid' kyianyna erotomana,* by Anonim, 4–6. L'viv: Kal'variia, 2004.

Bitel, Lisa M. *Land of Women: Tales of Sex and Gender in Early Ireland.* Ithaca and London: Cornell University Press, 1996.

Bodie, Joshua A., William W. Beeman, and Manoj Monga. "Psychogenic Erectile Dysfunction." *The International Journal of Psychiatry in Medicine* 33, no. 3 (2003): 273–93.

Bodnar, Andrii. "Zamist' peredmovy." Introduction to *Mal'va Landa,* by Iurii Vynnychuk, 5–7. L'viv: Piramida, 2004.

Borshchak, Il'ko, and Rene Martel'. *Ivan Mazepa; Zhyttia i poryvy velykoho het'mana.* Translated by Mykhailo Rudnyts'kyi. Kyïv: Radians'kyi pys'mennyk, 1991.

Brande, David. "Making Yourself a Body Without Organs: The Cartography of Pain in Kathy Acker's *Don Quixote*." *Genre* 24, no. 3 (1991): 191–209.

Breadley, Anthony, and Maryann Gialanella Valiulis, eds. *Gender and Sexuality in Modern Ireland.* Amherst, Massachusetts: University of Massachusetts Press, 1997.

Breuilly, John. *Nationalism and the State.* Manchester: Manchester University Press, 1982.

Briukhovets'kyi, V'iacheslav. *Lina Kostenko: Narys tvorchosti.* Kyïv: Dnipro, 1990.

Büchner, Georg. *Woyzeck.* Translated by John Mackendrick. London: Methuen, 1979.

———. *Complete Works and Letters.* Edited by Walter Hinderer and Henry J. Schmidt. Translated by Henry J. Schmidt. New York: Continuum, 1986.

Butler, Judith. *Bodies That Matter: On the Discursive Limits of 'Sex'.* New York and London: Routledge, 1993.

Cairns, David, and Shaun Richards. "'Woman' in the Discourse of Celticism." *Canadian Journal of Irish Studies* 13, no. 1 (1987): 43–60.

———. *Writing Ireland: Colonialism, Nationalism and Culture.* Manchester: Manchester University Press, 1988.

———. "Tropes and Traps." In *Gender in Irish Writing,* edited by Toni O'Brien Johnson and David Cairns, 128–37. Milton Keynes, Philadelphia: Open University Press, 1991.

Canon-Roger, Françoise. "John Banville's *Imagines* in 'The Book of Evidence.'" *European Journal of English Studies* 4, no. 1 (2000): 25–38.

Cantarella, Eva. "Dangling Virgins: Myth, Ritual, and the Place of Women in Ancient Greece." In *The Female Body in Western Culture: Contempora-*

198   MARYNA ROMANETS

ry Perspectives, edited by Susan Rubin Suleiman, 57–67. Cambridge, Massachusetts, and London: Harvard University Press, 1985.

Carson, Ciaran. "The Insular Celts." In *Contemporary Irish Poetry*, edited by Anthony Bradley, 396. Berkeley: University of California Press, 1988.

Carter, Angela. *The Sadeian Woman and the Ideology of Pornography*. New York: Pantheon Books, 1978.

Caws, Mary Ann. "Ladies Shot and Painted: Female Embodiment in Surreal Art." In *The Female Body in Western Culture: Contemporary Perspectives*, edited by Susan Rubin Suleiman, 262–87. Cambridge, Massachusetts, and London: Harvard University Press, 1985.

Chambers, Ann. *Granuaile: The Life and Time of Grace O'Malley c. 1530–1603*. Dublin: Wolfhound Press, 1998.

Chasnyk, Oleksandr. "Universal'ne i spetsyfichne v prostorovo-chasovii symvolitsi ukraïns'koho ta irlands'koho tradytsiinoho mystetstva (porivnial'no-semiotychnyi analiz)." Candidate diss., Kharkivs'ka derzhavna akademiia kul'tury, 2001.

Cheetham, Mark A. *Abstract Art Against Autonomy: Infection, Resistance, and Cure Since the 1960s*. Cambridge and New York: Cambridge University Press, 2006.

Chernetsky, Vitaly. "The Trope of Displacement and Identity Construction in Post-Colonial Ukrainian Fiction." *Journal of Ukrainian Studies* 27, nos. 1–2 (2002): 216–32.

———. *Mapping Postcommunist Cultures: Russia and Ukraine in the Context of Globalization*. Montreal: McGill-Queen's University Press, 2007.

Cherkasenko, S. "Z ukraïns'koho zhytia." *Literaturno-naukovyi vistnyk* 17, no. 65 (1914): 582–95.

Clark, J. C. D. *The Language Of Liberty, 1660–1832: Political Discourse and Social Dynamics in the Anglo-American World*. Cambridge: Cambridge University Press, 1994.

Conquest, Robert. *The Nation Killers: The Soviet Deportation of Nationalities*. New York: Macmillan, 1970.

Crighton, J. L. "Anatomy and Subversion: 150th Anniversary of Georg Büchner's Death." *British Medical Journal* 294 (1987): 489–91.

Cronin, Michael. *Translating Ireland: Translation, Languages, Cultures*. Cork: Cork University Press, 1996.

De Paor, Liam, ed. *Milestones in Irish History*. Cork and Dublin: Mercier, 1986.

Deane, Seamus. *A Short History of Irish Literature*. London: Hutchinson, 1986.

Deleuze, Gilles. "Coldness and Cruelty." Translated by Jean McNeil. In his *Masochism*, 8–138. New York: Zone Books, 1991.

———. *The Fold: Leibniz and the Baroque*. Translated by Tom Conley. Minneapolis and London: University of Minnesota Press, 1993.

———. *Essays Critical and Clinical*. Translated by Daniel W. Smith and Michael A. Greco. Minneapolis: University of Minnesota Press, 1997.

———. *Desert Islands and Other Texts: 1953–1974*. Edited by David Lapoujade. Translated by Michael Taormina. New York: Semiotext(e), 2004.

———. *Two Regimes of Madness: Texts and Interviews 1975–1995*. Edited by David Lapoujade. Translated by Ames Hodges and Mike Taormina. New York and Los Angeles: Semiotext(e), 2006.

Deleuze, Gilles, and Félix Guattari. *Anti-Oedipus: Capitalism and Schizophrenia*. Translated by Robert Hurley, Mark Seem, and Helen R. Lane. Minneapolis: University of Minnesota Press, 1983.

———. *Kafka: Toward a Minor Literature*. Translated by Dana Polan. Minneapolis: University of Minnesota Press, 1986.

———. *A Thousand Plateaus: Capitalism and Schizophrenia*. Translated by Brian Massumi. Minneapolis: University of Minnesota Press, 1987.

Deresh, Liubko. "Kollazhnykh del master." *Stolichnyie novosti*, May 18–24, 2004. http://www.cn.com.ua/N309/culture/personage/personage.html (accessed April 9, 2007).

Derrida, Jacques. *Memoirs of the Blind: The Self-Portrait and Other Ruins*. Translated by Pascale-Anne Brault and Michael Naas. Chicago and London: University of Chicago Press, 1993.

———. *Monolingualism of the Other; or, The Prosthesis of Origin*. Translated by Patrick Mensah. Stanford, California: Stanford University Press, 1998.

D'hoker, Elke. "Portrait of the Other as a Woman with Gloves: Ethical Perspectives in John Banville's *The Book of Evidence*." *Critique* 44, no. 1 (2002): 23–37.

Dibrova, Volodymyr. "Prynts Hamlet Khams'koho povitu." *Krytyka*, May 2001, no. 5: 26–28.

Dontsov, Dmytro. "Poetyka ukraïns'koho Risordzhimentu (Lesia Ukraïnka)." In *Ukraïns'ke slovo: Khrestomatiia ukraïns'koï literatury ta literaturnoï krytyky XX st.*, vol. 1, edited by Vasyl' Iaremenko and Ievhen Fedorenko, 149–83. Kyïv: Ros', 1994.

Doroshenko, Dmytro. "Rozvytok nauky ukraïnoznavstva u XIX—na pochatku XX st. ta ïï dosiahnennia." In *Ukraïns'ka kul'tura*, edited by Dmytro Antonovych, 26–39. Kyïv: Lybid', 1993.

Dotsenko, R. I. "Irlands'ka literatura." In *Ukraïns'ka literaturna entsyklopediia*, vol. 2, edited by I. O. Dzeverin et al., 331–32. Kyïv: Ukraïns'ka radians'ka entsyklopediia im. M. P. Bazhana, 1990.

Dyer, Geoff. "Between the Lines." *Guardian*, September 2, 2006. http://arts.guardian.co.uk/features/story/0,,1863044,00.html (accessed February 3, 2007).

"Dyke pole." In *Ukraïns'ka radians'ka entsyklopediia*. 2nd ed. Vol. 3, 344. Kyïv: Holovna redaktsia URE, 1979.

Dyshkant, Vadym. "Ukraïns'ki pys'mennyky ne zhyvut' z literatury." *Den'*, November 4, 2004. http://www.day.kiev.ua/290619?idsource=126816&mainlang=ukr (accessed March 14, 2007).

Eliade, Mircea. *Rites and Symbols of Initiation: The Mysteries of Birth and Rebirth*. New York: Harper and Row, 1965.

———. *Symbolism, the Sacred, and the Arts*. New York: Crossroad, 1986.

Féral, Josette. "Performance and Theatricality: The Subject Demystified." Translated by Terese Lyons. In *Mimesis, Masochism, and Mime: The Politics of Theatricality in Contemporary French Thought*, edited by Timothy Murray, 289–300. Ann Arbor: University of Michigan Press, 1997.

FitzSimon, Betsey Taylor, and James H. Murphy, eds. *The Irish Revival Reappraised*. Dublin: Four Courts Press, 2004.

Fleischmann, Ruth. "The Insularity of Irish Literature: Cultural Subjugation and the Difficulties of Reconstruction." In *The Internationalism of Irish Literature and Drama*, edited by Joseph McMinn, 309–19. Gerrards Cross: Colin Smyth, 1992.

Foster, R. F. *Modern Ireland, 1600–1972*. London: Penguin, 1989.

Foucault, Michel. "What Is an Author?" In *The Foucault Reader*, edited by Paul Rabinow, 101–20. New York: Pantheon Books, 1984.

————. *Mental Illness and Psychology*. Translated by Alan Sheridan. Berkeley, Los Angeles, and London: University of California Press, 1987.

Freiburg, Rudolf, and Jan Schnitker, eds. *"Do you consider yourself a postmodern author?": Interviews with Contemporary English Writers*. Münster: LIT, 1999.

Fuss, Diana. *Identification Papers: Readings on Psychoanalysis, Sexuality, and Culture*. London and New York: Routledge, 1995.

Gandhi, Leela. *Postcolonial Theory: A Critical Introduction*. New York: Columbia University Press, 1998.

Garratt, Robert F. *Modern Irish Poetry: Tradition and Continuity from Yeats to Heaney*. Berkeley and Los Angeles: University of California Press, 1989.

Genocchio, Benjamin. "Discourse, Discontinuity, Difference: The Question of 'Other' Spaces." In *Postmodern Cities and Spaces*, edited by Sophie Watson and Katherine Gibson, 35–56. Cambridge, Massachusetts: Blackwell, 1995.

Gibson, Ian. *The Erotomaniac: The Secret Life of Henry Spencer Ashbee*. Cambridge, Massachusetts: Da Capo, 2001.

Gilman, Sander L. "Büchner and Madness: Schizophrenia in Georg Büchner's *Lenz* and *Woyzeck*." *Bulletin of the History of Medicine* 74, no. 1 (2000): 165–66.

Girard, René. *Violence and the Sacred*. Translated by Patrick Gregory. Baltimore: John Hopkins University Press, 1979.

————. *Things Hidden since the Foundation of the World*. Translated by Stephen Bann and Michael Metteer. London: Athlone Press, 1987.

————. "From Mimetic Desire to the Monstrous Double." Translated by Patrick Gregory. In *Mimesis, Masochism and Mime: The Politics of Theatricality in Contemporary French Thought*, edited by Timothy Murray, 87–111. Ann Arbor: University of Michigan Press, 1997.

Green, Miranda. *Dictionary of Celtic Myth and Legend*. London: Thames and Hudson, 1992.

————. *Celtic Goddesses: Warriors, Virgins and Mothers*. New York: George Braziller, 1996.

Greenfield, Liah. "Transcending the Nation's Worth." In *The Worth of Nations: The Boston, Melbourne, Oxford Conversazioni on Culture and Society*, edited by Claudio Véliz, 43–56. Boston: Boston University, University Professors, 1993.

Gregory, Augusta. "The Felons of Our Land." *Cornhill Magazine*, May 1900, no. 47: 622–34.

Grosz, Elizabeth. "Women, *Chora*, Dwelling." In *Postmodern Cities and Spaces*, edited by Sophie Watson and Katherine Gibson, 47–58. Cambridge, Massachusetts: Blackwell, 1995.

Guattari, Félix. *Chaosophy*. Edited by Sylvère Lotringer. New York: Semiotext(e), 1995.

Haberstroh, Patricia Boyle. *Women Creating Women: Contemporary Irish Women Poets*. Syracuse: Syracuse University Press, 1996.

Halenko, Oleksandr. "Vytivky ukraïns'koho oriientalizmu." *Krytyka*, April 1999, no. 4: 11–17.

Hand, Derek. *John Banville: Exploring Fictions*. Dublin: Liffey Press, 2002.

Harvey, David C., et al. *Celtic Geographies: Old Culture, New Times*. London and New York: Routledge, 2002.

Hawkins, Anne Hunsaker. *Reconstructing Illness: Studies in Pathography*. 2nd ed. West Lafayette, Indiana: Purdue University Press, 1999.

Heaney, Seamus. *North*. London: Faber, 1975.

———. *Preoccupations: Selected Prose 1968–78*. London: Faber, 1980.

———. *The Haw Lantern*. New York: Farrar Straus Girous, 1987.

Herr, Cheryl. "The Erotics of Irishness." *Critical Inquiry* 17 (1990): 1–34.

Hinshelwood, R. D. "Psychoanalysis as Natural Philosophy." *Philosophy, Psychiatry, and Psychology* 12, no. 4 (2005): 325–29.

Hooper, Glen, and Colin Graham, eds. *Irish and Postcolonial Writing: History, Theory, Practice*. Basingstoke: Palgrave Macmillan, 2002.

Howe, Stephen. *Ireland and Empire: Colonial Legacies in Irish History and Culture*. Oxford and New York: Oxford University Press, 2000.

Hoyt, Charles Alva. *Witchcraft*. 2nd ed. Carbondale and Edwardsville: Southern Illinois University Press, 1989.

Human Sexuality: An Encyclopedia. Edited by Vern L. Bullough and Bonnie Bullough. New York and London: Garland, 1994.

Hutchinson, John. *The Dynamics of Cultural Nationalism: The Gaelic Revival and the Creation of the Irish Nation State*. London: Allen & Unwin, 1987.

Iaremenko, Vasyl'. "Zrada: Shel'muvannia istoriieiu v ukraïns'komu varianti." *Slovo*, September 1992, no. 14: 2–3.

Iashchenko, Leopol'd. *Derzhavna zasluzhena kapela bandurystiv Ukraïns'koï RSR.* Kyïv: Muzychna Ukraïna, 1970.

Ieshkilev, Volodymyr, and Iurii Andrukhovych, eds. *Mala ukraïns'ka entsyklopediia aktual'noï literatury.* Ivano-Frankivs'k: Lileia-NV, 1998.

———. "Votstsekurhiia bet: Komentari do 'vnutrishn'oï entsyklopediï' romanu Izdryka 'Votstsek.'" In Izdryk. *Votstsek & Votstsekurhiia*, 150–83. L'viv: Kal'variia, 2002.

Imhof, Rüdiger. *John Banville: A Critical Introduction.* Dublin: Wolfhound Press, 1997.

Innes, C. L. *Woman and Nation in Irish Literature and Society, 1880–1935.* Athens, Georgia: University of Georgia Press, 1993.

Istoriia Rusiv. Translated by Ivan Drach. L'viv: Atlas, 1991.

"Iurii Vynnychuk." *Potiah 76: Tsentral'no-ievropeis'kyi literaturnyi chasopys*, 2002, no. 1: 131.

Izdryk. *Votstsek.* Ivano-Frankivs'k: Lileia-NV, 1997.

———. *Ostriv KRK ta inshi istoriï.* Ivano-Frankivs'k: Lileia-NV, 1998.

———. *Podviinyi Leon: Istoriia khvoroby.* Ivano-Frankivs'k: Lileia-NV, 2000.

———. *Wozzeck.* Translated by Marko Pavlyshyn. Edmonton and Toronto: Canadian Institute of Ukrainian Studies Press, 2006.

Kabbani, Rana. *Europe's Myth of Orient: Devise and Rule.* London: Macmillan, 1986.

Kaufman, Leonid. Afterword to *Divchyna z lehendy: Marusia Churai*, 81–104. Kyïv: Dnipro, 1974.

Kaup, Monika. *Mad Intertextuality: Madness in Twentieth-Century Women's Writing.* Trier: WVT, 1993.

Kearney, Richard. *Postnationalist Ireland: Politics, Culture, Philosophy.* London and New York, 1997.

Kee, Robert. *The Most Distressful Country.* Vol. 1 of *The Green Flag: A History of Irish Nationalism.* London: Quartet Books, 1976.

———. *Ourselves Alone.* Vol. 3 of *The Green Flag: A History of Irish Nationalism.* London: Quartet Books, 1976.

Keen, Sam. "The Rite of War and the Warrior Psyche." In *Gender Images: Reading for Composition*, edited by Melita Schaum and Connie Flanagan, 616–26. Boston and Toronto: Hougton Mifflin Company, 1992.

Kiberd, Declan. *Inventing Ireland: The Literature of the Modern Nation*. Cambridge, Massachusetts: Harvard University Press, 1995.

———. *Irish Classics*. London: Granta Books, 2000.

King, Geoff. *Mapping Reality: An Exploration of Cultural Cartographies*. New York: St. Martin's Press, 1996.

Kinsella, Thomas. Introduction to *The Tain*. Translated by Thomas Kinsella, ix-xvi. Oxford: Oxford University Press; Dublin: Dolmen Press, 1969.

Knapp, Gerhard P. "Lenz, (1835 [post 1839])." *The Literary Encyclopedia*, 14 March, 2003. http://www.litencyc.com/php/sworks.php?rec=true&UID=1 0378 (accessed April 1, 2007).

Kohut, Zenon E. *Russian Centralism and Ukrainian Autonomy: Imperial Absorption of the Hetmanate, 1760s–1830s*. Cambridge, Massachusetts: Harvard University Press, 1988.

Korniienko, Nelli. "Les' Kurbas i zasady ukraïns'koho avanhardu." *Dzerkalo tyzhnia*, February 3–9, 2007. http://www.zn.kiev.ua/ie/razdel/633/3730/ (accessed February 4, 2007).

Koscharsky, Halyna. *Tvorchist' Liny Kostenko z pohliadu poetyky ekspresyvnosti*. Kyiv: KM Academia, 1994.

Kostenko, Lina. *Nepovtornist': Virshi. Poemy*. Kyïv: Molod', 1980.

———. *Marusia Churai: Istorychnyi roman u virshakh*. Kyïv: Dnipro, 1982.

———. *Sad netanuchykh skul'ptur: Virshi. Poema-balada. Dramatychni poemy*. Kyïv: Radians'kyi pys'mennyk, 1987.

———. *Humanitarna aura natsiï abo defekt holovnoho dzerkala: Lektsiia, prochytana v Natsional'nomu universyteti "Kyievo-Mohylians'ka akademiia" 1 veresnia 1999 r.* Kyïv: KM Academia, 1999.

———. *Berestechko: Istorychnyi roman*. Kyïv: Ukraïns'kyi pys'mennyk, 1999.

Kovtun, E. F., and Charlotte Douglas. "Kazimir Malevich." *Art Journal* 41, no. 3 (1981): 234–41.

Krishnaswamy, Revathi. *Effeminism: The Economy of Colonial Desire*. Ann Arbor: University of Michigan Press, 1998.

Kristeva, Julia. *Black Sun: Depression and Melancholia*. Translated by Leon S. Roudies. New York: Columbia University Press, 1989.

Kryp'iakevych, Ivan. *Istoriia Ukraïny*. L'viv: Svit, 1990.

Lapins'kyi, Ihor. "Sho neiasno? Vidvaha, nasnaha i zvytiaha Lesia Podervian-s'koho." Introduction to *Heroi nashoho chasu,* by Les' Poderv'ians'kyi, 5–9. L'viv: Kal'variia, 2000.

Lazarus, Neil, ed. *The Cambridge Companion to Postcolonial Literary Studies*. Cambridge: Cambridge University Press, 2004.

"*Leabhar Gabhála / The Book of Invasions*." *Royal Irish Academy / Acadamh Ríoga hÉireann: Library & Catalogue*. http://www.ria.ie/library+catalogu e/gabhala.html (accessed February 15, 2007).

Le Brun, Annie. *Sade: A Sudden Abyss*. Translated by Camille Naish. San Francisco: City Light Books, 1990.

Lee, J. J. *Ireland, 1912–1985: Politics and Society*. Cambridge, New York, and Oakleigh: Cambridge University Press, 1992.

Lewes, Darby. *Nudes From Nowhere: Utopian Sexual Landscapes*. Lanham, Boulder, New York, and Oxford: Rowman and Littlefield, 2000.

Lindstrom, Thais S. *A Concise History of Russian Literature*. Vol. 2. New York: New York University Press, 1978.

Lloyd, David. *Anomalous States: Irish Writing and the Post-Colonial Moment*. Dublin: Lilliput Press, 1993.

———. "Ireland After History." In *A Companion to Postcolonial Studies*, edited by Henry Schwarz and Santeeta Ray, 377–95. Malden, Massachusetts, and Oxford: Blackwell, 2000.

———. "Regarding Ireland in a Post-Colonial Frame." *Cultural Studies* 15, no. 1 (2001): 12–32.

Long, Jim. "Kazimir Malevich: Suprematism." *The Brooklyn Rail: Critical Perspectives on Arts, Politics, and Culture*, September 2003. http://www. thebrooklynrail.org/arts/sept03/malevich.html (accessed April 13, 2007).

Longley, Michael. *Poems 1963–1983*. Edinburgh: Salamander; Dublin: Gallery, 1985.

Loomba, Ania. *Colonialism/Postcolonialism*. 2nd ed. London and New York: Routledge, 2005.

Looper, Matthew G. "The Pathology of Painting: Tuberculosis as a Metaphor in the Art of Kazimir Malevich" *Configurations* 3, no. 1 (1995): 27–46.

Lowe, Jeremy. "Contagious Violence and the Spectacle of Death in *Táin Bó Cúailnge*." In *Language and Tradition in Ireland: Continuities and Dis-*

placements, edited by Maria Tymoczko and Colin Ireland, 84–100. Amherst and Boston: University of Massachusetts Press, 2003.

Luchuk, Ivan. "Sumburni prypushchennia (pisliaslovo redaktora)." Afterword to *Spovid' kyianyna erotomana*, by Anonim, 139–42. L'viv: Kal'variia, 2004.

Lyotard, Jean François. *The Postmodern Condition: A Report on Knowledge*. Translated by Geoff Bennington and Brian Massumi. Minneapolis: University of Minnesota Press, 1984.

Mac Cana, Proinsias. *Celtic Mythology*. London: Hamlyn, 1970.

Makarov, Anatolii. "Istoriia—sestra poeziï." *Ukraïns'ka mova i literatura v shkoli* 10 (1980): 24–38.

———. "Krasa barokko." *Khronika 2000: Ukraïns'kyi kul'turolohichnyi al'manakh*, 1992, no. 1: 80–116.

———. *Svitlo ukraïns'koho baroko*. Kyïv: Mystetstvo, 1994.

Makhnovets', L. Ie., ed. *Davnia literatura (XI–persha polovyna XVIII st.)*. Vol. 1 of *Istoriia ukraïns'koï literatury*. Kyïv: Naukova dumka, 1967.

Makhun, Serhii. "Slaves in the Sublime Porte: Slavic Factor at the Court of Suleiman I." *Den'*. http://www.day.kiev.ua/DIGEST/2002/01/culture/cu14.htm (accessed November 23, 2005).

Malone, Christopher T. "Writing Home: Spatial Allegories in the Poetry of Seamus Heaney and Paul Muldoon." *ELH: English Literary History* 67, no. 4 (2000): 1083–1109.

Maravall, José Antonio. *Culture of the Baroque: Analysis of a Historical Structure*. Translated by Terry Cochran. Minneapolis: University of Minnesota Press, 1986.

Markale, Jean. *Women of the Celts*. Translated by A. Mygind, C. Hauch, and P. Henry. London: Gordon Cremonesi, 1975.

Martin, Elizabeth Frances. "Painting the Irish West: Nationalism and the Representation of Women." *New Hibernia Review* 7, no. 1 (2003): 31–44.

Massey, Doreen. *Space, Place, and Gender*. Minneapolis: University of Minnesota Press, 1994.

Matthews, Caitlín, and John Matthews. *British and Irish Mythology: An Encyclopaedia of Myth and Legend*. London: Diamond, 1988.

Matthews, Steven. *Irish Poetry: Politics, History, Negotiation. The Evolving Debate, 1969 to the Present*. London: Macmillan, 1997.

McBride, Lawrence W., ed. *Reading Irish Histories: Texts, Contexts, and Memory in Modern Ireland*. Dublin: Four Courts Press, 2003.

McDiarmid, Lucy. "Questions and Answers: Nuala Ní Dhomhnaill." *Irish Literary Supplement* 6, no. 2 (1987): 41–43.

McDonald, Peter. "Michael Longley's Homes." In *The Chosen Ground: Essays on the Contemporary Poetry of Northern Ireland*, edited by Neil Corcoran, 63–83. Bridgend: Seren Books; Chester Springs: Dufour, 1992.

McMinn, Joseph. *John Banville: A Critical Study*. Dublin: Gill and Macmillan, 1991.

———. *The Supreme Fictions of John Banville*. Manchester and New York: Manchester University Press, 1999.

McWilliams Consalvo, Deborah. "The Lingual Ideal in the Poetry of Nuala Ní Dhomhnaill." *Éire-Ireland* 30, no. 2 (1995): 148–61.

Melchior-Bonnet, Sabine. *The Mirror: A History*. Translated by Katharina H. Jewett. New York and London: Routledge, 2001.

Moloney, Karen Marguerite. *Seamus Heaney and the Emblems of Hope*. Columbia: University of Missouri Press, 2007.

Moore, David Chioni. "Is the Post- in Postcolonial the Post- in Post-Soviet? Towards a Global Postcolonial Critique." In *Postcolonialisms: An Anthology of Cultural Theory and Criticism*, edited by Gaurav Desai and Supriya Nair, 514–38. Oxford: Berg, 2005.

Moreton, Cole. *Hungry for Home: Leaving the Blaskets: A Journey from the Edge of Ireland*. New York: Penguin, 2001.

Muldoon, Paul. *Why Brownlee Left*. London and Boston: Faber, 1980.

———. *Madoc: A Mystery*. New York: Farrar, 1991.

Müller, Anja. "'You Have Been Framed': The Function of Ekphrasis for the Representation of Women in John Banville's Trilogy (*The Book of Evidence, Ghosts, Athena*)." *Studies in the Novel* 36, no. 2 (2004): 186–205.

Murphy, Neil. *Irish Fiction and Postmodern Doubt: An Analysis of the Epistemological Crisis in Modern Irish Fiction*. Lewiston, New York: Edwin Mellen, 2004.

Murphy, Richard. *New Selected Poems*. London and Boston: Faber, 1989.

Myloradovych, V. P. "Zametki o malorusskoi demonologii." In *Ukraïntsi: narodni viruvannia, povir'ia, demonolohiia*, edited by A. P. Ponomariova, T. V. Kosmina, and O. O. Buriak, 407–29. Kyïv: Lybid', 1992.

Nagy, Joseph Falaky. *Conversations with Angels and Ancients: Literary Myths of Medieval Ireland*. Ithaca and London: Cornell University Press, 1997.

Narys istoriï "Prosvity". L'viv, Kraków, and Paris, 1993.

Nash, Catherine. "Remapping the Body/Land: New Cartographies of Identity, Gender, and Landscape in Ireland." In *Writing Women and Space: Colonial and Postcolonial Geographies*, edited by Alison Blunt and Gillian Rose, 225–50. New York: Guilford, 1994.

Ní Dhomhnaill, Nuala. *Selected Poems / Rogha Dánta*. Translated by Michael Hartnett. Dublin: Raven Arts Press, 1988.

———. "Dominic Larkin Interviewing Nuala Ní Dhomhnaill." *An Nasc* 3, no. 1 (1990): 26.

———. *The Astrakhan Cloak*. Translated by Paul Muldoon. Winston-Salem, North Carolina: Wake Forest University Press, 1993.

———. *Pharaoh's Daughter*. Revised edition. Translated by Ciaran Carson et al. Winston-Salem, North Carolina: Wake Forest University Press, 1993.

———. "Why I Choose to Write in Irish, The Corpse That Sits Up and Talks Back." *The New York Times Books Review*, January 8, 1995, 3, 27–28.

———. "Nuala Ní Dhomhnaill: Interviewed by Lucy McDiarmid and Michael J. Durkan." In *Writing Irish: Selected Interviews with Irish Writers from the Irish Literary Supplement*, edited by James P. Myers, Jr., 99–113. Syracuse: Syracuse University Press, 1999.

———. *The Water Horse*. Translated by Eiléan Ní Chuilleanáin and Medbh McGuckian. Oldcastle: Gallery Press, 2000.

———. "Travelling through Liminal Spaces: An Interview with Nuala Ní Dhomhnaill by Loretta Qwarnström." *Nordic Irish Studies* 3, no. 1 (2004): 65–73.

Nic Dhiarmada, Bríona. "Going For It—And Succeeding." *Irish Literary Supplement* 12, no. 2 (1993): 3–4.

———. "Tradition and the Female Voice in Contemporary Gaelic Poetry." *Women's Studies International Forum* 11, no. 4 (1988): 387–93.

Niranjana, Tejaswini. *Siting Translation: History, Post-Structuralism, and the Colonial Context*. Berkeley, Los Angeles, and Oxford: University of California Press, 1992.

Noyes, John K. *The Mastery of Submission: Inventions of Masochism*. Ithaca and London: Cornell University Press, 1997.

O'Connor, Coilin. "John Banville: Using Words to Paint Pictures of 'Magical' Prague." *Radio Prague*, July 30, 2006. http://www.radio.cz/en/article/815 11 (accessed April 5, 2007).

O'Connor, Mary. "Breaking the Rules: Nuala Ní Dhomhnaill's Language Strategies." In *Cross-Addressing: Resistance Literature and Cultural Borders*, edited by John C. Hawley, 67–85. New York: State University of New York Press, 1996.

O'Sullivan, Sean, ed. and trans. *Folktales of Ireland*. Chicago: University of Chicago Press, 1966.

Oliver, Lisi. "Forced and Unforced Rape In Early Irish Law." In *Proceedings of the Harvard Celtic Colloquium, 13, 1993*, edited by Barbara Hillers, Pamela Hopkins, and Jerry Hunter, 93–106. Cambridge, Massachusetts: Harvard University Press, 1993.

Pavlychko, Solomia. *Natsionalizm, seksual'nist', oriientalizm: Skladnyi svit Ahatanhela Kryms'koho*. Kyïv: Osnovy, 2000.

Pavlyshyn, Marko. "Ukraïns'ka kul'tura z kutu postmodernizmu (Ukrainian culture in postmodern perspective)." In *Ukraine in the 1990s: Proceedings of the First Conference of the Ukrainian Studies of Australia*, edited by J. E. M. Clarke and Marko Pavlyshyn, 38–49. Melbourne: Monash University, Slavic Section, 1992.

———. "Post-Colonial Features in Contemporary Ukrainian Culture." *Australian Slavonic and Eastern European Studies* 6, no. 2 (1992): 41–55.

———. *Kanon ta iconostas: Ukraïns'ka moderna literatura*. Kyïv: Chas, 1997.

———. "*Wozzeck* IV." Introduction to *Wozzeck,* by Izdryk, vii–xxi. Edmonton and Toronto: Canadian Institute of Ukrainian Studies Press, 2006.

The Phenomenon of the Ukrainian Avant-Garde, 1910–1935 / Le Phenomene de L'avant-garde ukrainienne, 1910–1935 / Феномен українського авангарду, 1910–1935. Winnipeg: Winnipeg Art Gallery, 2002.

Peirce, Leslie P. *The Imperial Harem: Women and Sovereignty in the Ottoman Empire*. New York and Oxford: Oxford University Press, 1993.

Poddae, Prem, and David Johnson, eds. *A Historical Companion to Postcolo-nial Thought in English*. New York: Columbia University Press, 2005.

Poderv'ians'kyi, Les'. *Heroi nashoho chasu*. L'viv: Kal'variia, 2000.

Pokal'chuk, Iurii. *Te, shcho na spodi*. L'viv: Kal'variia, 1998.

———. *Ozernyi viter*. Ivano-Frankivs'k: Lileia-NV, 2002.

———. *Shablia i strila*. Kharkiv: Folio, 2003.

———. *Zaboroneni ihry*. Kharkiv: Folio, 2005.

Putzel, Steven D. "Fluid Disjunction in Paul Muldoon's 'Immram' and 'The More a Man Has the More a Man Wants.'" *Papers on Language and Lit-erature* 32, no. 1 (1996): 85–108.

"Pys'mennyky rozdavaly knyzhky poviiam na Okruzhnii u Kyievi." *Hazeta po-ukraïns'ky*, March 9, 2007. http://www.gpu.ua/index.php?&id=153164 (accessed March 19, 2007).

Rancour-Laferriere, Daniel. *The Slave Soul of Russia: Moral Masochism and the Cult of Suffering*. New York and London: New York University Press, 1995.

Remy, Johannes. "The Valuev Circular and Censorship of Ukrainian Publica-tions in the Russian Empire (1863–1876): Intention and Practice." *Cana-dian Slavonic Papers* 49, nos. 1–2 (2007): 87–110.

Riabchuk, Mykola. "Ukraine without Ukrainians?" In *Towards an Intellectual History of Ukraine: An Anthology of Ukrainian Thought from 1710 to 1995*, edited by Ralph Lindheim and George S. N. Luckyj, 400–403. To-ronto: University of Toronto Press, 1996.

———. *Vid Malorosiï do Ukraïny: paradoksy zapizniloho natsiietvorennia*. Ky-ïv: Krytyka, 2000.

———. *Dylemy ukraïns'koho Fausta: hromadians'ke suspil'stvo i rozbudova derzhavy*. Kyïv: Krytyka, 2000.

———. *Dvi Ukraïny: real'ni mezhi, virtual'ni viiny*. Kyïv: Krytyka, 2003.

Richards, David. *Georg Büchner's Woyzeck*. Rochester, New York: Cadmen House, 2001.

Robinson, Douglas. *Translation and Taboo*. DeKalb, Illinois: Northern Illinois University Press, 1996.

Romanchuk, Oleh. "Derzhava *contra* kul'tura." *Universum*. http://www.un iversum. org.ua/journal/2004/rom_3.html (accessed February 1, 2007).

Romanets', Oleksa, ed. *Narodne viche Bukovyny, 1918–1993*. Chernivtsi: Prut, 1994.

Rooth, Judith. *A Lure of Knowledge: Lesbian Sexuality and Theory*. New York: Columbia University Press, 1991.

Rose, Gillian. *Feminism and Geography: The Limits of Geographical Knowledge*. Minneapolis: University of Minnesota Press, 1993.

Said, Edward E. *Culture and Imperialism*. New York: Vintage Books, 1993.

Saunders, David. "Russia's Nationality Policy: The Case of Ukraine (1847–1941)." *Journal of Ukrainian Studies* 29, nos. 1–2 (2004): 399–419.

Schuchard, Ronald. "The Legacy of Yeats in Contemporary Irish Poetry." *Irish University Review* 34, no. 2 (2004): 291–314.

Schwartz, Hillel. *The Culture of the Copy: Striking Likeness, Unreasonable Facsimiles*. New York: Zone Books, 1996.

Serbyn, R. "Lenine et la question ukrainienne en 1914: le discours 'separatiste' de Zurich." *Pluriel* 25 (1981): 77–89.

Sewell, Frank. "Between Two Languages: Poetry in Irish, English and Irish English." In *The Cambridge Companion to Contemporary Irish Poetry*, edited by Matthew Campbell, 149–68. Cambridge: Cambridge University Press, 2003.

Shapovalenko, T. V., ed. *Poeziia Liny Kostenko v chasakh perekhidnykh i vichnykh*. Kyïv: KM Academia, 2005.

Shevchuk, Valerii. *Renesans. Rannie baroko*. Vol. 1 of *Muza Roksolans'ka: Ukraïns'ka literatura XVI–XVII stolit'*. Kyïv: Lybid', 2004.

———. *Rozvynene baroko. Piznie baroko*. Vol. 2 of *Muza Roksolans'ka: Ukraïns'ka literatura XVI–XVIII stolit'*. Kyïv: Lybid', 2005.

Siegel, Sandra. "Literature and Degeneration: The Representation of 'Decadence.'" In *Degeneration: The Dark Side of Progress*, edited by J. Edward Chamberlin and Sander L. Gilman, 199–219. New York: Columbia University Press, 1985.

Sigel, Lisa Z. *Governing Pleasures: Pornography and Social Change in England, 1815–1914*. New Brunswick, New Jersey, and London: Rutgers University Press, 2005.

Slemon, Stephen. "Monuments of Empire: Allegory/Counter-Discourse/Post-Colonial Writing." *Kunapipi* 9, no. 3 (1987): 1–16.

Smal'-Stots'kyi, Roman. "Do povnoho obrusieniia (Peresliduvannia ukraïns'koï movy Moskvoiu)." *Slovo*, February 1992, no. 1: 2–3.

Smith, Anthony D. *National Identity*. Reno: University of Nevada Press, 1991.

Smyrniv, Volodymyr. "Istorychna poetyka Liny Kostenko." *Journal of Ukrainian Studies* 12, no. 2 (1987): 3–25.

Sofronova, L. O. "Kyïvs'kyi shkil'nyi teatr i problemy ukraïns'koho barokko." In *Ukraïns'ke literaturne barokko*, edited by O. V. Myshanych, 109–30. Kyïv: Naukova dumka, 1987.

Sperber, Jonathan. *The European Revolutions, 1848–1851*. New York: Cambridge University Press, 1994.

Spivak, Gayatri Chakravorty. *Outside in the Teaching Machine*. New York and London: Routledge, 1993.

The Spivak Reader. Edited by Donna Landry and Gerald MacLean. London and New York: Routledge, 1996.

Squire, Charles. *The Mythology of the British Islands: An Introduction to Celtic Myth, Legend, Poetry, and Romance*. London: Blackie and Son, 1905.

Stanchak, Ol'ha. "Blits-interv'iu z Iuriiem Pokal'chukom." *Dzyga: Literatura*. http://dzyga.com.ua/interv/pocalchuk.htm (accessed March 13, 2007).

Steiner, George. "Büchner Lives On." *Timesonline. TLS: Times Literary Supplement*, December 13, 2006. http://www.tls.timesonline.co.uk/article/0,,25341-2501658,00.html (accessed April 1, 2007).

Stenohrama hromads'kykh slukhan' vid 5 hrudnia: obhovorennia zakonoproektu "Pro rozvytok i zastosuvannia mov v Ukraïni." 10.12.2003 | 10:42 | Upravlinnia zv'iazkiv z hromadskistiu SKMU. http://www.kmu.gov.ua/control/uk/publish/article?art_id=3646619&cat_id=38176 (accessed February 1, 2007).

Stepanenko, Mykhailo. "Kolo Marusi Churai: Trahedia bezsmertnoï ukraïnky." *Den'*, January 27, 2007. http://www.day.kiev.ua/176126/ (accessed February 11, 2007).

Struk, Danylo Husar. "The How, the What and the Why of *Marusia Churai*: A Historical Novel in Verse by Lina Kostenko." *Canadian Slavonic Papers* 32, no. 2 (1990): 148–65.

———. "Istorychnyi roman Liny Kostenko." *Suchasnist'*, 1990, no. 5: 26–41.

Subtelny, Orest. *Ukraine: A History*. 3rd ed. Toronto, Buffalo, and London: University of Toronto Press, 2000.

Sutton, Peter C. "Artificial Magic." In *Dalí's Optical Illusions*. Edited by Dawn Ades, 30–37. New Haven and London: Wadsworth Atheneum Museum of Art in association with Yale University Press, 2000.

The *Táin*. Translated from the Irish epic *Táin Bó Cuailnge* by Thomas Kinsella. Oxford: Oxford University Press; Dublin: Dolmen Press, 1969.

Taran, Liudmyla. *Enerhiia poshuku*. Kyïv: Radians'kyi pys'mennyk, 1986.

Theweleit, Klaus. *Male Fantasies: Women, Floods, Bodies, History*. Translated by Stephen Conway in collaboration with Erica Carter and Chris Turner. Vol. 1. Minneapolis: University of Minnesota Press, 1987.

Thieme, John. *Postcolonial Con-Texts: Writing Back to the Canon*. London and New York: Continuum, 2001.

Tobin, Daniel. *Passage to the Centre: Imagination and the Sacred in the Poetry by Seamus Heaney*. Kentucky: University Press of Kentucky, 1999.

Tomenko, Mykola. *Teoriia ukraïns'koho kokhannia*. Kyïv: Mizhnarodnyi turyzm, 2002.

Toolis, Kevin. "The Only Gaels in the World." *Guardian Unlimited*, March 19, 2000. http://books.guardian.co.uk/reviews/history/0,,148306,00.html (accessed March 29, 2007).

A Treasury of Irish Myth, Legend, and Folklore: Fairy and Folk Tales of the Irish Peasantry. Edited by William Butler Yeats. *Cuchulain of Muirthemne: The Story of the Men of the Red Branch of Ulster*. Translated by Lady Isabella Augusta Gregory. New York: Avenel Books, 1986.

Trinchii, Vadym. "Pro pornoetnohrafiiu." *Krytyka*, May 2001, no. 5: 24–26.

Turhan, Filiz. *The Other Empire: British Romantic Writings about the Ottoman Empire*. New York and London: Routledge, 2003.

Tymoczko, Maria. *Translation in a Postcolonial Context: Early Irish Literature in English Translation*. Manchester: St. Jerome Publishing, 1999.

Tymoczko, Maria, and Colin Ireland, eds. *Language and Tradition in Ireland: Continuities and Displacements*. Amherst and Boston: University of Massachusetts Press, 2003.

Ul'ianov, Anatolii. "Izdryk rezhet liudei." *Proza,* April 22, 2004. http://www.proza.com.ua/peoples/izdryk_rezhet_ljudej_2161.shtml (accessed April 9, 2007).

Vance, Norman. *Irish Literature: A Social History. Tradition, Identity and Difference*. Oxford: Basil Blackwell, 1990.

Velychenko, Stephen. "Identities, Loyalties and Service in Imperial Russia: Who Administered the Borderlands?" *The Russian Review* 54, no. 2 (1995): 188–208.

Vynnychuk, Iurii. *Zhytiie haremnoie.* L'viv: Piramida, 1996.

———. *Mal'va Landa.* L'viv: Piramida, 2004.

———. *Vesniani ihry v osinnikh sadakh.* L'viv: Piramida, 2005.

———. "Pro vse tse tiazhko rozkazaty." *Potiah 76: Tsentral'no-ievropeis'kyi literaturnyi chasopys*, no. 4. http://www.potyah76.org.ua/potyah/?t=28 (accessed March 16, 2007).

Wandor, M., ed. *On Gender and Writing.* London, Boston, Melbourne, and Henley: Pandora Press, 1983.

Waugh, Patricia, ed. *Literary Theory and Criticism: An Oxford Guide.* Oxford: Oxford University Press, 2006.

Welch, Robert. "Translation as Tribute." *Poetry Ireland Review* 34 (1992): 125–29.

Weretiuk, Oksana. "Filozofia porażki: *Beresteczko* Liny Kostenko." *Przegląd Humanistyczny*, 2006, no. 1: 123–36.

Wheatley, David. "'The Blank Mouth': Secrecy, Shibboleths, and Silence in Northern Irish Poetry." *Journal of Modern Literature* 25, no. 1 (2001): 1–16.

Wilson, Rebecca E. "Nuala Ní Dhomhnaill." In *Sleeping with Monsters: Conversations with Scottish and Irish Women Poets*, edited by Gillean Somerville-Arjat and Rebecca Wilson, 148–57. Edinburgh: Polygon, 1990.

Yermolenko, Galina. "Roxolana: 'The Greatest Empress of the East.'" *The Muslim World* 95, no. 2 (2005): 231–48.

Zabuzhko, Oksana. *Pol'ovi doslidzhennia z ukraïns'koho seksu.* Kyïv: Zhoda, 1996.

———. "Where There Are No Knights, a Robber Baron Will Turn Up." *Den'.* Http://www.day.kiev.ua/DIGEST/1999/28/culture/cul-1.htm (accessed November 23, 2005).

———. *Shevchenkiv mif Ukraïny: sproba filosofs'koho analizu.* Kyïv: Abrys, 1997.

———. *Khroniky vid Fortinbrasa: Vybrana eseïstyka 90-kh.* Kyïv: Fakt, 1999.

———. *Notre Dame d'Ukraine : Ukraïnka v konflikti mifolohii.* Kyïv: Fakt, 2007.

Zahurs'ka, El'vira. "Lehendy pro Marusiu Churai: Pravda i domysly pro ukraïns'ku narodnu poetesu." *Den'*, December 16, 2006. http://www.day.kiev.ua/174196/ (accessed February 11, 2007).

Zalizniak, Leonid. "Ukraïna—Rosiia: Rizni istorychni doli." *Starozhytnosti*, November 1991, no. 10: 1, 6–8.

Zhukovs'kyi, Arkadii, and Orest Subtel'nyi. *Narys istoriï Ukraïny*. L'viv: Naukove tovarystvo imeni T. Shevchenka, 1992.

Index

SOVIET AND POST-SOVIET POLITICS AND SOCIETY

Edited by Dr. Andreas Umland

ISSN 1614-3515

FORTHCOMING (MANUSCRIPT WORKING TITLES)

Andrei Rogatchevski
The National-Bolshevik Party
ISBN 3-89821-532-6

Zenon Victor Wasyliw
Soviet Culture in the Ukrainian Village
The Transformation of Everyday Life and Values, 1921-1928
ISBN 3-89821-536-9

Nele Sass
Das gegenkulturelle Milieu im postsowjetischen Russland
ISBN 3-89821-543-1

Julie Elkner
Maternalism versus Militarism
The Russian Soldiers' Mothers Committee
ISBN 3-89821-575-X

Alexandra Kamarowsky
Russia's Post-crisis Growth
ISBN 3-89821-580-6

Martin Friessnegg
Das Problem der Medienfreiheit in Russland seit dem Ende der Sowjetunion
ISBN 3-89821-588-1

Nikolaj Nikiforowitsch Borobow
Führende Persönlichkeiten in Russland vom 12. bis 20 Jhd.: Ein Lexikon
Aus dem Russischen übersetzt und herausgegeben von Eberhard Schneider
ISBN 3-89821-638-1

Martin Malek, Anna Schor-Tschudnowskaja
Tschetschenien und die Gleichgültigkeit Europas
Russlands Kriege und die Agonie der Idee der Menschenrechte
ISBN 3-89821-676-4

Taras Kuzio, Paul D'Anieri (Hrsg.)
Aspects of the Orange Revolution I: Regime Politics and Democratization in Ukraine
ISBN 3-89821-698-5

Bohdan Harasymiw, Oleh S. Ilnytzkyj (Hrsg.)
Aspects of the Orange Revolution II: Analyses of the 2004 Ukrainian Presidential Elections
ISBN 3-89821-699-3

Andreas Langenohl
Political Culture and Criticism of Society
Intellectual Articulations in Post-Soviet Russia
ISBN 3-89821-709-4

Thomas Borén
Meeting Places in Transformation
ISBN 3-89821-739-6

Lars Löckner
Sowjetrussland in der Beurteilung der Emigrantenzeitung 'Rul', 1920-1924
ISBN 3-89821-741-8

Ekaterina Taratuta
The Red Line of Construction
Semantics and Mythology of a Siberian Heliopolis
ISBN 3-89821-742-6

Bernd Kappenberg
Zeichen setzen für Europa
Der Gebrauch europäischer lateinischer Sonderzeichen in der deutschen Öffentlichkeit
ISBN 3-89821-749-3

David Rupp
Die Rußländische Föderation und die russischsprachigen Minderheiten im "Nahen Ausland"
ISBN 3-89821-778-7

Tim Bohse
Die Transformation der postsowjetischen russischen Lokalpolitik am Beispiel der Stadt Kaliningrad
ISBN 3-89821-782-5

Ingmar Bredies, Andreas Umland, Valentin Yakushik
Aspects of the Orange Revolution III
Studies on the 2004 Ukrainian Presidential Election
ISBN 978-389821-803-0

Ingmar Bredies, Andreas Umland, Valentin Yakushik
Aspects of the Orange Revolution IV
Studies on the 2004 Ukrainian Presidential Election
ISBN 978-389821-808-5

Ingmar Bredies, Andreas Umland, Valentin Yakushik
Aspects of the Orange Revolution V
Studies on the 2004 Ukrainian Presidential Election
ISBN 978-389821-809-2

Taras Kuzio
Aspects of the Orange Revolution VI
Post-Transitional Democratic Upheavals in Comparative Perspective
ISBN 978-389821-820-7

Julia Kusznir
Der politische Einfluss von Wirtschafts-eliten in russischen Regionen 1992 bis 2005
Eine Analyse am Beispiel der Erdöl und Erdgasindustrie
ISBN 978-389821-821-4

Alena Vysotskaya
Die Politik Russlands und Belarus hinsichtlich der Osterweiterung der Europäischen Union
Die Minderheitenfrage und das Problem der Freizügigkeit des Personenverkehrs
ISBN 978-389821-822-1

Siegbert Klee, Martin Sandhop, Oxana Schwajka, Andreas Umland
Elitenbildung in der Postsowjetischen Ukraine
ISBN 978-389821-829-0

Natalya Ketenci
The effect of location on the performance of Kazakhstani industrial enterprises in the transition period
ISBN 978-389821-831-3

Quotes from reviews of SPPS volumes:

On vol. 1 – *The Implementation of the ECHR in Russia*: "Full of examples, experiences and valuable observations which could provide the basis for new strategies."

Diana Schmidt, *Неприкосновенный запас*, 2005

On vol. 2 – *Putins Russland*: "Wipperfürth draws attention to little known facts. For instance, the Russians have still more positive feelings towards Germany than to any other non-Slavic country."

Oldag Kaspar, *Süddeutsche Zeitung, 2005*

On vol. 3 – *Die Übernahme internationalen Rechts in die russische Rechtsordnung*: "Hussner's is an interesting, detailed and, at the same time, focused study which deals with all relevant aspects and contains insights into contemporary Russian legal thought."

Herbert Küpper, *Jahrbuch für Ostrecht, 2005*

On vol. 5 – *Квадратные метры, определяющие сознание*: „Meerovich provides a study that will be of considerable value to housing specialists and policy analysts."

Christina Varga-Harris, *Slavic Review, 2006*

On vol. 6 – *New Directions in Russian International Studies*: "A helpful step in the direction of an overdue dialogue between Western and Russian IR scholarly communities."

Diana Schmidt, *Europe-Asia Studies*, 2006

On vol. 8 – *Nation-Building and Minority Politics in Post-Socialist States:* "Galbreath's book is an admirable and craftsmanlike piece of work, and should be read by all specialists interested in the Baltic area."

Andrejs Plakans, *Slavic Review*, 2007

On vol. 9 – *Народы Кавказа в Вооружённых силах СССР:* "In this superb new book, Bezugolnyi skillfully fashions an accurate and candid record of how and why the Soviet Union mobilized and employed the various ethnic groups in the Caucasus region in the Red Army's World War II effort."

David J. Glantz, *Journal of Slavic Military Studies*, 2006

On vol. 10 – *Русское Национальное Единство*: "A work that is likely to remain the definitive study of the Russian National Unity for a very long time."

Mischa Gabowitsch, *e-Extreme*, 2006

On vol. 14 – *Aleksandr Solzhenitsyn and the Modern Russo-Jewish Question*: "Larson has written a well-balanced survey of Solzhenitsyn's writings on Russian-Jewish relations."

Nikolai Butkevich, *e-Extreme*, 2006

On vol. 16 – *Der russische Sonderweg?:* "Luks's remarkable knowledge of the history of this wide territory from the Elbe to the Pacific Ocean and his life experience give his observations a particular sharpness and his judgements an exceptional weight."

Peter Krupnikow, *Mitteilungen aus dem baltischen Leben*, 2006

On vol. 17 – *История «Мёртвой воды»*: "Moroz provides one of the best available surveys of Russian neo-paganism."

Mischa Gabowitsch, *e-Extreme*, 2006

On vol. 18 – *Этническая и религиозная интолерантность в российских СМИ*: "A constructive contribution to a crucial debate about media-endorsed intolerance which has once again flared up in Russia."

Mischa Gabowitsch, *e-Extreme*, 2006

On vol. 25 – *The Ghosts in Our Classroom*: "This well-researched and incisive monograph, balanced and informed about Romanian education in general, should be required reading for those Eurocrats who have shaped Romanian spending priorities since 2000."

Tom Gallagher, *Slavic Review*, 2006

On vol. 26 – *The 2002 Dubrovka and 2004 Beslan Hostage Crises:* "Dunlop's analysis will help to draw Western attention to the plight of those who have suffered by these terrorist acts, and the importance, for all Russians, of uncovering the truth of about what happened."

Amy Knight, *Times Literary Supplement*, 2006

On vol. 29 – *Zivilgesellschaftliche Einflüsse auf die Orange Revolution*: „Strasser's study constitutes an outstanding empirical analysis and well-grounded location of the subject within theory."

Heiko Pleines, *Osteuropa*, 2006

On vol. 34 – *Postsowjetische Feiern*: "Mühlfried's book contains not only a solid ethnographic study, but also points at some problems emerging from Georgia's prevalent understanding of culture."

Godula Kosack, *Anthropos*, 2007

On vol. 35 – *Fascism Past and Present, West and East*: "Committed students will find much of interest in these sometimes barbed exchanges."

Robert Paxton, *Journal of Global History*, 2007

Series Subscription

Please enter my subscription to the series *Soviet and Post-Soviet Politics and Society*, ISSN 1614-3515, as follows:

❒ complete series   OR   ❒ English-language titles
                                                                          ❒ German-language titles
                                                                          ❒ Russian-language titles

starting with

❒ volume # 1

❒ volume # ___
        ❒ please also include the following volumes: #___, ___, ___, ___, ___, ___, ___
❒ the next volume being published
        ❒ please also include the following volumes: #___, ___, ___, ___, ___, ___, ___

❒ 1 copy per volume   OR   ❒ ___ copies per volume

<u>Subscription within Germany:</u>

You will receive every volume at 1st publication at the regular bookseller's price – incl. s & h and VAT.

Payment:

❒ Please bill me for every volume.

❒ Lastschriftverfahren: Ich/wir ermächtige(n) Sie hiermit widerruflich, den Rechnungsbetrag je Band von meinem/unserem folgendem Konto einzuziehen.

Kontoinhaber: _______________________________ Kreditinstitut: _______________________________

Kontonummer: _______________________________ Bankleitzahl: _______________________________

<u>International Subscription:</u>

Payment (incl. s & h and VAT) in advance for

❒ 10 volumes/copies (€ 319.80)   ❒ 20 volumes/copies (€ 599.80)

❒ 40 volumes/copies (€ 1,099.80)

Please send my books to:

NAME _______________________________ DEPARTMENT _______________________________
ADDRESS ____
POST/ZIP CODE _______________________________ COUNTRY _______________________________
TELEPHONE _______________________________ EMAIL _______________________________

date/signature ____

A hint for librarians in the former Soviet Union: Your academic library might be eligible to receive free-of-cost scholarly literature from Germany via the German Research Foundation. For Russian-language information on this program, see
http://www.dfg.de/forschungsfoerderung/formulare/download/12_54.pdf.

Please fax to: **0511 / 262 2201 (+49 511 262 2201)**
or mail to: *ibidem*-Verlag, Julius-Leber-Weg 11, D-30457 Hannover, Germany
or send an e-mail: ibidem@ibidem-verlag.de

ibidem-Verlag

Melchiorstr. 15

D-70439 Stuttgart

info@ibidem-verlag.de

www.ibidem-verlag.de
www.edition-noema.de
www.autorenbetreuung.de